COMMONWEALTH POLITICAL FACTS

By the same authors

EUROPEAN POLITICAL FACTS 1918–1973
EUROPEAN POLITICAL FACTS 1848–1918
EUROPEAN POLITICAL FACTS 1789–1848

By John Paxton

A DICTIONARY OF THE EUROPEAN ECONOMIC COMMUNITY

COMMONWEALTH POLITICAL FACTS

Chris Cook and John Paxton

Facts On File
119 West 57th Street, New York, N.Y. 10019

52648

First published 1979 by

FACTS ON FILE INC.

New York

Library of Congress Cataloging in Publication Data

Cook, Chris, 1945–
  Commonwealth political facts.

  Bibliography: p.
  Includes index.
  1. Commonwealth of Nations—Politics and government.
I. Paxton, John, joint author.   II. Title.
JN248.C63   1978   320.9′171′241   77–27355
ISBN 0–87196–378–7

Printed in Great Britain

CONTENTS

PREFACE

The Commonwealth is a remarkable and unique grouping of countries scattered throughout the continents of the world. The aim of this volume was to assemble readily accessible facts concerning these diverse countries, ranging from key ministers and election statistics to armed forces and diplomacy.

Such a broad world-wide coverage naturally encounters considerable editorial difficulties. Although the aim was comparability between countries, this was far from easy to achieve. India is different from the Gambia, or Antigua from Australia. It is hoped that the facts presented here will nonetheless provide the essential data that historians, political scientists and anyone studying current affairs are constantly searching for.

The editors are deeply grateful to many people and organisations for their help and advice. This book cannot avoid a heavy debt to David Butler, whose original *British Political Facts* pioneered this new type of reference book. Sheila Fairfield completed a marathon labour searching for facts; Philip Jones contributed a mass of material on trade unions and Stephen Brooks produced a wealth of information on defence matters.

We must also thank Jean Ali, Penny White and Jean Stone for excellent typing and untiring eyes for inconsistencies. Inevitably in reference books of this sort, some error and inconsistency can still appear. Both editors would welcome constructive criticism for future editions of this book.

Chris Cook
John Paxton

London and Bruton
March 1978

1 THE EVOLUTION OF THE COMMONWEALTH

The Commonwealth is a free association of the United Kingdom, Canada, Australia, New Zealand, India, Sri Lanka, Ghana, Nigeria, Cyprus, Sierra Leone, Jamaica, Trinidad and Tobago, Uganda, Kenya, Malaysia, Tanzania, Malawi, Malta, Zambia, The Gambia, Singapore, Guyana, Botswana, Lesotho, Barbados, Mauritius, Swaziland, Tonga, Fiji, Western Samoa, Nauru, Bangladesh, Bahamas, Grenada, Papua New Guinea, Seychelles and their dependent territories.

Up to July1925 the affairs of all the British Empire, apart from the United Kingdom and India, were dealt with by the Colonial Office. From that date a new secretaryship of state, for Dominion Affairs, became responsible for the relations between the United Kingdom and all the independent members of the Commonwealth.

In July 1947 the designations of the Secretary of State for Dominion Affairs and the Dominions Office were altered to 'Secretary of State for Commonwealth Relations' and 'Commonwealth Relations Office'. In the following month, on the independence of India and Pakistan, the India Office ceased to exist and the staff were transferred to the Commonwealth Relations Office, which then became responsible for relations with India and Pakistan.

The Colonial Office was merged with the Commonwealth Relations Office on 1 Aug 1966 to form the Commonwealth Office, and the post of Secretary of State for Commonwealth Relations became Secretary of State for Commonwealth Affairs. The post of Secretary of State for the Colonies was retained until 6 Jan 1967. The Commonwealth Office was merged with the Foreign Office on 17 Oct 1968.

The Secretary of State for Foreign and Commonwealth Affairs is now responsible for relations with the independent members of the Commonwealth, with the Associated States, with the protected state of Brunei and for the administration of the UK dependent territories, in addition to his responsibilities for relations with foreign countries.

On 18 Apr 1949, when the Republic of Ireland Act 1948 came into force,

Southern Ireland ceased to be a member of the Commonwealth.

The Imperial Conference of 1926 defined Great Britain and the Dominions, as they were then called, as

autonomous communities within the British Empire, equal in status, in no way subordinate one to another in any aspect of their domestic or foreign affairs, though united by a common allegiance to the Crown, and freely associated as members of the British Commonwealth of Nations.

On 11 Dec 1931 the Statute of Westminster, which by legal enactment recognized the status of the Dominions as defined in 1926, became law. Each of the Dominions, which then included Canada, Australia, New Zealand, South Africa and Newfoundland (which in 1949 became a Canadian Province) had signified approval of the provisions of the Statute.

THE BRITISH EMPIRE

Main Territories under British Rule in 1900

	Original Entry into British Rule and Status in 1900
Aden	Colony (1839) and adjacent protectorate
Antigua	Colony (1663)
Ascension	Admiralty administered territory (1815)
Australia	First settled 1788; 6 self-governing colonies (1855 and later)
Bahamas	First settled 1646; Colony (1783)
Barbados	Settled 1627; Colony (1662)
Basutoland	Protectorate (1871); Colony (1884)
Bechuanaland	Protectorate (1885)
Bermuda	First settled 1609; Colony (1684)
British Guiana	Ceded Colony (1814)
British Honduras	First settled 1638; Colony (separated from Jamaica 1884)
British North Borneo	Protectorate (1893)
British Solomon Islands	Protectorate (1893)
British Somaliland	Protectorate (1887)
Brunei	Protectorate (1888)
Burma	Indian province (1852)
Canada	Ceded Colonies from 1714 onwards; self-governing Federation (1867)
Cape of Good Hope	Ceded Colony (1814)

2

Cayman, Turks and Caicos Islands	Ceded (1670); Dependencies of Jamaica (1848)
Ceylon	Ceded Colony (1802)
	Original Entry into British Rule and Status in 1900
Christmas Island	Annexed (1888)
Cocos-Keeling Islands	Annexed (1857)
Cook Islands	Protectorate (1888)
Cyprus	British Administered territory (1878)
Dominica	Colony (1763)
East African Protectorate	Protectorate (1895)
Egypt	Occupied by British since 1882
Falkland Islands	Colony (1874)
Fiji	Colony (1874)
Gambia	Settlement began 1618; Colony (1843) and adjacent Protectorate (1888)
Gibraltar	Ceded Colony (1713)
Gilbert and Ellice Islands	Protectorate (1892)
Gold Coast	Settlement began 1750; Colony (1821 and 1874)
Grenada	Ceded Colony (1763)
Hong Kong	Ceded Colony (1843)
India	Settlement began 1601; Indian Empire (1876)
Ireland	Union with Great Britain (1801)
Jamaica	Colony (seized 1655 and ceded 1670)
Labuan	Colony (1848) governed by North Borneo Company (1890)
Lagos	Colony (1861)
Leeward Isles	Colonies federated (1871)
Malay States	9 Protectorates, 4 of which were federated
Maldive Islands	Protectorate (1887)
	Original Entry into British Rule and Status in 1900
Malta	Ceded Colony (1814)
Mauritius	Ceded Colony (1814)
Montserrat	First settled (1642) as Colony
Natal	Colony (1843)
New Zealand	Self-governing Colony (1854)
Newfoundland	Settlement began 1623; Self-governing colony (1855)
Nigeria	Protectorates (1900)[1]

[1] Colony of Lagos joined Southern Nigeria 1906. Protectorates of Northern and Southern Nigeria joined 1914.

3

Norfolk Island	Settled 1788; under New South Wales (1896)[2]
Northern Rhodesia	Chartered Company territory (1889)
Nyasaland	Protectorate (1891)
Papua	Protectorate (1884)[3] Colony (1888)
Pitcairn	Settled 1790; Colony (1898)
St Christopher (St Kitts) and Nevis	Colony (1625)
St Helena	Administered by East India Co. 1673; Colony (1833)
St Lucia	Ceded Colony (1814)
St Vincent	Ceded Colony (1763)
Sarawak	Protectorate (1888)
Seychelles	Dependency of Mauritius (1810)
Sierra Leone	Colony (1808) and adjacent Protectorate (1896)
Singapore	Under Indian Government 1824; part of Straits Settlements (1867)
Southern Rhodesia	Chartered Company (1889) Original Entry into British Rule and Status in 1900
Straits Settlements (Singapore, Penang, Malacca)	Colonies (1867)
Sudan	Condominium with Egypt (1899)
Swaziland	Protectorate (1903)
Tonga	Protectorate (1900)
Trinidad and Tobago	Ceded (1802 and 1814) Colony (combined 1899)
Tristan da Cunha	British settlement (1815)
Uganda	Protectorate
Virgin Islands	Colonies (1666)
Windward Isles	Colonies (1763 and 1814, federated in 1885)
Zanzibar	Protected State (1890)

FROM EMPIRE TO COMMONWEALTH:
A CHRONOLOGY OF DATES OF INDEPENDENCE
1947–1977

15 Aug 47	India
4 Feb 48	Ceylon (now Sri Lanka)

[2] Became dependency of Australian Government 1914.
[3] Administered by Australia since 1906. United with New Guinea 1940.

4

6 Mar 57	Ghana (formerly Gold Coast)
31 Aug 57	Federation of Malaya (renamed Federation of Malaysia on 16 Sep 63)
16 Aug 60	Cyprus
1 Oct 60	Nigeria
27 Apr 61	Sierra Leone
9 Dec 61	Tanganyika (renamed Tanzania on 26 Apr 64 when she joined with Zanzibar)
1 Jan 62	Western Samoa
6 Aug 62	Jamaica
31 Aug 62	Trinidad and Tobago
9 Oct 62	Uganda
10 Dec 63	Zanzibar (joined with Tanganyika on 26 Apr 64 to form Tanzania)
12 Dec 63	Kenya
6 July 64	Malawi (formerly Nyasaland)
21 Sep 64	Malta
24 Oct 64	Zambia (formerly Northern Rhodesia)
18 Feb 65	The Gambia
9 Aug 65	Singapore (withdrew from Federation of Malaysia)
26 May 66	Guyana (formerly British Guiana)
30 Sep 66	Botswana (formerly Bechuanaland)
4 Oct 66	Lesotho (formerly Basutoland)
30 Nov 66	Barbados
12 Mar 68	Mauritius
6 Sep 68	Swaziland
31 Jan 68	Nauru
4 June 70	Tonga
10 Oct 70	Fiji
4 Feb 72	Bangladesh
10 July 73	Bahamas
7 Feb 74	Grenada
16 Sep 75	Papua New Guinea
29 June 76	Seychelles

All these countries became members of the Commonwealth on independence, except for Cyprus, Western Samoa and Bangladesh which joined on 13 Mar 1961, 28 Aug 1970 and 18 Mar 1972 respectively.

COMMONWEALTH COUNTRIES WHICH SUBSEQUENTLY BECAME REPUBLICS

All these countries accept the Queen as the symbol of the free association of its independent member nations and as such the Head of the Commonwealth.

26 Jan 50	India
29 June 60	Ghana
16 Aug 60	Cyprus
9 Dec 62	Tanganyika (became Tanzania on the unification of Tanganyika and Zanzibar)
1 Oct 63	Nigeria
24 Oct 64	Zambia
12 Dec 64	Kenya
9 Aug 65	Singapore
6 July 66	Malawi
30 Sep 66	Botswana
8 Sep 67	Uganda
31 Jan 68	Nauru
23 Feb 70	Guyana
24 Apr 70	The Gambia
19 Apr 71	Sierra Leone
16 Dec 72	Bangladesh
22 May 72	Sri Lanka (formerly Ceylon)
13 Dec 74	Malta
29 June 76	Seychelles

FORMER MEMBERS OF THE COMMONWEALTH WHO NO LONGER BELONG

18 Apr 49	Southern Ireland (on coming into force of Republic of Ireland Act)
31 May 61	South Africa withdrew on becoming a Republic
30 Jan 72	Pakistan withdrew from the Commonwealth

6

A NOTE ON THE CONSTITUTIONAL EVOLUTION
OF THE COMMONWEALTH

The Colonial Laws Validity Act, 1865: The Act stated that colonies always had the right to amend their own constitutions 'in such matter and form as may from time to time be required by any Act of Parliament, Letters Patent, Orders in Council or Colonial Laws for the time being in force in the said Colony'. It confirmed the overriding supremacy of the British Parliament in legislation but limited the categories of colonial laws that could be invalidated by the doctrine of repugnancy.

This doctrine was founded on the assumption that the British Parliament had full power to legislate for the colonies, and since the colonists had taken English law with them then they could pass no law in their colonial legislatures that was in conflict with or repugnant to English law.

In practice the British Parliament seldom acted on the doctrine; the Act of 1865 confirmed already existing attitudes.

Powers of Reservation: The Governor could reserve for the Royal Assent any bill passed by a colonial legislature. Obligatory reservation was exercised under statute until 1926. Discretionary reservation was exercised in accordance with the advice of Dominion ministers. Reserved bills were discussed by the British Government and Colonial governments together to try to find a solution. The British Government's veto was exercised occasionally until 1926.

Powers of constitutional amendment: Before 1865 only limited powers were granted to colonial parliaments. The British North America Act of 1867 gave the provincial but not the federal legislatures power to amend; this disability was removed by the second British North America Act of 1949. On the establishment of the Commonwealth of Australia in 1901 and the Union of South Africa in 1909, both constitutions included provision for their own amendment, except, in South Africa, for the powers of the House of Assembly and the provincial councils.

British powers to legislate for the colonies: In domestic matters these were exercised only where the colony lacked the constitutional power to act for itself; the legislation was only passed with the colony's consent. In foreign or intro-imperial matters a convention grew up that the local legislature should consent to an imperial measure coming into force in its own territory. The Imperial Conference of 1911 agreed procedures for international agreements affecting the Dominions as, for example,

7

that the Dominions should be afforded an opportunity for consultation when framing the instructions to be given to British delegates at future meetings of the Hague conference and that conventions affecting the Dominions provisionally assented to at that conference shall be circulated among the Dominion Governments for their consideration.

From 1926 Dominions had their own representation in foreign countries. From 1923 they were free to negotiate treaties with foreign states, and were not to be bound by any British or imperial treaty which they had not signed.

Parliamentary institutions common to Commonwealth countries: In all the legislatures the majority party forms the bond between the legislature and the executive; the executive has close control of legislation and expenditure; if there are two chambers then one has unquestioned primacy; the opposition is recognized as constitutional part of the system of government; the cabinet system is used; the lower house has a Speaker.

Governments are dependent on the support of a majority in one chamber only, the lower, which is elected.

The Imperial Conference 1926: Britain and the Dominions were defined as 'autonomous communities within the British Empire, equal in status' not subordinate to each other and united by their common allegiance to the Crown.

The Statute of Westminster 1931: Dominions were listed as Canada, Australia, New Zealand, South Africa, Newfoundland and the Irish Free State.

The Colonial Laws Validity Act should not apply to any law made by the Parliament of a Dominion hereafter.

The doctrine of 'repugnancy' was abolished.

Dominions might enact laws with extra-territorial operation.

No act of the British Parliament might apply to a Dominion unless the text of the act says that the Dominion has requested it.

The Dominions' power to legislate should not include the power to amend constitutions of Canada, Australia and New Zealand, other than by existing provisions.

The office of Governor General: A Governor General was originally the representative of the British Government in matters where that government and local ministers might clash, but this role gradually died out. He remained a channel of communication between the Colonial and British Governments, and came to be appointed on the advice of Colonial ministers. The 1926 Imperial Conference defined his position.

8

The Governor General in a Dominion is the representative of the Crown, holding in all essential respects the same position in relation to the administration of public affairs in a Dominion as is held by H. M. the King in Great Britain, and that he is not the representative or agent of H. M. Government in Great Britain or of any department of that government.

The 1930 Imperial Conference agreed that the Governor General be appointed on local advice.

COMMONWEALTH PRIME MINISTERS' MEETINGS, 1900–

(Commonwealth Heads of Government Meetings, 1971–)
(All have taken place in London unless otherwise stated)

30 June–11 Aug 02	Colonial Conference
15 Apr – 9 May 07	Colonial Conference
23 May–20 June 11	Imperial Conference
Mar– May 17	Imperial War Conference
June– Aug 18	Imperial War Conference
1 Oct– 8 Nov 23	Imperial Conference
19 Oct–23 Nov 26	Imperial Conference
1 Oct–14 Nov 30	Imperial Conference
14 May–15 June 37	Imperial Conference
1 –16 May 44	Commonwealth Prime Ministers' Meeting
23 Apr–23 May 46	Commonwealth Prime Ministers' Meeting
11 –22 Oct 48	Commonwealth Prime Ministers' Meeting
21 –28 Apr 49	Commonwealth Prime Ministers' Meeting
4 –12 Jan 51	Commonwealth Prime Ministers' Meeting
3 – 9 June 53	Commonwealth Prime Ministers' Meeting
31 Jan– 8 Feb 55	Commonwealth Prime Ministers' Meeting
27 June– 6 July 56	Commonwealth Prime Ministers' Meeting
26 June– 5 July 57	Commonwealth Prime Ministers' Meeting
3 –13 May 60	Commonwealth Prime Ministers' Meeting
8 –17 Mar 61	Commonwealth Prime Ministers' Meeting
10 –19 Sep 62	Commonwealth Prime Ministers' Meeting
8 –13 July 64	Commonwealth Prime Ministers' Meeting
17 –25 Jan 65	Commonwealth Prime Ministers' Meeting
6 –15 Sep 66	Commonwealth Prime Ministers' Meeting
7 –15 Jan 69	Commonwealth Prime Ministers' Meeting
14 –22 Jan 71	Commonwealth Heads of Government Meeting Singapore

| 2 | –10 Aug 73 | Commonwealth Heads of Government Meeting Ottawa |
| 29 Apr–6 May 75 | | Commonwealth Heads of Government Meeting Kingston, Jamaica |

Certain other meetings of comparable status have been held

20 June–5 Aug 21	Conference of Prime Ministers and London Representatives of the United Kingdom, the Dominions, and India	London
July– Aug 32	Imperial Economic Conference	Ottawa
4 –13 Apr 45	British Commonwealth Meeting	London
27 Nov–11 Dec 52	Commonwealth Economic Conference	London
11 –12 Jan 66	Commonwealth Prime Ministers' Meeting	Lagos

Commonwealth Secretariat. In the communiqué issued at the end of the Commonwealth Prime Ministers' Conference in July 1964, instructions were given for the preparation of proposals for the establishment of a Commonwealth Secretariat. These proposals were approved at the Commonwealth Prime Ministers' Conference in June 1965.

| Secretary-General | – | Aug 65–Jun 75 | A. Smith (Canada) |
| | | Jul 75– | S. S. Ramphal (Guyana) |

Associated States. The Caribbean islands of Antigua, St Christopher-Nevis-Anguilla, Dominica, Grenada and St Lucia entered into a new form of association with Britain in Feb 1967. St Vincent became an association state on 27 Oct 1969. Each has control of its internal affairs, with the right to amend its own constitution (including the power to end the associated status and declare itself independent). Britain continues to be responsible for external affairs and defence. Grenada became independent, within the Commonwealth, on 7 Feb 1974.

Dependent Territories. Territories dependent on the United Kingdom comprise dependent territories, a protectorate and a condominium. A dependent territory is a territory belonging by settlement, conquest or annexation to the British Crown. A protectorate is a territory not formally annexed but in which, by treaty, grant and other lawful means the Crown has power and jurisdiction.

United Kingdom dependencies administered through the Foreign and Commonwealth Office comprise, in the Far East: Hong Kong (dependent territory); in the Indian Ocean: British Indian Ocean Territory (dependent territory); in the Mediterranean: Gibraltar (dependent territory); in the Atlantic Ocean: Falkland Islands and dependencies (dependent territory), British Antarctic Territory (dependent territory), St Helena and dependencies of Tristan da Cunha and Ascension Island (dependent territory); in the Caribbean: Bermuda, Belize, Montserrat, British Virgin Islands, Cayman Islands, Turks and Caicos Islands (dependent territories); in the Western Pacific: Solomon Islands (protectorate), Gilbert Islands, Tuvalu, Pitcairn (dependent territories), New Hebrides (Anglo-French Condominium).

The case of Anguilla. The Island of Anguilla, although technically still a part of the State of St Christopher-Nevis-Anguilla, is administered as a dependent territory and now has its own Constitution and Ministerial form of Government. The Anguilla (Constitution) Order 1976 (made under the Anguilla Act 1971) came into operation on 10 Feb. 1976. Provision is made in the constitution for a Legislative Assembly, comprising 7 elected members, 2 nominated members and 3 *ex-officio* members, and for an Executive Council comprising the Chief Minister, 2 other Ministers and 2 *ex-officio* members. The constitution provides for the Executive authority of Anguilla to be exercised by HM Commissioner. The constitution of St Kitts-Nevis-Anguilla now no longer applies in and in relation to Anguilla.

While constitutional responsibility to Parliament for the government of the dependent territories rests with the Secretary of State for Foreign and Commonwealth Affairs, the administration of the territories is carried out by the Government of the territories themselves.

Brunei is a sovereign state in treaty relationship with Great Britain, whereby Great Britain is responsible for the conduct of external affairs and has a consultative responsibility for defence. It has never been a dependent territory, and in 1971 ceased to be a protected state. In 1978 the relationship between UK and Brunei was under review.

The case of Nauru. To cater for the special circumstances of Nauru, a 'special membership' of the Commonwealth was devised in close consultation with the independent Government of Nauru.

Nauru has the right to participate in all functional activities of the Commonwealth and to receive appropriate documentation in relation to them as well as the right to participate in non-Governmental Commonwealth organizations. Nauru is not represented at meetings of Commonwealth Heads of Government, but may attend Commonwealth meetings at ministerial or official level, in such fields as education, medical cooperation, finance and other functional and technical areas as the Nauruan Government desires. It is eligible for Commonwealth technical assistance.

11

2 HEAD OF COMMONWEALTH, HEADS OF STATE, GOVERNORS GENERAL, GOVERNORS AND HIGH COMMISSIONERS

DATE OF ACCESSION

Victoria	20 June 1837
Edward VII	22 Jan 1901
George V	6 May 1910
Edward VIII	20 Jan 1936
George VI	11 Dec 1936
Elizabeth II	6 Feb 1952

As Head of Commonwealth the Royal Style and Titles of Queen Elizabeth II are: In Australia: 'Elizabeth the Second, by the Grace of God Queen of Australia and Her other Realms and Territories, Head of the Commonwealth'. In the Bahamas: 'Elizabeth the Second, by the Grace of God, Queen of the Commonwealth of the Bahamas and of Her other Realms and Territories, Head of the Commonwealth'. In Barbados: 'Elizabeth the Second, by the Grace of God, Queen of Barbados and of Her other Realms and Territories, Head of the Commonwealth'. In Canada: 'Elizabeth the Second, by the Grace of God of the United Kingdom, Canada and Her other Realms and Territories Queen, Head of the Commonwealth, Defender of the Faith'. In Fiji: 'Elizabeth the Second, by the Grace of God, Queen of Fiji and of Her other Realms and Territories, Head of the Commonwealth'. In Grenada: 'Elizabeth the Second, by the Grace of God, Queen of the United Kingdom of Great Britain and Northern Ireland and of Grenada and Her other Realms and Territories, Head of the Commonwealth'. In Jamaica:

'Elizabeth the Second, by the Grace of God of Jamaica and of Her other Realms and Territories Queen, Head of the Commonwealth'. In Mauritius: 'Elizabeth the Second, Queen of Mauritius and of Her other Realms and Territories, Head of the Commonwealth'. In New Zealand: 'Elizabeth the Second, by the Grace of God Queen of New Zealand and Her Other Realms and Territories, Head of the Commonwealth, Defender of the Faith'. In Papua New Guinea: 'Elizabeth the Second, Queen of Papua New Guinea and Her other Realms and Territories, Head of the Commonwealth'. In the United Kingdom: 'Elizabeth the Second, by the Grace of God of the United Kingdom of Great Britain and Northern Ireland and of Her other Realms and Territories Queen, Head of the Commonwealth, Defender of the Faith'.

ADEN

Political Residents

1899–1901	O'M. Creagh
1901–4	P. J. Maitland
1904–6	H. M. Mason
1906–10	E. De Brath
1910–15	J. A. Bell
1915–16	C. H. Price
1916–20	J. M. Stewart
1920–5	T. E. Scott
1925–8	J. H. K. Stewart
1928–31	G. S. Symes
1931–2	B. R. Reilly

Chief Commissioner and Resident

1932–7	B. R. Reilly

Governors

1937–40	B. R. Reilly
1940–4	J. H. Hall
1944–51	R. S. Champion
1951–6	T. Hickinbotham
1956–60	W. H. T. Luce
1960–3	C. H. Johnston

13

AJMER-MERWARA

Chief Commissioners

1898–1905	A. H. T. Martindale
1905–18	E. G. Colvin
1918–19	J. M. Smith
1919–25	R. E. Holland
1925–7	S. B. A. Patterson
1927–32	L. W. Reynolds
1932–7	G. D. Ogilvie
1937–44	A. C. Lothian
1944–7	H. R. Shivdasani

ANDAMAN AND NICOBAR ISLANDS

Chief Commissioners

1894–1904	R. C. Temple
1904–6	W. R. H. Merk
1906–13	H. A. Browning
1913–20	M. W. Douglas
1920–3	H. C. Beadon
1923–31	M. L. Ferrar
1931–5	J. W. Smyth
1935–8	W. A. Cosgrave
1938–42	C. F. Waterfall
1942–5	(under Japan)
1945–6	C. F. Waterfall
1946–7	N. K. Paterson

ANGLO-EGYPTIAN SUDAN

Governors General

1899–1916	F. R. Wingate
1916–24	L. O. F. Stack
1924–6	G. F. Archer
1926–34	J. L. Maffey
1934–40	G. S. Symes
1940–7	H. J. Huddleston
1947–54	R. G. Howe
1954–5	A. K. Helm

ANTIGUA

Administrators
1936	H. E. Bader
1936–41	J. D. Harford
1941–4	H. Boon
1944–6	F. S. Harcourt
1946–7	L. S. Greening
1947–54	R. St. J. O. Wayne
1954–8	A. Lovelace
1958–64	I. G. Turbott
1964–6	D. J. G. Rose
1966–7	W. E. Jacobs

Governors
1967–	W. E. Jacobs

ASHANTI

Resident
1896–1902	D. W. Stewart

Chief Commissioners
1902–4	D. W. Stewart
1905–20	F. C. Fuller
1920–3	C. H. Harper
1923–31	J. Maxwell
1931–3	H. S. Newlands
1933–6	F. W. F. Jackson
1936–41	H. C. Stevenson
1941–6	E. G. Hawkesworth
1946–51	C. O. Butler
1951–2	W. H. Beaton

Regional Officers
1952–4	W. H. Beaton
1954–5	A. J. Loveridge
1955–7	A. C. Russell

ASSAM

Commissioners
1896–1902   H. J. S. Cotton
1902–5   J. B. Fuller

EAST BENGAL AND ASSAM

Lieutenant Governors
1905–6   J. B. Fuller
1906–11   L. Hare
1911–12   C. S. Bayley

ASSAM

Chief Commissioners
1912–18   A. Earle
1918–21   N. D. B. Bell

Governors
1921   N. D. B. Bell
1921–2   W. S. Marris
1922–7   J. H. Kerr
1927–32   E. L. L. Hammond
1932–7   M. Keane
1937–42   R. N. Reid
1942–7   A. G. Clow

AUSTRALIA

Governors General
1901–3   J. A. L. Hope, Earl of Hopetoun
1903–4   H. Tennyson, Baron Tennyson
1904–8   H. S. Northcote, Baron Northcote
1908–11   W. H. Ward, Earl of Dudley
1911–14   T. Denman, Baron Denman
1914–20   R. C. M. Ferguson, Viscount Novar
1920–5   H. W. Forster, Baron Forster
1925–30   J. L. Baird, Baron Stonehaven
1931–6   I. A. Isaacs

16

(continued

AUSTRALIA (*continued*)

Governors General

1936–44	A. G. A. Hore-Ruthven, Baron Gowrie
1945–7	Henry William Frederick Albert, Duke of Gloucester
1947–53	W. J. McKell
1953–9	W. J. Slim
1959–61	W. S. Morrison, Viscount Dunrossil
1961–5	W. P. Sidney, Viscount de l'Isle
1965–9	R. G. Casey, Baron Casey
1969–74	P. M. C. Hasluck
1974–	J. Kerr

High Commissioners

1936–41	Sir G. Whiskard
1941–6	Sir R. Cross
1946–52	E. J. Williams
1952–6	Sir S. Holmes
1956–9	P. A. R. Carrington
1959–65	Lieut-Gen. Sir W. Oliver
1965–71	Sir C. Johnston
1971–6	Sir M. James
1976	Sir D. C. Tebbitt

COMMONWEALTH OF THE BAHAMAS

Governors

1898–1904	Sir G. T. Carter
1904–12	Sir W. Grey-Wilson
1912–14	Sir G. B. Haddon-Smith
1914–20	Sir W. L. Allardyce
1920–6	Sir H. E. S. Cordeaux
1926–32	Sir C. W. J. Orr
1932–6	Sir B. E. Clifford
1936–40	Sir C. C. F. Dundas
1940–5	Edward Alfred Christian, Duke of Windsor
1945–50	Sir W. L. Murphy
1950–1	Sir G. R. Sandford
1951–3	Gen. Sir R. A. Neville
1953–6	T. D. Knox, Earl of Ranfurly
1956–60	Sir O. R. Arthur

17

(continued

COMMONWEALTH OF THE BAHAMAS (*continued*)

Governors
1960–4	Sir R. Stapledon
1964–8	Sir R. F. A. Grey
1968–72	Lord Thurlow
1973	Sir J. W. Paul
1973–	M. Butler

High Commissioners
1973–5	C. J. Treadwell
1975–	P. Mennell

BAHRAIN

Political Agents
1900–4	J. C. Gaskin
1904–9	F. B. Prideaux
1909–10	C. F. Mackenzie
1910–11	S. G. Knox
1911–12	D. L. R. Lorimer
1912–14	A. P. Trevor
1914–16	T. H. Keyes
1916–17	T. C. W. Fowle
1917–18	P. G. Loch
1918	G. A. G. Mungavin
1918–19	A. G. Phillips
1919–21	H. R. P. Dickson
1921–6	C. K. Daly
1926–9	C. C. J. Barrett
1929–32	C. G. Prior
1932–7	P. G. Loch
1937	T. Hickinbotham
1937–40	H. Weightman
1940–1	R. G. E. W. Alban
1941–3	E. B. Wakefield
1943–5	T. Hickinbotham
1945–7	E. B. Wakefield
1947–51	C. J. Pelly
1951–2	W. S. Laver

18

(*continued*

BAHRAIN (*continued*)

Political Agents

1952–5	J. W. Wall
1955–9	C. A. Gault
1959–62	E. P. Wiltshire
1962–5	J. P. Tripp
1965–9	A. D. Parsons
1969–71	A. J. Stirling

BALUCHISTAN

Chief Commissioners

1896–1900	H. S. Barnes
1900–4	C. E. Yate
1905–7	A. L. P. Tucker
1907–9	A. H. McMahon
1909–11	C. Archer
1911–17	J. Ramsay
1917–19	H. R. C. Dobbs
1919–22	A. B. Dew
1922–7	F. W. Johnston
1927–31	H. B. St. John
1931–8	A. N. L. Cater
1938–9	A. E. B. Parsons
1939–43	H. A. Metcalfe
1943–6	W. R. Hay
1946	C. G. Prior
1946–7	H. M. Poulton
1947–8	A. D. F. Dundas
1948–9	C. A. G. Savidge

BANGLADESH

High Commissioners

1972–5	A. A. Golds
1975–	B. G. Smallman

19

BARBADOS

Governors

1891–1900	Sir J. S. Hay
1900–4	Sir F. Hodgson
1904–11	Sir G. Carter
1911–18	Sir L. Probyn
1918–25	Sir C. O'Brien
1925–33	Sir W. Robertson
1933	H. S. Newlands
1933–8	Sir M. Young
1938–41	Sir E. J. Waddington
1941–7	Sir G. Bushe
1947–9	Sir H. Blood
1949–53	Sir A. Savage
1953–9	Sir R. Arundell
1959–66	Sir J. Stow

Governors General

1966–7	Sir J. Stow
1967–76	Sir W. Scott
1976–	Sir D. Ward

High Commissioners

1966–71	J. S. Bennett
1971–3	D. A. Roberts
1973–	C. S. Roberts

BELIZE (formerly British Honduras)

Governors

1897–1904	D. Wilson
1904–6	E. B. Sweet-Escott
1906–13	E. J. E. Swayne
1913–18	W. Collet
1918–19	W. H. Bennett
1919–25	E. Hutson
1925–32	J. A. Burdon
1932–4	H. B. Kittermaster
1934–40	A. C. M. Burns

20

(*continued*

BELIZE (*continued*)

Governors

1940–7	J. A. Hunter
1947–8	E. G. Hawkesworth
1948–52	R. H. Garvey
1952–5	P. M. Renison
1955–61	C. H. Thornley
1961–6	P. H. G. Stallard
1966–74	J. W. Paul
1974–6	R. N. Posnett
1976–	P. D. McEntee

BENGAL

Lieutenant Governors

1898–1903	J. Woodburn
1903–8	A. H. L. Fraser
1908–12	E. N. Baker

Governors

1912–17	Baron Carmichael
1917–22	Earl of Ronaldshay
1922–7	V. A. G. R. Bulwer-Lytton, Earl of Lytton
1927–30	F. S. Jackson
1930–2	H. L Stephenson
1932–7	J. Anderson
1937–9	M. H. R. K. Hugesson, Baron Brabourne
1939–44	J. A. Herbert
1944–6	R. G. Casey
1946–7	F. J. Burrows

BERMUDA

Governors

1896–1902	G. D. Barker
1902–4	H. LeG. Geary
1904–7	R. M. Stewart
1907–8	J. H. Wodehouse

21

(*continued*

BERMUDA (*continued*)

Governors

1908–12	F. W. Kitchener
1912–17	G. M. Bullock
1917–22	J. Willcocks
1922–7	J. J. Asser
1927–31	L. J. Bols
1931–6	T. Astley-Cubitt
1936–9	R. J. T. Hildyard
1939–41	D. J. C. K. Bernard
1941–3	F. Knollys
1943–6	D. G. B. Cecil, Marquess of Exeter
1946–9	R. Leatham
1949–55	A. Hood
1955–9	J. D. Wooddall
1959–64	J. A. Gascoine
1964–72	J. R. Robinson, Baron Martonmere
1973	R. Sharples
1973–7	E. H. C. Leather
1977–	P. Ramsbotham

BIHAR

BIHAR AND ORISSA

Lieutenant Governors

1912–15	C. S. Bayley
1915–19	E. A. Gait

Governors

1919–20	E. A. Gait
1920–2	S. P. Sinha, Baron Sinha
1922–7	H. Wheeler
1927–32	H. L. Stephenson
1932–6	J. D. Sifton

22

(*continued*

BIHAR

Governors

1936–7	J. D. Sifton
1937–9	M. G. Hallett
1939–43	T. A. Stewart
1943–6	T. G. Rutherford
1946–7	H. Dow

BOMBAY

Governors

1899–1903	H. S. Northcote
1903–7	C. W. C. Baillie, Baron Lamington
1907–13	G. S. Clarke, Baron Sydenham
1913–18	F. Freeman-Thomas, Marquess of Willingdon
1918–23	G. A. Lloyd, Baron Lloyd
1923–8	L. O. Wilson
1928–33	F. H. Sykes
1933–7	M. H. R. K. Hugesson, Baron Brabourne
1937–43	L. R. Lumley, Earl of Scarbrough
1943–7	D. J. Colville

BOTSWANA (formerly Bechuanaland)

Commissioners

1897–1901	H. J. Goold-Adams
1901–6	R. C. Williams
1907–16	F. W. Panzera
1916–17	E. C. F. Garraway
1917–23	J. C. Macgregor
1923–7	J. Ellenberger
1928–30	R. M. Daniel
1930–7	C. F. Rey
1937–42	C. N. Arden-Clarke
1942–6	A. D. F. Thompson
1946–50	A. Sillery
1950–3	E. B. Beetham

23

(continued

BOTSWANA (*continued*)

Commissioners
1953–5	W. F. MacKenzie
1955–9	M. O. Wray
1959–65	R. P. Fawcus
1965–6	H. S. Norman-Walker

High Commissioners
1966–9	J. S. Gandee
1969–73	G. D. Anderson
1973–	Miss E. J. Emery

BRITISH INDIAN OCEAN TERRITORY

Commissioners
1965–6	J. E. Asquith, Earl of Oxford and Asquith
1966	H. S. Norman-Walker

BRITISH NEW GUINEA

Administrators
1914–15	W. Holmes
1915–17	S. A. Pethebridge
1917–18	S. S. Mackenzie
1918–20	G. J. Johnston
1920–1	T. Griffiths
1921–33	E. A. Wisdom
1933–4	T. Griffiths
1934–42	W. R. McNicoll
1942–5	(under Japan)

24

(*continued*

PAPUA NEW GUINEA

Administrators

1945–52	J. K. Murray
1952–67	D. M. Cleland
1967–	D. O. Hay

BRITISH NORTH BORNEO

Governors

1895–1900	L. P. Beaufort
1900–1	H. Clifford
1901–4	E. W. Birch
1904–12	E. P. Gueritz
1912–15	C. W. C. Parr
1915–22	A. C. Pearson
1922–5	W. H. Rycroft
1925–6	A. C. Pearson
1926–9	J. L. Humphreys
1929–33	A. F. Richards
1933–7	D. J. Jardine
1937–42	C. R. Smith
1942–5	(under Japan)
1946–9	E. F. Twining
1949–54	H. R. Hone
1954–60	R. E. Turnbull
1960–3	W. A. C. Goode

BRITISH SOMALILAND

Consuls General

1898–1901	J. H. Sadler
1902–5	E. J. E. Swayne

Administrators

1905–10	H. E. S. Cordeaux
1910–11	W. H. Manning
1911–14	H. A. Byatt

Commissioner

1914–19	G. F. Archer

25

(*continued*

BRITISH SOMALILAND (*continued*)

Governors

1919–22	G. F. Archer
1922–6	G. H. Summers
1926–32	H. B. Kittermaster
1932–9	A. S. Lawrance
1939–41	V. G. Glenday
1941–3	A. R. Chater
1943–8	G. T. Fisher
1948–54	G. Reece
1954–9	T. O. Pike
1959–60	D. B. Hall

BRUNEI

Residents

1906–7	M. S. H. McArthur
1907–8	H. Chevallier
1908	M. S. H. McArthur
1908–9	J. F. Owen
1909–13	H. Chevallier
1913–15	F. W. Douglas
1915–16	E. B. Maundrell
1916–21	G. E. Cator
1921–3	L. A. Allen
1923–6	E. E. F. Pretty
1926–7	O. E. Venables
1927–8	E. E. F. Pretty
1928–31	P. A. B. McKerron
1931–4	T. F. Carey
1934–7	R. E. Turnbull
1937–40	J. G. Black
1940–1	E. E. Pengilly
1941–5	(under Japan)
1946–8	W. J. Peel
1948–51	E. E. F. Pretty
1951–4	J. C. H. Barcroft
1954–8	J. O. Gilbert
1958–9	D. C. White

(*continued*

BRUNEI (*continued*)

High Commissioners

1959–63	D. C. White
1963	A. M. Mackintosh
1963–5	E. O. Laird
1965–8	F. D. Webber
1968–72	A. R. Adair
1972–5	P. Gautrey
1975–	J. A. Davidson

BURMA

Lieutenant Governors

1897–1903	F. W. R. Fryer
1903–5	H. S. Barnes
1905–10	H. T. White
1910–15	H. Adamson
1915–18	S. H. Butler
1918–23	R. H. Craddock

Governors

1923–7	S. H. Butler
1927–33	C. A. Innes
1933–6	H. L. Stephenson
1936–41	A. C. Douglas
1941–2	R. H. Dorman-Smith
1942–5	(under Japan)
1945–6	R. H. Dorman-Smith
1946	H. F. Knight
1946–8	H. E. Rance

CANADA

Governors General

1898–1904	G. J. Elliot-Murray-Kynynmond, Earl of Minto
1904–11	A. H. G. Grey, Earl Grey
1911–16	A. W. P. Albert, Duke of Connaught

27

(*continued*

CANADA (*continued*)

Governors General

1916–21	V. C. Cavendish, Duke of Devonshire
1921–6	J. H. G. Byng, Baron Byng
1926–31	F. Freeman-Thomas, Marquess of Willingdon
1931–5	V. B. Ponsonby, Earl of Bessborough
1935–40	J. Buchan, Baron Tweedsmuir
1940–6	A. A. Cambridge, Earl of Athlone
1946–52	H. R. L. G. Alexander, Viscount Alexander
1952–9	V. Massey
1959–67	G. P. Vanier
1967–74	D. R. Michener
1974–	J. Léger

High Commissioners

1928–35	Sir W. Clark
1935–8	Sir F. Floud
1938–41	Sir G. Campbell
1941–6	M. MacDonald
1946–52	Sir A. Clutterbuck
1952–6	Sir A. Nye
1956–61	Sir S. Garner
1961–3	D. Heathcoat-Amory
1963–8	Sir H. Lintott
1968–70	Sir C. Crowe
1970–4	P. T. Hayman
1974–	Sir J. Johnston

CAPE COLONY

Governors/High Commissioners

1897–1900	A. Milner, Viscount Milner

Governors

1900–1	A. Milner, Viscount Milner
1901–10	W. F. Hely-Hutchinson

CAYMAN ISLANDS

Commissioners

1900–6	F. S. Sanguinetti
1906–7	C. H. Y. Slader
1907–13	G. S. S. Hirst
1913–16	A. C. Robinson
1916–19	C. E. Mellish
1919–29	H. H. Hutchings
1929–31	G. H. Frith
1931–4	E. A. Weston
1934–41	A. W. Cardinall
1941–6	J. P. Jones
1946–52	I. O. Smith
1952–6	A. M. Gerrard
1956–8	A. H. Donald

Administrators

1958–60	A. H. Donald
1960–4	J. Rese
1964–8	J. A. Cumber
1968–71	A. C. E. Long
1971–4	K. R. Crook
1974–	T. Russell

CENTRAL PROVINCES AND BERAR

Chief Commissioners

1898–1902	D. C. J. Ibbetson
1902	A. H. L. Fraser
1902–4	J. P. Hewett
1904–5	F. S. P. Lely
1905–6	J. O. Miller
1906–7	S. Ismay
1907–12	R. H. Craddock
1912–19	B. Robertson
1919–21	F. G. Sly

Lieutenant Governors

1921–5	F. G. Sly
1925–33	M. S. D. Butler
1933–8	H. C. Gowan

29

(continued

CENTRAL PROVINCES AND BERAR (*continued*)

Lieutenant Governors
1938	H. Bomford
1938–40	F. V. Wylie
1940–6	H. J. Twynam
1946–7	F. C. Bourne

COOK ISLANDS

Residents
1898–1901	W. E. Gudgeon

Resident Commissioners
1901–9	W. E. Gudgeon
1909–13	J. E. Smith
1913–16	H. W. Northcroft
1916–21	F. W. Platts
1921–3	J. G. L. Hewitt
1923–37	H. F. Ayson
1937–8	S. J. Smith
1938–43	H. F. Ayson
1943–51	W. Tailby
1951–60	G. Nevill
1960–5	A. O. Dare

High Commissioners
1965	A. O. Dare
1965–	L. J. Davis

COORG

Chief Commissioners
1896–1903	D. Robertson
1903–5	J. A. Bourdillon
1905–10	S. M. Fraser
1910–16	H. Daly
1916–20	H. V. Cobb

(*continued*

COORG (*continued*)

Chief Commissioners

1920–5	W. P. Barton
1925–30	S. E. Pears
1930–3	R. J. C. Burke
1933–7	C. T. C. Plowden
1937–40	J. D. Gordon
1940–3	J. W. Pritchard
1943–7	B. Chengappa

CYPRUS

High Commissioners

1898–1904	W. F. H: Smith
1904–11	C. A. King-Harman
1911–15	H. J. Goold-Adams
1915–20	J. E. Clauson
1920–5	M. Stevenson

Governors

1925–6	M. Stevenson
1926–32	R. Storrs
1932–3	R. E. Stubbs
1933–9	H. R. Palmer
1939–41	W. D. Battershill
1941–6	C. C. Woolley
1946–9	R. T. H. Fletcher, Baron Winster
1949–53	A. B. Wright
1953–5	R. P. Armitage
1955–8	J. Harding
1958–60	H. M. Foot

Representative

1960	W. A. W. Clark

Counsellor

1960	I. F. Porter

31

(*continued*

CYPRUS (*continued*)

High Commissioners

1961–4	W. A. W. Clark
1964–5	Maj.-Gen. W. H. A. Bishop
1965–7	Sir D. Hunt
1967–9	Sir N. Costar
1969–71	P. E. Ramsbotham
1971–3	R. H. G. Edmonds
1973–5	S. J. L. Olver
1975–	D. McD. Gordon

DELHI

Chief Commissioners

1912–18	W. M. Hailey
1918–24	C. A. Barron
1924–6	E. R. Abbott
1926–8	A. M. Stow
1928–32	J. P. Thompson
1932–7	J. N. G. Johnson
1937–40	E. M. Jenkins
1940–5	A. V. Askwith
1945–7	W. Christie

DOMINICA

Administrators

1899–1905	H. H. J. Bell
1905–13	W. D. Young
1914	E. R. Drayton
1915–19	A. W. Mahaffy
1919–23	R. Walter
1923–30	E. C. Eliot
1931–3	W. A. Bowring
1933–7	H. B. Popham
1938–45	J. S. Neill
1946–52	E. P. Arrowsmith
1952–9	H. L. Lindo
1959–67	A. Lovelace

(continued

DOMINICA (*continued*)

Governors
1967	G. C. Guy
1967–	L. Cools-Lartigue

EGYPT

Residents/Consuls General
1883–1907	E. Baring, Baron Cromer
1907–11	J. E. Gorst
1911–14	H. H. Kitchener, Earl Kitchener

High Commissioners
1914	M. Chatham
1914–16	A. H. MacMahon
1916–19	F. R. Wingate
1919–22	E. H. H. Allenby, Viscount Allenby

FALKLAND ISLANDS

Governors
1897–1904	W. Grey-Wilson
1904–15	W. L. Allardyce
1915–20	W. D. Young
1920–7	J. Middleton
1927–31	A. M. Hodson
1931–5	J. O'Grady
1935–41	H. H. Heaton
1941–6	A. W. Cardinall
1946–54	G. M. Clifford
1954–7	O. R. Arthur
1957–64	E. P. Arrowsmith
1964–70	C. D. T. Haskard
1971–5	E. G. Lewis
1975–6	N. A. I. French
1976–	J. R. W. Parker

33

FEDERATED MALAY STATES

Residents General

1896–1904	F. A. Swettenham
1904–10	W. T. Taylor
1910–11	A. H. Young

Chief Secretaries

1911–20	E. L. Brockman
1920–6	W. G. Maxwell
1926–30	W. Peel
1930–2	C. W. H. Cochrane
1932–4	A. Caldecott
1934–5	M. B. Shelley
1935–6	M. Rex

Federal Secretaries

1936–9	C. D. Ahearne
1939–42	H. Fraser

High Commissioners

1963	Sir G. Tory
1963–6	A. H. Head
1966–71	Sir M. Walker
1971–4	Sir J. Johnston
1974–	Sir E. Norris

FIJI

Governors

1897–1902	G. T. M. O'Brien
1902–4	H. M. Jackson
1904–11	E. F. Im Thurn
1911–12	F. H. May
1912–18	E. B. Sweet-Escott
1918–25	C. H. Rodwell

34

(continued

FIJI (*continued*)

Governors

1925–9	E. Hutson
1929–35	A. M. Fletcher
1936–8	A. F. Richards
1938–42	H. C. J. Luke
1942–5	P. E. Mitchell
1945–8	A. W. Grantham
1948–52	L. B. Freeston
1952–8	R. H. Garvey
1958–63	K. P. Maddocks
1963–8	F. D. Jakeway
1968–	R. S. Foster

Governor General

1973	Ratu Sir G. Cakobau

High Commissioners

1970–4	J. R. Williams
1974–	J. S. Arthur

THE GAMBIA

Administrators

1891–1900	R. B. Llewelyn
1900–1	G. C. Denton

Governors

1901–11	G. C. Denton
1911–14	H. L. Gallwey
1914–20	E. J. Cameron
1920–7	C. H. Armitage
1927–8	J. Middleton
1928–30	E. B. Denham
1930–3	H. R. Palmer
1933–6	A. F. Richards
1936–42	W. T. Southorn
1942–7	H. R. Blood
1947–9	A. B. Wright

35

(continued

THE GAMBIA (*continued*)

Governors

1949–58	P. Wyn-Harris
1958–62	E. H. Windley
1962–5	J. W. Paul

Governors General

1965–6	J. W. Paul
1966–	F. M. Singhateh

High Commissioners

1965–8	G. E. Crombie
1968–72	J. G. W. Ramage
1972–5	J. R. W. Parker
1975–	M. H. G. Rogers

GHANA (formerly Gold Coast)

Governors

1897–1900	F. M. Hodgson
1900–4	M. Nathan
1904–10	J. P. Rodger
1910–12	J. J. Thorburn
1912–19	H. Clifford
1919–27	F. G. Guggisberg
1927–32	A. R. Slater
1932–4	T. S. W. Thomas
1934–41	A. W. Hodson
1941–8	A. C. M. Burns
1948–9	G. H. Creasy
1949–57	C. N. Arden-Clarke

(*continued*

GHANA

Governor General
1957–60   W. F. Hare, Earl of Listowel

High Commissioners
1957–9	Sir I. Maclennan
1959–61	A. W. Snelling
1961–4	Sir G. de Freitas
1964–7	H. Smedley
1967–70	H. K. Matthews
1970–5	H. S. H. Stanley
1975–	F. Mills

GIBRALTAR

Governors

1893–1900	R. Biddulph
1900–5	G. S. White
1905–10	F. W. E. Forestier-Walker
1910–13	A. Hunter
1913–18	H. S. G. Miles
1918–23	H. L. Smith-Dorrien
1923–8	C. C. Monro
1928–33	A. J. Godley
1933–8	C. H. Harington
1938–9	E. Ironside
1939–41	C. Liddell
1941–2	J. S. S. P. Vereker, Viscount Gort
1942–4	N. Mason-Macfarlane
1944–7	R. Eastwood
1947–52	K. A. Anderson
1952–5	G. H. MacMillan
1955–8	H. Redman
1958–62	C. F. Keightley
1962–5	A. D. Ward

(continued

GIBRALTAR (*continued*)

Governors

1965–9	G. W. Lathbury
1969–73	V. C. Begg
1973–	J. Grandy

GILBERT AND ELLICE ISLANDS

Resident Commissioners

1892–1901	C. R. Swayne
1901–9	W. T. Campbell
1909–13	J. Q. Dickson
1913–21	E. C. Eliot
1921–6	H. R. McClure
1926–33	A. F. Grimble
1933–41	J. C. Barley
1941–6	V. Fox-Strangways
1946–9	H. E. Maude
1949–52	W. J. Peel
1952–61	M. L. Bernacchi
1961–	V. J. Andersen

GOLD COAST, NORTHERN TERRITORIES

Chief Commissioners

1899–1904	A. H. Morris
1905–10	A. E. G. Watherston
1910–20	C. H. Armitage
1921–4	A. J. Philbrick
1924–30	A. H. C. Walker-Leigh
1930–3	F. W. F. Jackson
1933–42	W. J. A. Jones
1942–6	G. H. Gibbs
1947–8	W. H. Ingrams
1948–50	E. N. Jones
1950–3	G. N. Burden

38

(*continued*

GOLD COAST, NORTHERN TERRITORIES (*continued*)

Regional Officers
1953–4   A. J. Loveridge
1954–7   S. MacDonald-Smith

GOLD COAST COLONY

Chief Commissioners
1945–50   T. R. O. Mangin
1950–3   A. J. Loveridge

GRENADA

Administrators
1892–1915   E. R. Drayton
1915–30   H. Ferguson
1930–5   H. R. R. Blood
1935–40   W. L. Heape
1940–2   C. H. V. Talbot
1942–51   G. C. Green
1951–7   W. Macmillan
1957–62   J. M. Lloyd
1962–4   L. A. Pinard
1964–7   I. G. Turbott

Governors
1967–8   I. G. Turbott
1968–74   H. L. Bynoe
1974   L. V. de Gale

High Commissioner
1974–   C. E. Diggines

39

GUYANA (formerly British Guiana)

Governors

1898–1901	W. J. Sendall
1901–4	J. A. Swettenham
1904–12	F. M. Hodgson
1912–17	W. Egerton
1918–23	W. Collet
1923–5	G. Thomson
1925–8	C. H. Rodwell
1928–30	F. G. Guggisberg
1930–5	E. B. Denham
1935–7	G. A. Northcote
1937–41	W. E. Jackson
1941–7	G. J. Lethem
1947–53	C. C. Woolley
1953–5	A. W. L. Savage
1955–9	P. M. Renison
1959–64	R. F. A. Grey
1964–6	R. E. Luyt

GUYANA

Governors General

1966	R. E. Luyt
1966–9	D. J. G. Rose
1969–70	E. Luckhoo (Acting)

High Commissioners

1966–7	T. L. Crosthwaite
1967–70	K. G. Ritchie
1970–5	W. S. Bates
1975–	P. Gautrey

HONG KONG

Governors

1898–1903	H. A. Blake
1904–7	M. Nathan

40

(continued

HONG KONG (*continued*)

Governors
1907–12	F. J. D. Lugard
1912–19	F. H. May
1919–25	R. E. Stubbs
1925–30	C. Clementi
1930–5	W. Peel
1935–7	A. Caldecott
1937–40	G. A. Northcote
1940–1	E. F. Norton
1941	M. A. Young

Governor (under Japan)
1941–5	R. Isogai

Governors (under Great Britain)
1945–7	M. A. Young
1948–58	A. W. Grantham
1958–64	R. B. Black
1964–71	D. C. C. Trench
1971–	C. M. MacLehose

INDIA

Viceroys
1899–1905	G. N. Curzon, Marquess Curzon
1905–10	G. J. Elliot-Murray-Kynynmond, Earl of Minto
1910–16	C. Hardinge, Baron Hardinge
1916–21	F. J. N. Thesiger, Baron Chelmsford
1921–6	R. D. Isaacs, Marquess of Reading
1926–31	E. F. L. Wood-Halifax, Baron Irwin
1931–6	F. Freeman-Thomas, Marquess of Willingdon
1936–43	V. A. Hope, Marquess of Linlithgow
1943–7	A. P. Wavell, Viscount Wavell
1947	L. F. Mountbatten, Earl Mountbatten

Governors General
1947–8	L. F. Mountbatten, Earl Mountbatten
1948–50	C. Rajagopalachari

41

(*continued*

INDIA (*continued*)

Presidents

1948–50	C. Rajagopalachari
1950–62	R. Prasad
1962–7	S. Radakrishnan
1967–9	Z. Hussain
1969–74	V. V. Giri
1974–7	F. A. Ahmed
1977–	N. S. Reddy

High Commissioners

1946–8	Sir T. Shone
1948–52	Lt.-Gen. Sir A. Nye
1952–5	Sir A. Clutterbuck
1955–60	M. MacDonald
1960–5	Sir P. Gore-Booth
1965–8	J. Freeman
1968–71	Sir M. James
1971–3	Sir T. Garvey
1973–6	Sir M. Walker
1977–	Sir J. A. Thompson

IRAQ

MESOPOTAMIA

Civil Commissioners

1914–17	P. Z. Cox
1917–20	A. T. Wilson

IRAQ

High Commissioners

1920–3	P. Z. Cox
1923–8	H. R. C. Dobbs
1928–9	G. F. Clayton
1929–32	F. H. Humphrys

IRISH FREE STATE

Governors General

1922–8	T. M. Healy
1928–32	J. McNeill
1932–6	D. Ua Buachalla (D. Buckley)

JAMAICA

Governors

1898–1904	A. W. L. Hemming
1904–7	J. A. Swettenham
1907–13	S. H. Olivier
1913–18	W. H. Manning
1918–24	L. Probyn
1924–6	S. H. Wilson
1926–32	R. E. Stubbs
1932–4	A. R. Slater
1934–8	E. B. Denham
1938–43	A. F. Richards
1943–51	J. Huggins
1951–7	H. M. Foot
1957–62	K. W. Blackburne

Governors General

1962	K. W. Blackburne
1962–73	C. C. Campbell
1973–	F. Glasspole

High Commissioners

1962–5	Sir A. Morley
1965–70	J. D. Murray
1970–3	E. N. Larmour
1973–	J. D. Hennings

KENYA

BRITISH EAST AFRICA

Commissioners

1896–1900	A. H. Hardinge
1900–4	C. N. E. Eliot
1904–5	D. W. Stewart
1905–6	J. H. Sadler

Governors

1906–9	J. H. Sadler
1909–12	E. P. C. Girouard
1912–19	H. C. Belfield
1919–20	E. Northey

KENYA

Governors

1920–2	E. Northey
1922–5	R. T. Coryndon
1925–31	E. M. Grigg
1931–7	J. A. Byrne
1937–40	H. R. Brooke-Popham
1940–4	H. Monck-Mason Moore
1944–52	P. E. Mitchell
1952–7	E. Baring
1957–9	F. Crawford
1959–63	P. M. Renison
1963–4	M. J. MacDonald

Representative

1963	H. S. H. Stanley

High Commissioners

1963–5	Sir G. de Freitas
1965–6	M. J. MacDonald
1966–8	Sir E. Peck
1968–72	E. G. Norris
1972–5	A. A. Duff
1975–	S. J. G. Fingland

KUWAIT

Political Agents

1904–9	S. G. Knox
1909–15	W. H. I. Shakespear
1915–16	W. G. Grey
1916–18	R. E. A. Hamilton
1918	P. G. Loch
1918–20	D. V. MacCollum
1920–30	J. C. More
1930–6	H. R. P. Dickson
1936–9	G. S. H. DeGaury
1939–41	A. C. Galloway
1941–3	T. Hickinbotham
1943–5	M. O. Tandy
1945–7	A. C. Galloway
1947–51	H. G. Jakins
1951–5	C. J. Pelly
1955–7	G. W. Bell
1957–9	A. S. Halford
1959–61	J. C. B. Richmond

LEEWARD ISLANDS

Governors

1895–1901	F. Fleming
1901–2	H. M. Jackson
1902–4	G. Strickland
1904–6	C. C. Knollys
1906–12	E. B. Sweet-Escott
1912–16	H. H. J. Bell
1916–21	E. M. Merewether
1921–9	E. E. Twisleton-Wykeham-Fiennes
1929–36	T. R. St Johnston
1936–41	G. J. Lethem
1941–3	D. J. Jardine
1943–8	L. B. Freeston
1948–50	O. R. Baldwin, Earl Baldwin
1950–7	K. W. Blackburne
1957–60	A. T. Williams

LESOTHO (formerly Basutoland)

Resident Commissioners

1893–1901	G. Y. Lagden
1901–15	H. C. Sloley
1916–17	R. T. Coryndon
1917–26	E. C. F. Garraway
1926–35	J. C. R. Sturrock
1935–42	E. C. S. Richards
1942–6	C. N. Arden-Clarke
1947–51	A. D. F. Thompson
1951–5	E. P. Arrowsmith
1955–61	A. G. T. Chaplin
1961–6	A. F. Giles

High Commissioners

1966–70	I. B. Watt
1970–3	H. G. M. Bass
1973–6	M. J. Moynihan
1976–	R. H. Hobden

MADRAS

Governors

1896–1901	A. E. Havelock
1901–6	O. A. V. Russell, Baron Ampthill
1906–11	A. Lawley
1911–12	T. D. Gibson-Carmichael, Baron Carmichael
1912–19	J. Sinclair, Baron Pentland
1919–24	F. Freeman-Thomas, Marquess of Willingdon
1924–9	G. J. Goschen, Viscount Goschen
1929–34	G. F. Stanley
1934–40	T. W. Erskine, Viscount Erskine
1940–6	A. O. J. Hope, Baron Rankeillour
1946–7	A. E. Nye

MALAWI (formerly Nyasaland)

Commissioners/Consuls-General
1896–1907   A. Sharpe

Governors
1907–10   A. Sharpe
1911–13   W. H. Manning
1913–23   G. Smith
1923–9   C. C. Bowring
1929–32   T. S. Whitelegge Thomas
1932–4   H. W. Young
1934–9   H. B. Kittermaster
1939–42   H. C. D. C. Mackenzie-Kennedy
1942–7   E. C. S. Richards
1948–56   G. F. T. Colby
1956–61   R. P. Armitage
1961–6   G. S. Jones

High Commissioners
1964–7   D. L. Cole
1967–71   T. S. Tull
1971–3   W. R. Haydon
1973–   K. G. Ritchie

MALAYA/MALAYSIA

High Commissioners
1946–8   G. E. J. Gent
1948–51   H. L. G. Gurney
1952–4   G. W. R. Templer
1954–7   D. C. McGillivray
1957–63   G. W. Tory
1963–6   A. H. Head
1966–71   M. Walker
1971–4   J. B. Johnston
1974–   E. G. Norris

Governor General
1946–8   M. J. McDonald

47

MALTA

Governors

1899–1903	F. W. Grenfell, Baron Grenfell
1903–7	C. M. Clarke
1907–9	H. F. Grant
1909–15	H. M. L. Rundle
1915–19	P. S. Methuen, Baron Methuen
1919–24	H. C. Plumer, Baron Plumer
1924–7	W. N. Congreve
1927–31	J. P. DuCane
1931–6	D. G. Campbell
1936–40	C. Bonham-Carter
1940–2	W. G. Dobbie
1942–4	J. S. S. P. Vereker, Viscount Gort
1944–6	E. C. Screiber
1946–9	F. C. Douglas
1949–54	G. H. Creasy
1954–9	R. E. Laycock
1959–62	G. Grantham
1962–4	M. H. Dorman

Governors General

1964–71	M. H. Dorman
1971–4	A. Mamo

High Commissioners

1964–5	Sir E. Wakefield
1965–7	Sir J. Martin
1967–70	Sir G. Tory
1970–2	Sir D. Watson
1972–4	J. O. Moreton
1974–6	W. R. Haydon
1976–	N. Aspin

MAURITIUS

Governors

1897–1903	C. Bruce
1904–11	C. Boyle

48

(continued

MAURITIUS (*continued*)

Governors

1911–16	J. R. Chancellor
1916–25	H. H. J. Bell
1925–30	H. J. Read
1930–7	W. E. Jackson
1937–42	B. E. Clifford
1942–9	H. C. D. C. Mackenzie-Kennedy
1949–53	H. R. R. Blood
1953–9	R. Scott
1959–62	C. M. Deverell
1962–8	J. S. Rennie

Governors General

1968	J. S. Rennie
1968–	A. L. Williams

High Commissioners

1968–70	A. Wooller
1970–3	P. A. Carter
1973–	A. H. Brind

MONTSERRAT

Commissioners

1889–1900	E. Baynes
1900–6	F. H. Watkins
1906–18	W. B. Davidson-Houston
1918–22	C. F. Condell
1922–9	H. W. Peebles
1929–32	H. H. Hutchings
1932–46	T. E. P. Haynes
1946–9	H. Burrowes
1949–56	C. Ross

Administrators

1956–60	A. F. Dawkins
1960–4	D. A. Wiles
1964–71	D. R. Gibbs
1971–4	W. H. Thompson
1974–6	N. D. Matthews
1977–	G. W. Jones

49

(*continued*

MONTSERRAT (*continued*)

Governor
1974   W. H. Thompson

NATAL

Governors
1893–1901   W. F. Hely-Hutchinson
1901–7   H. E. McCallum
1907–9   M. Nathan
1909–10   P. S. Methuen, Baron Methuen

NAURU

Administrators
1921–7   T. Griffiths
1927–33   W. A. Newman
1933–8   R. C. Garsia
1938–42   F. R. Chalmers
1942–5   (under Japan)
1945–9   M. Ridgway
1949   H. H. Reeve
1949–53   R. S. Richards
1953–4   J. K. Lawrence
1954–8   R. S. Leydin
1958–62   J. P. White
1962–6   R. S. Leydin
1966–8   L. D. King

NEWFOUNDLAND

Governors
1898–1901   H. E. McCallum
1901–4   C. Boyle
1904–9   W. Macgregor

50

(*continued*

NEW FOUNDLAND (*continued*)

Governors

1909–13	R. C. Williams
1913–17	W. E. Davidson
1917–22	C. A. Harris
1922–8	W. L. Allardyce
1928–32	J. Middleton
1933–5	D. M. Anderson
1936–46	H. T. Walwyn
1946–9	G. Macdonald

NEW HEBRIDES CONDOMINIUM

Resident Commissioners

1902–7	E. G. Rason
1907–24	M. King
1924–7	G. W. B. Smith-Rewse
1927–40	G. A. Joy
1940–50	R. D. Blandy
1950–5	H. J. M. Flaxman
1955–62	J. S. Rennie
1962–6	A. M. Wilkie
1966–	C. H. Allan

NEW ZEALAND

Governors

1897–1904	U. M. J. Knox, Earl of Ranfurly
1904–10	W. L. Plunket, Baron Plunket
1910–12	J. P. Dickson-Poynder, Baron Islington
1912–17	A. W. D. S. Foljambe, Earl of Liverpool

Governors General

1917–20	A. W. D. S. Foljambe, Earl of Liverpool
1920–4	J. R. Jellicoe, Earl Jellicoe
1924–30	C. Fergusson
1930–5	C. Bathurst, Viscount Bledisloe

51

(*continued*

NEW ZEALAND (*continued*)

Governors General

1935–41	G. V. A. Monckton-Arundell, Viscount Galway
1941–5	C. L. N. Newall, Viscount Newall
1945–52	B. C. Freyberg
1952–7	C. W. M. Norrie, Baron Norrie
1957–62	C. J. Lyttelton, Viscount Cobham
1962–7	B. E. Fergusson
1967–72	A. E. Porritt
1972–77	D. Blundell
1977–	K. Holyoake

High Commissioners

1939–45	Sir H. Batterbee
1945–9	Sir P. Duff
1949–53	Sir R. Price
1953–7	Gen. Sir G. Scoones
1957–9	H. G. C. Mallaby
1959–64	F. E. Cumming-Bruce
1964–9	Sir I. Maclennan
1969–73	Sir A. Galsworthy
1973–6	D. A. Scott
1976	H. Smedley

NIGERIA

LAGOS

Governors

1899–1904	W. Macgregor
1904–6	W. Egerton

NIGER COAST PROTECTORATE

Commissioner

1896–1900	R. D. R. Moor

SOUTHERN NIGERIA

High Commissioners

1900–4	R. D. R. Moor
1904–12	W. Egerton
1912–14	F. J. D. Lugard

(continued

NORTHERN NIGERIA

High Commissioners

1900–7	F. J. D. Lugard
1907–9	E. P. C. Girouard
1909–12	H. H. J. Bell
1912–14	F. J. D. Lugard

NIGERIA

Governors

1914–19	F. J. D. Lugard
1919–25	H. Clifford
1925–31	G. Thomson
1931–5	D. C. Cameron
1935–42	B. H. Bourdillon
1942–3	A. C. M. Burns
1943–8	A. F. Richards
1948–54	J. S. Macpherson

Governors General

1954–5	J. S. Macpherson
1955–60	J. Robertson
1960–3	N. Azikiwe

NIGERIA, SOUTHERN PROVINCES

Lieutenant Governors

1914–20	A. G. Boyle
1920–5	H. C. Moorhouse
1925–9	U. F. Ruxton
1929–30	C. W. Alexander
1930–5	W. Buchanan-Smith

Chief Commissioner

1935–9	W. E. Hunt

NIGERIA, NORTHERN REGION

Lieutenant Governors

1914–17	C. L. Temple
1917–21	H. S. Goldsmith
1921–5	W. F. Gowers
1925–30	H. R. Palmer
1930–2	C. W. Alexander

53

(continued

NIGERIA (*continued*)

Chief Commissioners

1933–7	G. S. Browne
1937–43	T. S. Adams
1943–7	J. R. Patterson
1948–51	E. W. Thompstone

Lieutenant Governors

1951–2	E. W. Thompstone
1952–4	B. E. Sharwood-Smith

Governors

1954–7	B. E. Sharwood-Smith
1957–62	G. W. Bell

NIGERIA, EASTERN REGION

Chief Commissioners

1939–43	G. G. Shute
1943–8	F. B. Carr
1948–51	J. G. Pyke-Nott

Lieutenant Governors

1951–2	J. G. Pyke-Nott
1952–4	C. J. Pleass

Governors

1954–6	C. J. Pleass
1956–60	R. de Stapledon

NIGERIA, WESTERN REGION

Chief Commissioners

1939–46	G. C. Whiteley
1946–51	T. C. Hoskyns-Abrahall

Lieutenant Governors

1951	T. C. Hoskyns-Abrahall
1951–4	H. F. Marshall

Governor

1954–60	J. D. Rankine

(continued

NIGERIA (*continued*)

High Commissioners

1960–4	A. H. Head
1964–7	Sir F. Cumming-Bruce
1967–9	Sir D. Hunt
1969–71	Sir L. Glass
1971–4	Sir C. Pickard
1974–6	Sir M. Le Quesne
1976	Sir S. Falle

NIUE

Resident Commissioners

1901–2	S. P. Smith
1902–7	C. F. Maxwell
1907–18	H. G. Cornwall
1918–20	G. N. Morris
1920–2	J. C. Murray Evison
1922–6	G. N. Morris
1926–31	A. A. Luckham
1931–42	W. M. Bell
1942–3	J. P. McMahon-Box
1943–53	C. H. W. Larsen
1953–6	J. M. McEwen
1956–8	A. O. Dare
1958–62	D. W. R. Heatley
1962–8	L. A. Shanks
1968–	S. D. Wilson

NORFOLK ISLAND

Administrators

1898–1903	C. M. King
1903–7	W. Drake
1907–13	C. S. Elliot

(continued

NORFOLK ISLAND (*continued*)

Administrators

1913—20	M. V. Murphy
1920—4	J. W. Parnell
1924—6	E. T. Leane
1926	H. S. Edgar
1926—7	M. V. Murphy
1927—8	V. C. M. Sellheim
1928	H. S. Edgar
1928—9	C. E. Herbert
1929—32	A. J. Bennett
1932—7	C. R. Pinney
1937—46	C. Rosenthal
1946—53	A. Wilson
1953—8	C. H. B. Norman
1958—62	R. S. Leydin
1962—4	R. H. Wordsworth
1964—6	R. B. Nott
1966—8	R. Marsh
1968—	R. N. Dalkin

NORTH-WEST FRONTIER PROVINCE

Chief Commissioners

1901—8	H. A. Deane
1908—19	G. O. Roos-Keppel
1919—21	A. H. Grant
1921—4	J. L. Maffey
1924—30	H. N. Bolton
1930—1	S. E. Pears
1931—2	R. E. H. Griffith

Governors

1932—7	R. E. H. Griffith
1937—46	G. Cunningham
1946—7	O. K. Caroe
1947—8	G. Cunningham
1948—9	A. D. F. Dundas

ORANGE RIVER COLONY

Governors
1902–5	A. Milner, Viscount Milner
1905–7	W. W. Palmer, Earl of Selborne
1907–10	H. J. Goold-Adams

Lieutenant Governor
1901–7	H. J. Goold-Adams

ORISSA

Governors
1936–41	J. A. Hubback
1941–6	W. H. Lewis
1946–7	C. M. Trivedi

PALESTINE

High Commissioners
1920–5	H. L. Samuel
1925–8	H. C. O. Plumer
1928–31	J. R. Chancellor
1931–8	A. G. Wauchope
1938–44	H. A. MacMichael
1944–6	J. S. S. P. Vereker, Viscount Gort
1946–8	A. G. Cunningham

PAPUA

Lieutenant Governors
1898–1903	G. R. LeHunte
1903–4	C. S. Robinson
1904–7	F. R. Barton
1907–40	J. H. P. Murray

(continued

PAPUA (*continued*)

Administrators
1940–2   H. L. Murray
1942–5   B. M. Morris

PAPUA NEW GUINEA

Administrators
1945–52   J. K. Murray
1952–67   D. M. Cleland
1967–   D. O. Hay

PERSIAN GULF

Chief Political Residents
1897–1900   M. J. Meade
1900–4   C. A. Kemball
1904–20   P. Z. Cox
1920–4   A. P. Trevor
1924–7   F. B. Prideaux
1927–9   L. B. H. Haworth
1929   C. C. J. Barrett
1929–32   H. V. Biscoe
1932–9   T. C. W. Fowle
1939–46   C. G. Prior
1946–53   W. R. Hay
1953–8   B. A. B. Burrows
1958–61   G. H. Middleton
1961–6   W. H. T. Luce
1966–   R. S. Crawford

PITCAIRN ISLAND

Presidents of the Council
1898–1904   J. R. McCoy
1904   W. A. Young

(continued

PITCAIRN ISLAND (*continued*)

Chief Magistrates

1904–6	J. R. McCoy
1907	A. H. Young
1908	W. A. Young
1909	E. McCoy
1910–19	G B. Christian
1920	C. R. P.Christian
1921	F. Christian
1922	C. R. P. Christian
1923–4	E. A. Christian
1925	C. R. P. Christian
1926–9	E. A. Christian
1930–1	A. H. Young
1932	E. A. Christian
1933–4	C. R. P. Christian
1935–9	E. A. Christian
1940	A. D. Young
1941	F. M. Christian
1942	C. R. P. Christian
1943	F. M. Christian
1944	C. R. P. Christian
1945–8	H. N. Young
1949	C. R. P. Christian
1950–1	W. C. Christian
1952–4	J. L. Christian
1955–7	C. R. P. Christian
1958–60	W. C. Christian
1961–6	J. L. Christian
1967–	P. Young

PUNJAB

Lieutenant Governors

1897–1902	W. M. Young
1902–7	C. M. Rivaz

(continued

PUNJAB (*continued*)

Lieutenant Governors
1907–8	D. C. J. Ibbetson
1908–11	L. W. Dane
1911–13	J. M. Douie
1913–19	M. F. O'Dwyer
1919–21	E. D. Maclagan

Governors
1921–4	E. D. Maclagan
1924–8	W. M. Hailey
1928–33	G. F. de Montmorency
1933–8	H. W. Emerson
1938–41	H. D. Craik
1941–6	B. J. Glancy
1946–7	E. M. Jenkins

RHODESIA (formerly Southern Rhodesia)

Administrators
1897–1914	W. H. Milton
1914–23	F. D. P. Chaplin

Governors
1923–8	J. R. Chancellor
1928–34	C. H. Rodwell
1934–42	H. J. Stanley
1942–4	E. Baring
1944–6	W. C. Tait
1947–53	J. N. Kennedy
1954–9	P. B. R. W. William-Powlett
1959–65	H. V. Gibbs

RHODESIA AND NYASALAND

Governors General
1953–7   J. J. Llewellin, Baron Llewellin
1957–63   S. Ramsay, Earl of Dalhousie

High Commissioners
1953–5   I. M. R. Maclennan
1955–61   M. R. Metcalf
1961–3   C. J. M. Alport
1963   J. B. Johnston

SAINT HELENA

Governors
1897–1903   R. A. Sterndale
1903–11   H. L. Gallwey
1912–20   H. E. S. Cordeaux
1920–5   R. F. Peel
1925–32   C. H. Harper
1932–8   S. S. Davis
1938–41   H. G. Pilling
1941–7   W. B. Gray
1947–54   G. A. Joy
1954–8   J. D. Harford
1958–62   R. E. Alford
1962–8   J. O. Field
1968–71   D. A. P. Murphy
1971   T. Oates

SAINT KITTS-NEVIS-ANGUILLA

Administrators
1899–1904   C. T. Cox
1904–6   R. Bromley
1906–16   T. L. Roxburgh

61

(continued

SAINT KITTS-NEVIS-ANGUILLA (*continued*)

Administrators

1916–25	J. A. Burdon
1925–9	T. R. St Johnston
1929–31	T. C. Macnaghten
1931–40	D. R. Stewart
1940–7	J. D. Harford
1947–9	L. S. Greening
1949	F. M. Noad
1949–56	H. Burrowes
1956–66	H. A. C. Howard
1966–7	F. A. Phillips

Governors

1967–9	F. A. Phillips
1972–5	M. P. Allen
1975	P. E. Inniss

ANGUILLA

Commissioners

1969	A. Lee
1969	J. A. Cumber
1969	W. H. Thompson
1974	A. C. Watson

SAINT LUCIA

Commissioners

1900–2	H. L. Thompson
1902–5	G. Melville
1905–8	P. C. Cork
1909–14	E. J. Cameron
1914–15	W. D. Young
1915–18	C. G. Murray
1918–27	W. B. Davidson-Houston
1928–35	C. W. Doorly
1935–8	E. W. Baynes
1938–44	A. A. Wright
1944–6	E. F. Twining

62

(continued

SAINT LUCIA (*continued*)

Commissioners
1947–53	J. M. Stow
1953–8	J. K. Thorp

Administrators
1958–62	J. E. Asquith, Earl of Oxford and Asquith
1962–7	G. J. Bryan

Governors
1967–71	F. J. Clarke
1974	I. Simmons
1974–	A. M. Lewis

SAINT VINCENT

Administrators
1895–1901	H. L. Thompson
1901–9	E. J. Cameron
1909–15	C. G. Murray
1915–23	R. P. Lobb
1923–9	R. Walter
1929–33	H. W. Peebles
1933–6	A. F. Grimble
1936–8	A. A. Wright
1938–41	W. B. Gray
1941–4	A. E. Beattie
1944–8	R. H. Garvey
1948–55	W. F. Coutts
1955–61	A. F. Giles
1961–6	S. H. Graham
1966–7	J. L. Chapman
1967–9	H. George

Governors
1969–70	H. George
1970–6	R. G. John
1977–	S. D. Gun-Murro

SARAWAK

Governors
1946–9   C. N. Arden-Clarke
1949   D. G. Stewart
1949–59   A. F. Abell
1959–63   A. N. Waddell

SEYCHELLES

Administrators
1899–1903   E. B. Sweet-Escott

Governors
1903–04   E. B. Sweet-Escott
1904–12   W. E. Davidson
1912–18   C. R. M. O'Brien
1918–21   E. E. Twisleton-Wykeham-Fiennes
1922–7   J. A. Byrne
1927   M. Stevenson
1928–34   D. M. G. Honey
1934–6   G. J. Lethem
1936–42   A. F. Grimble
1942–7   W. M. Logan
1947–51   P. S. Selwyn-Clarke
1951–3   F. Crawford
1953–8   W. Addis
1958–61   J. K. Thorp
1961–7   J. E. Asquith, Earl of Oxford and Asquith
1967–9   H. S. Norman-Walker
1969–73   B. Greatbatch
1973–6   C. H. Allan

SIERRA LEONE

Governors
1894–1900   F. Cardew
1900–4   C. A. King-Harman
1904–11   L. Probyn
1911–16   E. M. Merewether

64

(continued

SIERRA LEONE (*continued*)

Governors

1916–22	R. J. Wilkinson
1922–7	A. R. Slater
1927–31	J. A. Byrne
1931–4	A. M. Hodson
1934–7	H. Monck-Mason Moore
1937–41	D. J. Jardine
1941–8	H. C. Stevenson
1948–53	G. B. Stooke
1953–6	R. D. Hall
1956–61	M. H. Dorman

Governors General

1961–2	M. H. Dorman
1962–8	H. J. L. Boston
1968–	B. Tejan-Sie

High Commissioners

1961–3	J. B. Johnston
1963–6	D. J. C. Crawley
1966–9	S. J. G. Fingland
1969–72	S. J. L. Olver
1972–	I. B. Watt

SIND

Commissioners

1891–1900	H. E. M. James
1900–2	R. Giles
1902–3	A. Cumine
1903–4	H. C. Mules
1904–5	J. W. P. Muir-Mackenzie
1905–12	A. D. Younghusband
1912–16	W. H. Lucas
1916–20	H. S. Lawrence
1920–5	J. L. Rieu
1925–6	P. R. Cadell
1926–9	W. F. Hudson

65

(continued

SIND (*continued*)

Commissioners
1929–31	G. A. Thomas
1931–5	R. E. Gibson
1935–6	G. F. S. Collins

Governors
1936–41	L. Graham
1941–6	H. Dow
1946–7	R. F. Mudie

SINGAPORE

Governors
1946–52	F. C. Gimson
1952–5	J. F. Nicoll
1955–7	R. B. Black
1957–9	W. A. C. Goode

Representative
1965	J. V. Rob

High Commissioners
1965–8	J. V. Rob
1968–70	A. J. de la Mare
1970–4	S. Falle
1974–	J. P. Tripp

SOLOMON ISLANDS

Resident Commissioners
1896–1915	C. M. Woodford
1915–17	F. J. Barnett
1917–21	C. R. M. Workman
1921–9	R. R. Kane
1929–39	F. N. Ashley
1939–43	W. S. Marchant
1943–50	O. C. Noel
1950–3	H. G. Gregory-Smith

SOUTH AFRICA

High Commissioners
1901–5	A. Milner, Viscount Milner
1905–10	W. W. Palmer, Earl of Selborne
1910–31	(under Union of South Africa)
1931–5	H. J. Stanley
1935–40	W. H. Clark
1940–1	W. C. Huggard
1941–4	W. G. A. Ormsby-Gore, Baron Harlech
1944	W. C. Huggard
1944–51	E. Baring
1951–5	J. H. le Rougetel
1955–8	P. Liesching
1959–63	J. P. R. Maud
1963–4	H. S. Stephenson

SOUTH ARABIAN FEDERATION

High Commissioners
1959–60	W. H. T. Luce
1960–3	C. H. Johnston
1963–5	G. K. N. Trevaskis
1965–7	R. G. Turnbull
1967–	H. Trevelyan

SRI LANKA (formerly Ceylon)

Governors
1895–1903	J. W. Ridgeway
1903–7	H. A. Blake
1907–13	H. E. McCallum
1913–16	R. Chalmers
1916–18	J. Anderson
1918–25	W. H. Manning
1925–7	H. Clifford
1927–31	H. J. Stanley
1931–3	G. Thomson

67

(*continued*

SRI LANKA (*continued*)

Governors

1933–7	R. E. Stubbs
1937–44	A. Caldecott
1944–8	H. Monck-Mason Moore

Governors General

1948–9	H. Monck-Mason Moore
1949–55	H. Ramsbotham, Viscount Soulbury
1955–62	O. E. Goonetilleke
1962–	W. Gopallawa

High Commissioners

1948–51	Sir W. Hankinson
1951–7	Sir C. Syers
1957–62	A. F. Morley
1962–6	C. M. Walker
1966–9	F. S. Tomlinson
1969–73	A. M. Mackintosh
1973–6	H. Smedley
1976	D. P. Aiers

STRAITS SETTLEMENTS

Governors

1899–1901	J. A. Swettenham
1901–04	F. A. Swettenham
1904–11	J. Anderson
1911–19	A. H. Young
1919–28	L. N. Guillemard
1928–30	H. Clifford·
1930–6	C. Clementi
1936–42	T. S. W. Thomas
1942–5	(under Japan)

SWAZILAND

Resident Commissioners

1907–16	R. T. Coryndon
1917–28	D. M. G. Honey
1928–35	T. A. Dickson
1935–7	A. G. Marwick
1937–42	C. L. Bruton
1942–6	E. K. Featherstone
1946–50	E. B. Beetham
1950–6	D. L. Morgan
1956–63	B. A. Marwick
1963–8	F. A. Loyd

High Commissioners

1968–72	P. Gautrey
1972–5	E. G. Le Tocq
1975–	J. A. E. Miles

TANZANIA (formerly Tanganyika and Zanzibar)

TANGANYIKA

Governors

1916–24	H. A. Byatt
1924–31	D. C. Cameron
1931–3	G. S. Symes
1933–8	H. A. MacMichael
1938–42	M. A. Young
1942–5	W. E. Jackson
1945–9	W. D. Battershill
1949–58	E. F. Twining
1958–61	R. G. Turnbull

High Commissioner

1961	N. Pritchard

ZANZIBAR

Consuls General

1894–1900	A. H. Hardinge
1900–4	C. N. E. Eliot

(continued

TANZANIA (*continued*)

Consuls General
1904–9   B. S. Cave
1909–13   E. Clarke

Residents
1914–22   F. B. Pearce
1922–4   J. H. Sinclair
1924–30   A. C. Hollis
1930–7   R. S. D. Rankine
1937–40   J. H. Hall
1941–6   H. G. Pilling
1946–51   V. G. Glenday
1952–4   J. D. Rankine
1954–60   H. S. Potter
1960–3   G. R. Mooring

High Commissioner
1963–4   T. L. Crosthwaite

TANGANYIKA AND ZANZIBAR

High Commissioners
1964   Sir N. Pritchard
1964   R. W. D. Fowler

TANZANIA

High Commissioners
1964–8   R. W. D. Fowler
1968–73   H. Phillips
1973–5   A. R. H. Kellas
1975–   M. Brown

TONGA

Consuls
1901–9   H. Hunter
1909–13   W. T. Campbell
1913–17   H. E. W. Grant

(*continued*

TONGA (*continued*)

Consuls

1917–26	I. McOwan
1926–37	J. S. Neill
1937–43	A. L. Armstrong
1943–9	C. W. T. Johnson
1949–54	J. E. Windrum
1954–7	C. R. H. Nott
1957–9	A. C. Reid
1959–65	E. J. Coode
1965–	A. C. Reid

Representative

1965	A. C. Reid

High Commissioners

1970–3	Sir A. Galsworthy
1973–	H. A. Arthington-Davy

TRANSJORDAN

Residents

1921–4	H. Philby
1924–39	C. H. F. Cox
1939–46	A. S. Kirkbride

TRANSVAAL

Governors

1902–5	A. Milner, Viscount Milner
1905–10	W. W. Palmer, Earl of Selborne

Lieutenant Governors

1902–5	A. Lawley
1905–6	R. Solomon

71

TRINIDAD AND TOBAGO

Governors

1897–1900	H. E. H. Jerningham
1900–04	C. A. Moloney
1904–09	H. M. Jackson
1909–16	G. R. LeHunte
1916–22	J. R. Chancellor
1922–4	S. H. Wilson
1924–30	H. A. Byatt
1930–6	A. C. Hollis
1936–8	A. M. Fletcher
1938–42	H. W. Young
1942–7	B. E. Clifford
1947–50	J. V. Shaw
1950–5	H. E. Rance
1955–60	E. B. Beetham
1960–2	S. Hochoy

Governors General

1962–73	S. Hochoy
1973	E. Clarke

High Commissioners

1962–6	N. E. Costar
1966–70	G. P. Hampshire
1970–3	R. C. C. Hunt
1973–	C. E. Diggines

TURKS AND CAICOS ISLANDS

Commissioners

1899–1901	G. P. St Aubyn
1901–5	W. D. Young
1905–14	F. H. Watkins
1914–23	G. W. Smith
1923–32	H. E. Phillips
1933–4	H. H. Hutchings
1934–6	F. C. Clarkson
1936–40	H. C. N. Hill

72

(continued

TURKS AND CAICOS ISLANDS (*continued*)

Commissioners

1940–6	E. P. Arrowsmith
1947–52	C. E. Wool-Lewis
1952–5	P. Bleackley
1955–8	I. E. G. Lewis
1958–9	G. C. Guy

Administrators

1959–65	G. C. Guy
1965	R. E. Wainwright
1965–7	J. A. Golding
1967–	R. E. Wainwright

UGANDA

Commissioners

1899–1902	H. H. Johnston
1902–5	J. H. Sadler

Governors

1905–10	H. H. J. Bell
1910–11	H. E. S. Cordeaux
1911–18	F. J. Jackson
1918–22	R. T. Coryndon
1922–5	G. F. Archer
1925–32	W. F. Gowers
1932–5	B. H. Bourdillon
1935–40	P. E. Mitchell
1940–4	C. C. F. Dundas
1944–52	J. H. Hall
1952–7	A. B. Cohen
1957–61	F. Crawford
1961–2	W. F. Coutts

Governor General

1962–3	W. F. Coutts

High Commissioners

1962–5	D. W. S. Hunt
1965–7	R. C. C. Hunt

(continued

UGANDA (*continued*)

High Commissioners

1967–70	D. A. Scott
1970–3	R. M. K. Slater
1973–	J. P. I. Hennessy

UNION OF SOUTH AFRICA

Governors General

1910–14	H. J. Gladstone, Viscount Gladstone
1914–20	S. C. Buxton, Earl Buxton
1920–3	H. R. H. the Prince Arthur of Connaught
1924–30	A. A. Cambridge, Earl of Athlone
1931–7	G. H. Villiers, Earl of Clarendon
1937–43	P. Duncan
1943–6	N. J. de Wet
1946–51	G. B. van Zyl
1951–9	E. Jansen
1959–61	C. R. Swart

UNITED PROVINCES OF AGRA AND OUDH

LIEUTENANT GOVERNORS, NORTH-WEST PROVINCES, AND
CHIEF COMMISSIONERS, OUDH

1895–1901	A. P. McDonnell
1901–2	J. J. D. LaTouche

UNITED PROVINCES OF AGRA AND OUDH

Lieutenant Governors

1902–7	J. J.D. LaTouche
1907–12	J. P. Hewett
1912–17	J. S. Meston
1917–21	S. H. Butler

Governors

1921–2	S. H. Butler
1922–7	W. S. Marris

74

(*continued*

UNITED PROVINCES OF AGRA AND OUDH (*continued*)

Governors

1927–8	A. P. Muddiman
1928–33	W. M. Hailey
1934–9	H. G. Haig
1939–45	M. G. Hallett
1945–7	F. V. Wylie

BRITISH VIRGIN ISLANDS

Administrators

1896–1903	N. G. Cookman
1903–10	R. S. Earl
1910–19	T. L. H. Jarvis
1919–22	H. W. Peebles
1922–3	R. Hargrove
1923–6	O. L. Hancock
1926–34	F. C. Clarkson
1934–46	D. P. Wailling
1946–54	J. A. C. Cruikshank
1954–6	H. A. C. Howard
1956–9	G. P. Allesbrook
1959–62	G. J. Bryan
1962–7	M. S. Staveley
1967–71	J. S. Thomson
1971–	D. G. Cudmore

Governors

1971–4	D. G. Cudmore
1974–	W. W. Wallace

WEIHAIWEI

Commissioners

1902–21	J. H. S. Lockhart
1921–3	A. P. Blunt
1923–7	W. R. Brown
1927–30	R. F. Johnston

WESTERN PACIFIC HIGH COMMISSION

High Commissioners

1877–1952	(see Fiji)
1952–5	Sir R. C. Stanley
1955–61	Sir J. Gutch
1961–4	Sir D. C. C. Trench
1964–8	Sir R. S. Foster
1968–	Sir M. D. I. Gass
1974	D. C. C. Luddington

WESTERN SAMOA

Administrators

1914–19	R. Logan
1920–3	R. W. Tate
1923–8	G. S. Richardson
1928–31	S. S. Allen
1931–5	H. E. Hart
1935–46	A. C. Turnbull
1946–8	F. W. Voelcker

High Commissioners

1948–9	F. W. Voelcker
1949–60	G. R. Powles
1960–2	J. B. Wright

WEST INDIES FEDERATION

Governor General

1958–62	P. G. T. Buchan-Hepburn, Baron Hailes

British Government Representatives

1967–70	C. S. Roberts
1970–2	J. E. Marnham
1972–	E. O. Laird

76

WINDWARD ISLANDS

Governors

1897–1900	C. A. Moloney
1900–6	R. B. Llewelyn
1906–9	R. C. Williams
1909–14	J. H. Sadler
1914–23	G. B. Haddon-Smith
1923–30	F. S. James
1930–5	T. A. Best
1935–7	S. M. Grier
1937–42	H. B. Popham
1942–8	A. F. Grimble
1948–53	R. D. Arundell
1953–5	E. B. Beetham
1955–60	C. M. Deverell

ZAMBIA (formerly Northern Rhodesia)

NORTH-EASTERN RHODESIA

Administrators

1898–1907	R. E. Codrington
1907–9	L. A. Wallace
1909–11	L. P. Beaufort

NORTH-WESTERN RHODESIA

Administrators

1897–1907	R. T. Coryndon
1907–8	R. E. Codrington
1909–11	L. A. Wallace

NORTHERN RHODESIA

Administrators

1911–21	L. A. Wallace
1921–3	D. P. Chaplin
1923–4	R. A. J. Goode

77

(continued

ZAMBIA (*continued*)

Governors

1924–7	H. J. Stanley
1927–32	J. C. Maxwell
1932–4	R. Storrs
1934–8	H. W. Young
1938–41	J. A. Maybin
1941–7	E. J. Waddington
1948–54	G. M. Rennie
1954–8	A. E. T. Benson
1958–64	E. D. Hone

High Commissioners

1964–7	W. B. L. Monson
1967–71	J. L. Pumphrey
1971–4	J. S. R. Duncan
1974–	F. S. Miles

3 CONSTITUTIONS AND PARLIAMENTS

ADEN

The territory was administered by a Political Resident with four assistant officers. Internal control was the ultimate responsibility of the India Office acting through the Government of India. Aden settlement was the responsibility of the Bombay government as was the Port Trust.

In 1932 Aden proper was separated from the Bombay Presidency and made into a separate province directly administered by the Government of India. The Protectorate was not directly administered but ruled by its own chiefs under the control of the Resident in Aden, on behalf of the Colonial Office.

Under the Aden Colony Order 1936 Aden became a colony in 1937. It was administered by a governor assisted by a nominated executive council. In 1947 a legislative council was established which had official and unofficial members. In the Protectorate the rulers of the two Hadhramaut states in the Eastern Protectorate adopted British resident advisers in 1938 and 1939. The other four Eastern states and those of the Western Protectorate continued to be governed by their rulers, but under the ultimate control of the Resident and Governor in Aden colony. In 1959 six of the Western rulers formed the Federation of Arab Emirates of the South, and four more joined them. At that time Aden colony had an elected majority on its legislative council, and ministers appointed to control government departments. Aden joined the South Arabian Federation in 1963. The Federation (formerly that of Arab Emirates of the South) held exclusive legislative and executive powers in certain respects and the state legislatures, including that of Aden, had concurrent power on agriculture, fisheries, roads, immigration, prisons, imports, exports, shipping, navigation (excluding ports and harbours) and insurance. Aden had 24 members in the federal parliament. Its own constitution of 1963 provided for a high commissioner representing the Sovereign who, in Council, retained power to legislate for peace and order. There was a council of ministers and legislative council of 16 elected, 2 *ex-officio* and 6 nominated members.

In 1967 the People's Republic of Southern Yemen was established (the same was subsequently changed to People's Democratic Republic of Yemen). It comprises Aden and the former protectorate of South Arabia.

AUSTRALIA

The former colonies of New South Wales, Victoria, Queensland, South Australia, Western Australia and Tasmania came together as the Commonwealth of Australia in 1901, under the Act of 1900. The Northern Territory — originally attached to South Australia — joined in its own right in 1911 and the federal territory for the capital was separated from New South Wales in the same year.

The federal parliament consisted of the Sovereign represented by a governor general, a senate and a house of representatives. The Senate had at least six members elected for each of the original states of the Commonwealth and sitting for six years; the house might, however, be dissolved earlier if there was serious disagreement with the lower house. The House of Representatives had approximately twice as many members, elected from each state in proportion to its non-aboriginal population and sitting for three years. For the first parliament, electoral qualifications were the same as those in force in each separate state for elections to its larger house; after the first parliament the franchise was standardised as universal adult suffrage. Voting has been compulsory since 1925.

The state parliaments retained residuary power in their respective territories and could legislate in any matter not exclusively reserved to the Federal Parliament, but if a state law was inconsistent with a federal law, federal law prevailed.

Executive power was exercised by the Governor General, assisted by an executive council of not more than nine Ministers of State who were members of and responsible to parliament.

The constitution could only be amended on submission to the electorate; a majority of states and a majority of all electors were needed to carry an amendment.

The Northern Territory was directly governed by the Commonwealth government. Other states had each a bicameral parliament and a governor. In New South Wales the upper house was appointed for life and the lower house elected on universal adult suffrage and (since 1918) proportional representation. In Victoria both houses were elected, the upper on a qualified franchise and the lower on universal adult suffrage after 1908, before which year only adult men voted. In Queensland the upper house was appointed for life and the lower elected on a franchise which was qualified until 1914. In South Australia the upper house was elected but could not be dissolved by the executive. The franchise for its electors was qualified by property or office. The House of Assembly was elected on universal adult suffrage. In Western Australia the Legislative Council was elected on a qualified suffrage and the House of Assembly on adult suffrage. Tasmania had a legislative council elected on a property franchise and not liable to be dissolved by the executive. The House of Assembly was elected on adult suffrage; proportional representation was introduced in 1907.

In 1922 the Northern Territory was granted a non-voting member in the House of Representatives of the Federal Parliament. Canberra received the same in 1948.

In 1922 the upper house in Queensland was abolished and later that of New South Wales was reformed as a body elected by parliament for twelve years.

Northern Territory remained directly governed under various bodies until 1947, when it gained a legislative council. This was reconstituted in 1959 and then had as members an administrator, 6 officials, 3 nominated non-officials and 8 elected members. An elected majority was introduced in 1968. A fully elected legislative assembly was introduced in 1974. All the ordinances passed by the Administrator's Council (5 members appointed from the legislative assembly) needed his assent and, in some cases, that of the Governor General. The territory's representative in federal parliament was given a vote.

ASCENSION ISLAND, SAINT HELENA AND TRISTAN DA CUNHA

St. Helena and its dependencies (Tristan and Ascension) were in 1900 a crown colony and two territories, independently and directly administered from Britain. St. Helena as a colony had a governor who ruled with an advisory council of five members. Ascension Island was ruled by the Lords Commissioners of the Admiralty and Tristan da Cunha had no form of government.

Ascension Island was annexed to St. Helena in 1922 and placed under the control of the Colonial Office. Tristan da Cunha received a Chief with three administrative officers in 1932; the Chief was chairman of an Island Council. An administrator was appointed in 1948.

In 1967 St. Helena received a legislative council consisting of the Governor, two official members and 12 elected members; government departments were run by committees of the Council, whose chairmen, together with the two official members, formed the Governor's Executive Council.

THE BAHAMAS

By 1900 the Bahamas were a colony administered by a governor with an executive council of 9 members and a legislative council of 9; both these bodies were nominated. There was also a representative assembly of 29 members elected on a property qualification. The Executive was not responsible to this body but to the Governor.

In 1959 the General Assembly Elections Act altered the franchise to the Assembly and members were returned on adult male suffrage with a limited second vote on property qualifications. Women received the vote in 1962. Internal self-government with cabinet responsibility was introduced in 1964. The Legislative Council was replaced by a senate of 16 members, of whom 9 were appointed on the advice of the Prime Minister, 4 on the advice of the leader of the opposition and 3 at the Governor's discretion. The House of Assembly had 38 elected members and sat for a term of 5 years, subject to dissolution by the Governor.

In 1973 the Bahamas became independent, remaining a constitutional monarchy with the Queen represented by a Governor General.

BARBADOS

By 1900 Barbados was a colony administered by a governor. There was an executive council, a legislative council of 9 members appointed by the crown and a house of assembly of 24 members elected annually on a limited franchise. Women obtained the vote in 1943.

In 1951 adult suffrage was introduced; the Legislative Council had 15 members and the House of Assembly still had 24, although they were elected for a three-year term.

In 1958 authority in internal affairs passed to the Cabinet of ministers; the Prime Minister was appointed by the Governor who then appointed the other ministers on the Prime Minister's recommendation. They and others formed the Executive Committee; the Legislative Council remained a nominated chamber with revisionary powers.

Full internal self-government followed in 1961, the legislature consisting of the Governor General, the Senate and the House of Assembly. The Senate had 21 members appointed by the Governor General, of whom 12 were appointed on the advice of the Prime Minister, 2 on the advice of the opposition leader and 7 at the Governor General's discretion. The House of Assembly was elected for a five-year term. There is a Privy Council to advise the Governor General in some of his functions; he appoints its members (11) after consultation with the Prime Minister. Independence within the Commonwealth followed in 1966, with the same form of government. The Sovereign continues to be head of state, represented by the Governor General.

BELIZE (formerly BRITISH HONDURAS)

By 1900 British Honduras was a crown colony administered by a governor and commander-in-chief, assisted by an executive council of 5 members (3 official) and a legislative council of 13 official and 5 unofficial members. Both bodies were nominated, the Legislative Council becoming partly elective in 1937.

The 1961 constitution provided for ministerial government and an increase in elected membership in the Legislative Assembly; it now had 18 elected, 5 nominated and 2 *ex officio* members, and the Executive Council had 2 officials and 6 unofficials of whom at least one was a nominated member of the Legislative Assembly.

The constitution of 1964 provided a bicameral legislature with a ministerial system and cabinet responsibility. The House of Representatives had 18 members elected on universal suffrage; the senate had 8 appointed members, 5 of them appointed on the advice of the Prime Minister, 2 on that of the opposition leader and 1 by the Governor. The Governor retained reserve powers on defence, external affairs, internal security and finance, for so long as British Honduras continued to receive British Government budgetary aid.

BERMUDA

By 1900 Bermuda was a crown colony with a governor, an executive council of 6 nominated members and a legislative council of 9. There was also a house of assembly with 36 members elected on a limited franchise. The franchise was extended to women in 1944.

The constitution of 1968 provided that the Governor should normally act on the advice of the Executive, whose members were appointed from the Legislative Council and House of Assembly membership on the recommendation of the government leader. The Governor retained powers on external affairs, police, defence and internal security. The House of Assembly was elected on universal adult suffrage, with 2 members from each of 20 constituencies.

BOTSWANA (BECHUANALAND until 1966)

The territory became a protectorate in 1895. It was governed by 3 chiefs, with a British Commissioner under the direction of a High Commissioner for British Southern Africa.

A constitution was granted in 1961 which provided for a legislative council with an elected majority; African members were indirectly elected, European and Asian members were directly elected by communal voting. There was an executive council with an official majority and unofficial members drawn from the Legislative Council. An African Council was set up to replace the old advisory council of the chiefs, and this elected from among its own members the African members of the Legislative Council. The protectorate became independent as a republic in 1966, with a constitution drafted in 1965 and still in force with minor amendments. Executive power is vested in the President who is responsible to the National Assembly and an *ex-officio* member of it. The legislature has one chamber, the Assembly, which has 36 members and a majority elected on adult suffrage. There is also a House of Chiefs to advise the government; it is composed of chiefs of 8 principal tribes and elected representatives of the sub-chiefs.

BRITISH NORTH BORNEO

The territory was held under grants from the Sultans of Brunei and Sulu by the British North Borneo Company, by a Royal Charter of 1881. Administration was by a governor in Borneo and a board of directors in London; the appointment of the governor was made with the approval of the Secretary of State for the Colonies. The territory was administered as five Residencies.

In 1946 the territory was joined with the island of Labuan and together formed a crown colony, which was administered by a governor. There was a legislative council of 22 nominated members of whom 12 were officials, and a nominated executive council of 5 official and 4 unofficial members.

In 1960 the constitution was amended to provide an unofficial majority in the legislative council, and equal official and unofficial membership in the executive council, under the Governor. The nominated members of the legislative council were taken from lists submitted by towns, districts, chiefs and chambers of commerce. In 1963 the territory joined Malaysia as the state of Sabah.

BRUNEI

The territory was placed under British protection in 1888. In 1906 the Sultan handed over the administration of the state to the British Resident by treaty; this arrangement stood until 1959 when it was replaced by the first written constitution. This provided a privy council to advise the Sultan, an executive council and a legislative council. The United Kingdom government remained responsible for defence and security, and a high commissioner advised the Sultan on these matters and on matters of internal security. The Legislative Council had 8 *ex officio* members, 6 officials appointed by the Sultan, 3 unofficials also appointed by him and 16 members to be elected from among district councillors on adult suffrage.

These institutions were replaced in 1962 by an emergency council (temporarily). In 1965 the constitution was amended to provide for a legislative council comprising a Speaker, 6 *ex officio* members, 5 nominated members and 10 elected members; the Executive Council became a council of ministers presided over by the Sultan and including the High Commissioner, 6 *ex officio* members and 4 other members drawn from the Legislative Council. One of the *ex officio* members of both Councils is the Mentri Besar, who is responsible to the Sultan for the administration of the state.

CANADA

Canada was united as a federal state by the British North America Act of 1867. All the provinces had joined the federation by 1905 except Newfoundland, which joined in 1949.

The federal constitution provides for a central parliament which consists of the Sovereign, the Senate and the House of Commons, and a separate parliament in each province consisting of a Lt. Governor as head of the executive and a single-chamber legislature, with ministers responsible to it. (Quebec and Nova Scotia had originally two chambers). The two territories are ruled by commissioners appointed by the central government and assisted by councils. The Yukon Council has 7 elected members; that of the Northwest Territories has 14, of whom 10 are elected and 4 appointed by central government.

The central parliament has power to make laws on all matters not assigned exclusively to the provincial parliaments. The central list includes defence, taxation, trade and commerce, navigation and shipping, fisheries, money and banking, bankruptcy, interest, copyright, marriage laws, criminal law and prisons, inter-province and international communications, unemployment insurance and any works for the general good of the nation. The following powers have been added by constitutional amendment: powers over the frequency and duration of Parliamentary sessions, power to amend the constitution except in regard to the division of powers between central and provincial parliaments, powers in regard to the rights guaranteed to the English and French languages and to certain religious denominations in education.

The British North America Act established a limited official bilingualism; an act of 1969, the Official Languages Act, established English and French as dual official languages for all purposes of parliament and government.

The functions of the executive and the legislature are decided as much by practice and tradition as by the written constitution. Executive power is exercised by the Governor General (appointed on the advice of the cabinet) as the Queen's representative, for a term of five to seven years. He is advised by the cabinet which is responsible to parliament.

The members of the Senate are appointed by the cabinet until retirement at 75; they were until 1965 appointed for life, by the Governor General, and until 1917 were 87 in number, representing each province according to population. Their number was then increased to 96 and is now 104. Constitutionally they have the same powers as the lower house, except that money bills must originate in the Commons.

The cabinet is responsible to the Commons, whose members are elected by single-member constituencies; no province may have fewer members in the Commons than in the Senate. The total number of members is redistributed after each census.

The British North America Act No. 2 was passed in 1949. It extended to the federal parliament the right to amend the constitution which had belonged to the provincial legislatures in respect of provincial constitutions since 1867.

THE CAYMAN ISLANDS

The islands were a dependency of Jamaica and administered by a Commissioner. In 1962 they were placed under the Colonial Office, together with the Turks and Caicos Islands. They had a legislative assembly consisting of the Administrator, between 2 and 3 official members, between 2 and 3 nominated members and 12 elected members. The Executive Council consisted of members chosen from the Legislative Assembly — 2 from among the official members, 1 from the nominated members and 2 from the elected members who also had to be elected to the Executive Council.

COOK ISLANDS

The group was annexed by New Zealand in 1901, having previously been a British dependency with a British Resident whose assent was required for all measures passed by the islands' legislature, which was set up in 1890. There was an executive council composed of chiefs. A New Zealand Act of 1915 provided that a minister of the New Zealand Executive should take special responsibility for the islands, and that Island Councils should be set up. Laws applying to the whole group may be made by the New Zealand parliament; ordinances by the central islands' legislature; ordinances applying to one island only may be made by that island's council. All ordinances require the assent of the Resident Commissioner. Niue Island was separately administered from 1903, by the same system.

The islands were made an internally self-governing territory in 1965 (Niue in 1974). The Resident Commissioner became High Commissioner representing the Queen; the Executive became a cabinet of responsible ministers. New Zealand retained responsibility for defence and external affairs.

THE FALKLAND ISLANDS

The Islands were a crown colony administered by a governor, who was assisted by an executive council and a legislative council, both having official and unofficial members. The latter also received four elected representatives in 1949, as well as its 3 *ex officio*, 3 official and 2 nominated unofficial members. In 1963 two members were elected to the Executive Council by the members of the Legislative Council.

FIJI

Fiji was a colony ceded to the British Government in 1874 and administered by a governor. He was assisted by an executive council of 4 official members and a legislative council with 6 official and 6 nominated unofficial members. By 1920 the Executive and Legislative Councils had increased by the addition of more nominated members to the Executive and seven elected and two native members to the Legislative Council.

The constitution of 1929 provided an executive council of 6 official and 2 nominated unofficial members, and a legislative council of up to 13 nominated

87

members, 3 native members, 6 European elected members (on a communal roll) and 3 Indian elected members (on a communal roll).

Under the constitutional amendments of 1937 the executive council was composed of 5 official and 4 nominated unofficial members, and the legislative council had 16 officials, 5 European members (3 of them elected and 2 nominated), 5 Fijian members (chosen by the Governor from among nominees of the Great Council of Chiefs) and 5 Indian members (3 elected and 2 nominated).

The Tikina or native councils had power to make by-laws affecting the Fijian population, and these had the force of law when sanctioned by the Secretary for Fijian affairs.

In 1961 unofficial members of the executive council were given supervisory powers over government departments.

In 1970 Fiji became independent with a constitution which provided for a new house of representatives; this had 12 Fijians, 12 Indians and 3 other members elected on communal rolls and 10 Fijians, 10 Indians and 5 general members elected on national rolls. There was a senate of 22 members, 8 of them nominated by the Council of Chiefs, 7 by the chief minister, 6 by the leader of the opposition and 1 by the Rotuma Island Council.

THE GAMBIA

Gambia was a crown colony and protectorate administered by a governor who was assisted by nominated executive and legislative councils, the latter having some unofficial members; it had its first elected member in 1946.

In 1960 a new constitution was promulgated following a general election on universal adult suffrage. It provided for a house of representatives of 27 elected members, 3 nominated and 4 official. The Executive Council consisted of four officials and six ministers appointed from among the elected and nominated members of the House. The first chief minister was appointed in 1961. Internal self-government was achieved in 1963 and full independence in 1965. The House of Representatives now had 32 elected members, four nominated non-voting members and four chiefs elected by the Chiefs in Assembly.

The Gambia became a republic in 1970, following a referendum.

GHANA (GOLD COAST until 1957)

The constitution of 1874 provided for an executive and a legislative council.

88

Both were nominated; the Legislative Council had 3 unofficial members. A governor ruled in conjunction with these two bodies.

The Constitution of 1925 provided the first unofficial elected representation (although a minority) in the Legislative Council. Elections in the municipalities were direct and in the provinces indirect. African Provincial Councils were also set up at this time for the East and West provinces.

In 1935 the Ashanti Confederacy Council was set up as the supreme Ashanti native authority; it was composed of chiefs and other Ashanti representatives. In 1936 the African Provincial Councils gained the right to send representatives to a Joint Provincial Council; a Northern Territories Provincial Council was added in 1946. A new constitution in 1946 provided that a central representative government should rule over Ashanti as well as the Gold Coast. The Legislative Council was given an elected African majority and now consisted of six official members, six unofficials nominated by the Governor (three African and three European) and 18 elected members of whom 9 were elected by the Joint Provincial Council, 4 by municipalities in the colony, 4 by the Ashanti Confederacy Council and 1 by the municipality of Kumasi in Ashanti. The Executive Council had 3 unofficial members and 8 officials of whom 1 was nominated, and the Governor still had the reserved power of veto and emergency action.

In 1949 a fresh constitution enlarged the Legislative Assembly (as the Legislative Council was now called) and its members were mainly elected by popular vote, either direct or indirect, over the whole country. There was a Speaker, 6 special members for commercial and mining interests, 3 officials, 34 members elected from the colony, 19 from Ashanti, 19 from the Northern Territories and the Northern Section of Togoland and 3 from the Southern Section. Members from the municipalities were elected directly and those from rural communities indirectly.

The Executive Council had a majority of Africans drawn from the Legislative Assembly as ministers in charge of government departments. The office of Prime Minister was created in 1952.

The constitution of 1954 provided the basis for independence in 1957. This created a single-chamber legislature with a cabinet of wholly African membership. The Assembly was entirely elected by adult suffrage in single-member constituencies on a population basis. It was presided over by a Speaker. The Governor still had some reserve powers and might ensure the passing of any bill essential to public order.

Ghana became independent in March 1957 and comprised the former Colony of the Gold Coast and the Trusteeship Territory of Togoland.

A republican constitution came into force in 1960, with a president as head of state. This constitution was suspended by the newly formed National Liberation Council in 1966; ministers were dismissed and parliament suspended, all political parties banned. A Presidential Commission was set up under a new constitution for the Second Republic in 1969; it had three members and was dissolved in 1970, being succeeded by a president. Political parties were reinstated in 1969 and a Council of State of 12 members was established together with the reinstated Legislative Assembly.

In 1972 the armed forces took over power from the civil government and established the National Redemption Council, suspending the constitution of 1969, abolishing the office of President and dissolving the Legislative Assembly. This National Redemption Council was replaced in 1975 by a Supreme Military Council, which is the highest legislative and administrative authority and has the head of state as its chairman; all other members are *ex officio*. The National Redemption Council was then reconstituted as a subordinate body, also composed of *ex officio* members. Government departments are headed not by ministers but by administrative commissioners.

GIBRALTAR

Gibraltar was a crown colony with a governor who exercised all functions of legislation and government. An executive council was established in 1922, composed of four official members and three unofficial members chosen by the Governor. A legislative council was established in 1950. It had 10 members; three officials, two appointed by the Governor and five elected.

In 1969 a new constitution established the Gibraltar House of Assembly, consisting of a Speaker appointed by the Governor, two official members and 15 elected. The Governor acted with the advice of a Gibraltar Council of five elected and four official members; the former were appointed from among the elected members of the Assembly after consultation with the leader of the government who was styled Chief Minister and presided over a Council of Ministers. Ministers dealt with matters of internal concern; external affairs remained the responsibility of Britain.

GILBERT ISLANDS (GILBERT AND ELLICE ISLANDS until 1975)

The islands were proclaimed a protectorate in 1892 and annexed as a colony in 1915. (Christmas Island was annexed in 1919). They were administered by a resident commissioner, with native officers on each of the main islands who conducted native affairs.

In 1967 the Governing Council and House of Representatives were established. The Council had 2 *ex officio* members, up to 3 appointed members and 5 elected members, one of whom had the title of Chief Elected Member. The House of Representatives had 2 *ex officio* members, up to 5 official appointed members and 23 members elected by universal adult suffrage. The 5 elected members of the Governing Council were elected by this House from among its own elected members. Both houses comprised the legislature. They were originally elected for a term of two years.

In 1972 the islands were transferred from the Western Pacific High Commission and placed under a governor who was responsible directly to the British Government. In 1974 the Council of Ministers and the House of Assembly were established. The House consisted of the Deputy Governor, Attorney-General and Financial Secretary and 28 members elected on universal adult suffrage. It sat for four years. The Council consisted of the same three officials, the Chief Minister elected by the elected members of the Assembly and six ministers appointed by the Governor on his advice.

The Ellice Islands were separated from the group in 1975 and took the name of Tuvalu. They were administered by a commissioner.

GUYANA (BRITISH GUIANA until 1966)

The colony was administered by a governor who was assisted by a court of policy and a combined court. The first had 7 official members and 8 elected on a limited franchise; the second added to these another 6 elected members representing financial interests. Executive and administrative power was held by the Governor and an executive council; the Combined Court alone had the power to levy taxes and manage the budget.

These institutions were removed by the constitution of 1928 and replaced by an executive and legislative council, the latter consisting of the Governor, 10 official and 19 unofficial members.

The constitution of 1953 provided for a new legislature consisting of a state council of nominated members; an executive council consisting of the Governor, 3 *ex officio* members, 1 member elected from the State Council and 6 from the House of Assembly; the House of Assembly of 24 elected and 3 *ex officio* members. The members of the Executive Council had ministerial status. Internal self-government came in 1961; there was a legislative assembly of 35 elected members and a nominated senate, the majority of members being appointed on the premier's advice.

Independence was gained in 1966. There was a unicameral parliament with members elected by the single-list system of proportional representation for a four-year term. In 1970 the country became a republic with a president as head of state.

91

HONG KONG

In 1900 Hong Kong was a crown colony (ceded by the Chinese in 1841, confirmed by the Treaty of Nanking in 1842 and with a Charter dated 1843). The administration was controlled by a governor, assisted by an executive council of 6 official and 2 unofficial members, and a legislative council of 7 official and 6 unofficial members. Of the 6 unofficials on the latter, 4 were nominated by the Crown, one by the Chamber of Commerce and one by the Justices of the Peace.

Hong Kong was under Japanese administration from 1941 until 1945. Apart from this period the system of government has remained the same, only the number of unofficial members on each council varying. By 1976 there were 8 unofficials on the Executive Council (still nominated) and 15 on the Legislative Council (still nominated).

INDIA

The Government of India Act of 1858 was still in force in 1900. Under it the country's British provinces were ruled by the Secretary of State in London and the Viceroy in India. The Secretary of State was assisted by a council of not less than 10 members, of whom at least 9 were persons who had lived for 10 years in India, and not more than 10 years previously. The members served for 10 years, and none of them could sit in Parliament. This Council had no initiative but it controlled the Indian budget and its majority approval was necessary for grants or appropriations.

In India the Viceroy was assisted by a council of 5 ordinary members each appointed by the Crown for 5 years, and the Commander-in-Chief. Administration was divided between 7 departments, each under a secretary; the Foreign Department was the responsibility of the Viceroy and the members of the council each had responsibility for one of the other departments. The Indian Councils Act of 1892 provided that for legislative purposes another 16 nominated members could be added to this council. In that form it legislated for all British India, all British subjects in the native states and all native Indian subjects of the crown wherever they lived. (The number of ordinary members of the council and the number of government departments under them varied with need.)

The control of central government over native states varied, but all Indian rulers had the advice of a British agent and none of them could declare war or peace, send ambassadors, maintain more than a specified military force or keep any European resident at court on their own authority, and they might be dethroned for misgovernment. Baluchistan was a dependency of India; Sikkim was a British protectorate.

A legislative assembly was established in 1921 as the lower of two legislative chambers, the upper house being a much extended council of state which replaced the Viceroy's council in its legislating form; the Viceroy's council continued as an executive body with members appointed by the crown to hold government departments.

The Council of State had 60 members of whom 33 were elected and 27 nominated, and of whom not more than 20 could be official. The Legislative Assembly had 145 members of whom 104 were elected and the rest nominated, and of whom 26 could be official members. The Council of State sat for five years and the Assembly for three; differences between them could be settled by joint session.

The British Provinces had their powers defined by the Government of India Act of 1919 which classified those subjects of legislation which were to be dealt with by central government, transferred to Indian ministers of provincial governments or reserved to the provincial governors-in-council. The subjects transferred to Indian ministers were: local self-government, medicine and public health, education, public works, agriculture, fisheries, cooperative societies, industries, excise, registration, adulteration, weights and measures, religious and charitable endowments. In all these the central government has no power to intervene except in the case of disagreement between two provinces or to safeguard the authority of central government. Each Province had a legislative council with at least 70% elected members and an executive council of up to 4 members appointed by the crown.

Provincial autonomy was extended by the Government of India Act of 1935 which made ministers responsible to provincial parliaments. It also made provision for an Indian federation, with the first constitution for the whole of India, but the provisions were not accepted. In 1947 the Indian Independence Act established India and Pakistan, each having a constituent assembly, and provided for the adoption of the 1935 Act as a provisional constitution for each state.

The constitution of the Republic of India came into force in 1950 and was amended in 1951. The previous provinces and states became states of the Union under an elected president, who holds office for five years and is elected by members of the central and state legislatures. Central parliament consists of the President and a bicameral legislature, the Council of States and the House of the People. The Council of States has indirectly elected members, the representatives of each state being elected by the elected members of the state legislature if there is one house or the elected members of the lower house if there are two. The Council of States is not liable to dissolution, but one third of its members retire every second year. The House of the People has directly elected members returned on adult suffrage for a five-year term, and some nominated members. The President is assisted by the Council of Ministers which includes a cabinet under the leadership of the Prime Minister who is the head of the majority party. It also includes ministers of state who are not in the cabinet, and deputy ministers. A minister who ceases to be a member of either house of parliament for six consecutive months may no longer be a minister.

The constitution divides legislation into a union list, a state list and a concurrent list. Central parliament can legislate on any subject in the state list if there is a national emergency, or in exceptional circumstances. The states have either one or two chambers of parliament, with the lower (or single) house sitting for five years, its members being elected on adult suffrage.

Seats in both the central and the state legislatures are specially allotted to scheduled castes and scheduled tribes; in 1975 there were 77 seats for the castes in the House of the People and 37 for the tribes; of the 3,563 state legislature seats there were 503 and 262 respectively.

THE IRISH FREE STATE

The constitution of 1922 established the country as a Dominion with a Governor General representing the King as head of state and head of the government. In 1936 the Irish parliament passed an amendment to the constitution which removed all reference to King and Governor General and replaced their authority with that of an executive authority merely empowering the King to act for the Irish Free State in appointing diplomats and consuls and in concluding external agreements.

In 1937 a new constitution proclaimed Eire a sovereign, independent state with a president; the 1936 Executive Authority (External Relations) Act, however, remained until 1949.

In 1949 the Ireland Act recognized that the Republic of Ireland had ceased to be part of His Majesty's Dominions, but should not be regarded as alien.

JAMAICA

The constitution of the colony was amended in 1884 and 1895 to provide a governor and privy council who administered with the aid of a legislative council which had 5 *ex officio* members, 6 nominated members and 14 members elected on a limited franchise for a five-year term. The number of nominated members might be increased to 10. A new constitution of 1944 provided for a house of representatives wholly elected on universal adult suffrage, and an executive council with an unofficial majority. The Legislative

94

Council became the upper house of parliament with 15 members. Ministerial government was introduced in 1953.

In 1959 a new constitution provided for internal self-government; the Legislative Council had an entirely unofficial membership, 18 appointed by the Governor to represent the parties in the House of Representatives and 2–3 nominated by the Prime Minister. The cabinet consisted of not less than 11 ministers drawn from both houses. No powers were reserved to the Governor.

Full independence followed in 1962. The Legislative Council was replaced by a senate of 21 members, 13 appointed on the advice of the Prime Minister and 8 on the advice of the opposition leader. The Governor General as representative of the crown was appointed by the crown on the advice of the Prime Minister.

Jamaica was a member of the West Indies Federation from 1957–62.

KENYA

The East Africa Protectorate was transferred from the authority of the Foreign Office to that of the Colonial Office in 1905. In 1906 it was placed under a governor and a commander-in-chief and was given an executive council of 4 members and a legislative council of 8 official and 4 unofficial members.

In 1919 the Legislative Council was altered to include 11 elected represen-tatives of the European settlers, 3 nominated members, 2 members representing the Indian community, 1 member representing the Arabs and enough official members to ensure an official majority. The Council was an advisory and consultative body; legislation was by ordinance of the governor with the council's consent.

The Protectorate territory was added to the Colony in 1920 and the two together formed a crown colony; the Protectorate territory had formerly been the property of the Sultan of Zanzibar.

In 1923 Asian members of the Legislative Council were elected on a communal vote. In 1927 a European representative of African interests was appointed.

Under the constitution of 1928 there was a 12-member executive council and a legislative council of 11 elected European members, 5 elected Indian members, 2 nominated unofficial members and one other to represent Arabs, 11 *ex officio* members and up to 9 nominated officials. Elected members were returned by communal franchise.

In 1946 the member system was introduced into the Executive Council, with individual members taking responsibility for their own groups of depart-ments. The Executive Council became a council of ministers in 1954, with half its members taken from the elected and representative members of the Legislative Council.

95

In 1957 African members were directly elected to the Legislative Council on a qualified franchise. The Council also had specially elected members for the various community interests in place of the communal representative.

The constitution of 1960 provided a legislative council of 65 elected members–53 of them elected in constituencies on a common roll and 12 elected by those 53. Of the members elected in constituencies 10 represented Europeans, 8 Asians and 2 Arabs; the rest of the seats were open seats. The Governor retained the right to nominate official members. There was also a council of ministers with 4 official and 8 unofficial members and an Arab representative who had the right to attend but not to vote. Most of the ministers were taken from among the unofficial members.

In 1963 internal self-government was introduced, with ministerial responsibility and restricted powers for the Governor; this was followed at the end of the year by full independence. The independent state had a house of representatives and a senate, and the Queen was acknowledged as head of state until December 1964 when Kenya became a republic under President Kenyatta. In 1966 the House of Representatives and the Senate were amalgamated into one national assembly; at that time the House of Representatives had 117 members elected on universal adult suffrage, 12 specially elected by the House and 1 *ex officio*. The Senate had 41 members elected on universal adult suffrage.

THE LEEWARD AND WINDWARD ISLANDS

At 1900 the Leeward Islands (Montserrat, St. Christopher and Nevis, Virgin Islands, Dominica and Antigua) had a governor for the whole group. He was assisted by a federal executive council nominated by the Crown and a federal legislative council of 10 nominated members and 10 members elected by the unofficial members of each territory's legislative council. Montserrat had a nominated legislative council; St. Christopher and Nevis had a nominated executive council and a legislative council of 10 officials and 10 nominated unofficials; the Virgin Islands had nominated executive and legislative councils; Dominica had a nominated executive council and legislative council; Antigua had a nominated legislative council.

The Windward Islands (Grenada, St. Lucia and St. Vincent) had a governor for the group but each territory had its own administration. Grenada had a legislative council of 6 officials nominated by the Governor and 6 unofficials nominated by the Crown. St. Vincent had an administrator assisted by a legislative council of 4 official and 4 nominated unofficial members. St. Lucia had an administrator and nominated executive and legislative councils.

In 1925 Dominica reverted to an elected council (having been governed by a

96

nominated body since 1898). The other Leeward islands retained nominated councils, but elected members were introduced into the councils of the Windward Islands. Dominica was transferred to the Windward Islands in 1940.

In 1951 the Windward Islands received a new constitution which provided for elected majorities in council, and universal adult suffrage.

The Leeward Islands' constitution was also amended in 1951. The Federal Executive Council and the General Legislative Council remained, with a representative majority on the latter chosen by the unofficial members of the individual legislatures from among their own elected members.

In 1960 the two groups ceased to be separately administered. Each territory had its own government; the executive councils consisted of an administrator, 1 official member and 5 unofficials including 4 ministers of whom one is Chief Minister. (Montserrat had 2 officials and 4 unofficials). Each legislative council had a majority elected on universal adult suffrage and 1 or 2 official members, and was presided over by a Speaker. The ministerial system had been practised in most territories since 1956.

In 1967 a new status was introduced: Statehood in Association with Britain. Each of the States is responsible for its internal affairs; Britain retains responsibility for external affairs and defence. This status applies to all the former territories (including Anguilla, which is a separate State in Association and no longer part of St. Christopher and Nevis) except Montserrat which remains a crown colony. There is a governor for each state, acting on the advice of its Prime Minister.

LESOTHO (BASUTOLAND until 1966)

Basutoland since 1884 was directly administered by a commissioner as a representative of the Crown; he was under the direction of a high commissioner for British Southern Africa in whom legislative power was vested and by whom it could be exercised by proclamation. The supreme native authority was the Paramount Chief. In 1910 a Basutoland council was established as an advisory body with no legislative power. The constitution of 1959 provided for a more representative Basutoland National Council of 80 members—half of them elected from among members of district councils. The District Councils were in turn elected on a common roll franchise. The other half of the National Council was composed of chiefs, members nominated by the Paramount Chief and official members. There was an executive council with advisory powers, half of the members being unofficial members of the National Council. The country became independent in 1966 as the Kingdom of Lesotho, with the Paramount Chief as king. Parliament consisted of a national assembly and a senate, the former being elected on universal adult suffrage and the latter composed of chiefs and members nominated by the King.

The constitution was suspended between 1970 and 1973, when parliamentary government was restored. Parliament began considering a new constitution.

MALAWI (NYASALAND until 1964, formerly BRITISH CENTRAL AFRICA)

The territory was made a protectorate in 1891 and administrated by a commissioner. In 1907 it became the Nyasaland Protectorate, with a governor who was assisted by executive and legislative councils, both nominated. Local legislation was by ordinance and the Governor had the right of veto.

A constitution granted in 1960 provided for a legislative council of 28 elected, 3 official and 2 nominated members. There were two electoral rolls— 20 members were elected on the lower roll and 8 on the upper, the electors having different qualifications.

The Executive Council had 5 official members and 5 unofficials chosen from among the elected members of the Legislative Council.

Self-government with a ministerial system was introduced in 1963 for all internal affairs. Full independence followed in 1964, and the country became a republic with a president as head of state in 1966; he is also head of the government and of the one political party.

MALAYSIA AND SINGAPORE

In 1900 the Crown Colony of the Straits Settlements comprised Singapore, Penang, Malacca, the Cocos Islands and Christmas Islands. There was an executive council of 8 official members and a legislative council of 9 official and 7 unofficial members of whom 5 were nominated by the Crown and 2 by Chambers of Commerce in Singapore and Penang. There was a governor, who was also high commissioner for the Federated Malay States of Perak, Selangor, Negri Sembilan and Pahang, which were a British protectorate.

In 1909 these two groups were joined by the five unfederated Malay states which Britain acquired by treaty from Thailand: Johore, Perlis, Kelantan, Kedah and Trengganu. In both groups and the unfederated states the rulers retained their sovereignty but agreed to abide by British advice except in matters of the Moslem religion and Malay custom. State councils were nominated by the rulers. The Federated States also had a federal council under the High Commissioner; the rulers were members of this until 1927, when they were replaced by unofficial members. The High Commissioner co-ordinated policy.

In 1946 there were constitutional proposals for a Malay Union, which were never fully implemented. At the same time Singapore was separated as a colony (*see* Singapore).

The Federation of Malaya came into being in 1948 and included all former territories except Singapore. The British sovereign and the Malay rulers delegated authority to a high commissioner, under whom was a central government with an executive and a legislative council. The Executive Council had an official majority, the Legislative Council an unofficial majority, not elected; it consisted of 14 officials, 11 representatives of states and settlements and 50 unofficials nominated to represent various interests. In 1951 the member system was introduced into the Legislative Council—that is, each department of government was the responsibility of one particular member of the house. In 1952 all these 'members' were included in the Executive Council; a Speaker was appointed to the Legislative Council in 1953.

Each separate state was still governed by its ruler, assisted by executive and legislative councils of non-elected members. The rulers accepted the High Commissioner's advice with the same exceptions as before, and the British sovereign exercised control over defence and external relations.

The constitution of 1955 altered the composition of the Legislative Council, which now had 52 elected members, 10 of whom were included on the Executive Council. All adult citizens could vote in Federal elections on a common electoral roll; candidates were elected directly by constituencies demarcated in 1954. The states and settlements also had unofficial elected majorities in the legislative councils; each state also had a council of state as well as an executive council.

By changes prior to independence in 1957 the British advisers to the states were withdrawn, non-elected ministers were replaced by elected ministers and the High Commissioner agreed to act on the advice of the Executive Council.

In 1957 Malaya became independent as a monarchy. Its head of state was the Yang di Pertuan Agong, elected by his fellow rulers for a five-year term; he chose his head of government who was the leader of the majority party in the legislature. The Queen was still acknowledged as head of the Commonwealth. The federal government had two houses of parliament with a federal list of legislation, a concurrent list and a state list; residual powers lay with the states. The upper house was a senate of 38 members, 22 elected by state legislatures (2 each) and 16 appointed. The new constitution provided that the first fully elected House of Representatives should sit within two years of independence.

The Federation joined with Singapore, North Borneo (Sabah) and Sarawak in 1963 to become Malaysia; the constitution was based on that of the

Federation of Malaya, with a ruler elected for five years and a bicameral legislature, the senate sitting for six and the House of Represenatives for five years, subject to dissolution by the head of state on his ministers' advice.

Singapore left Malaysia in 1965.

MALTA

The constitution of 1888 provided for a governor, assisted by an executive council and a council of government. In 1900 the Council of Government had six official and 13 elected members. The constitution of 1921 provided for an elected legislature to control internal affairs; it consisted of a legislative assembly of 32 members and a senate of 17 members. The Senate was partly, the Assembly wholly, elected on proportional representation. There was a responsible Ministry. The Governor retained power over external relations and trade, defence, coinage and immigration; he was assisted by an executive council of official members; this was later called the Nominated Council and the Executive Council became the Governor in session with the Ministers.

Responsible government was suspended between 1930 and 1932, and again briefly from 1933. The constitution of 1947 provided for a single chamber legislature elected directly on proportional representation. There was a privy council consisting of the Nominated and Executive Councils in joint session.

A state of emergency was declared in 1958 and the island was directly administered by the Governor until 1959, when the 1947 constitution was replaced by an interim constitution. A new constitution of 1961 gave internal self-government, Britain remaining responsible for external affairs and defence. Malta became independent in 1964. The independent state had a house of representatives of 50 elected members. The head of state was the President.

MAURITIUS

Under the constitution of 1885 Mauritius was a colony ruled by a governor and an executive council appointed by him; there was a legislature (the Council of Government) of 27 members, 10 of them elected on a limited franchise.

The constitution of 1947 provided an executive council of 4 official members, 2 appointed members and 4 members elected by the Legislative Council. The Legislative Council had a majority elected on universal franchise. Internal self-government was achieved in 1967 and independence in

1968; responsible ministerial government was introduced and the Legislative Assembly increased in size to 62 elected members and 8 community representatives. It sits for a five-year term.

NEW HEBRIDES CONDOMINIUM

The islands are administered by resident commissioners who are responsible to two high commissioners, one English and one French. The arrangement was laid down in the Anglo-French Convention of 1906 and in a protocol ratified in 1922.

NEW ZEALAND

The constitution of 1852, amended in 1875, was still in force in 1900. It provided for a governor and a bicameral general assembly of legislative council and house of representatives. Members of the Legislative Council were (if appointed before 1891) in office for life. If they were appointed after that date they sat for a seven-year term and could be reappointed at the end of it. European representatives in the House were elected on adult suffrage for three years; Maori representatives were elected by every adult Maori resident in a Maori electoral district. There was a system of ministerial government responsible to parliament.

The Governor (Governor General after 1917) had power to assent to bills or not, and to reserve bills for the pleasure of the Crown. He could draft bills for consideration in either house (except that money bills must be considered by the lower house first) and could return bills to either house for amendment.

The Legislative Council was abolished in 1951, leaving a one-chamber general assembly. Standing Orders of the house safeguard the right of Maoris to use their language in parliamentary business, and to have translations of anything specially affecting them. The voting age was lowered from 21 to 20 in 1969.

In practice the Governor General must be guided in all his actions by the advice of the Executive Council of responsible ministers.

NIGERIA

Lagos formed part of the Gold Coast Colony from which it was detached in

1886 as a separate colony and protectorate of Lagos. In 1899 the Royal Niger Company surrendered its charter to the crown and in 1900 its territories were formed into the two protectorates of Northern and Southern Nigeria. Another protectorate, that of the Niger Coast which had been formed in 1893, was added to Southern Nigeria.

Lagos was ruled by a governor assisted by a nominated executive and legislative council. Northern and Southern Nigeria were ruled by High Commissioners.

In 1906 Lagos and Southern Nigeria were combined into the Colony and Protectorate of Southern Nigeria and in 1914 Northern Nigeria joined them and the whole became the Colony and Protectorate of Nigeria. The Executive Council of Lagos colony was made the Executive Council of the whole territory; there was also a Nigerian Council which consisted of members of the Executive Council, other officials, 7 European representatives and 6 Africans. The Protectorate was redefined as the Northern and Southern Provinces, each under a lieutenant governor appointed by the crown and under the authority of the Governor.

In 1922 a legislative council was created which had power to legislate for the Colony and the Southern Provinces, laws affecting the Northern Provinces being enacted by the Governor. This council consisted of the Governor, the members of the Executive Council, other official members to make a total of not more than 30, 4 members elected by ratepayers in Lagos and Calabar, 6 members representing commercial interests and 7 representing African interests in areas not returning elected members. The Executive Council continued to consist entirely of officials until 1942.

The constitution of 1946 extended the authority of the Legislative Council to the whole of Nigeria, and established under it a house of chiefs and a house of assembly for the Northern Province; these together were called the Northern Regional Council. West and East Provinces were created and given houses of assembly which formed links between the native rulers and the Legislative Council; they were advisory bodies with a majority of unofficial members chosen by the native authorities.

In 1951 the Legislative Council was replaced by a house of representatives which had a majority of members elected indirectly. The regional Houses of Assembly were given powers in local legislation, and the West Province gained its own House of Chiefs. Elections were through electoral colleges; electors in the primary election needed residence and tax qualifications to elect members of a divisional college which in turn elected to provincial colleges. The provincial colleges elected members of each regional House of Assembly which then elected from among its own members those who would represent it in the House of Representatives. The Central Executive Council became a council of ministers, the ministers being drawn from the regions on the advice of regional legislatures. Officials remained in charge of defence, justice and finance. Ministers of the regions were nominated by regional lieutenant governors with the approval of the Houses of Assembly.

In 1954 Nigeria became a Federation. The Governor was replaced by a governor general and the regional lieutenant governors by governors. There was a federal house of representatives with a Speaker, 184 elected members, 3 officials and 6 special members. The Council of Ministers had authority over all matters on which the Federal House might legislate. The Federal House had exclusive power in external affairs, migration, citizenship, defence, external trade, customs and excise, currency, banks, loans, mining and communications. There was then a concurrent list, on which federal law prevailed in case of conflict. Elections to the Federal House varied with the regions. In the North there were indirect elections with franchise confined to adult male taxpayers. In the West there were direct elections and also in the East and in Lagos on adult suffrage.

The Southern Cameroons were at this time a region of the Federation with a house of assembly of mainly elected members and an executive council with an unofficial majority. In 1961 the region joined the Republic of Cameroon.

In 1960 there were further constitutional changes as preparation for independence. The Federal House of Representatives was elected in single-member constituencies, a senate was established with revisionary powers; its members were nominated by regional governments with the approval of the majority in each regional parliament, and there were 4 members for Lagos and 4 appointed by the Governor General. The regional parliaments consisted of a house of chiefs, an elected house of assembly (5 appointed members serving in the Northern regional House) and an executive council of Prime Minister and other ministers. Full independence followed in October of 1960, and Nigeria became a republic in 1963.

In 1966 the government was overthrown by a military *coup*, which was in turn suppressed by the head of the army, General Ironsi, who then suspended the constitution and set up a supreme military council. He abolished all political parties and tribal associations and dissolved the federal system of government. He was in his turn overthrown in July 1966 and the federal system was restored in September as the Federal Military Government.

In 1967 the Republic was divided into 12 states: 6 in the former Northern Region, 3 in the former Eastern Region, one in the West, a Mid-West state and a state of Lagos. Following this, the military governor of the Eastern region states seceded from the Federation and renamed the region as the Republic of Biafra; this led to civil war which ended with federal victory in 1970.

Central government is still a military government; local government is by native authorities of local government bodies controlled by state legislation.

NORTHERN RHODESIA (ZAMBIA from 1964) and SOUTHERN RHODESIA

Southern, North-Eastern and North-Western Rhodesia were, by an Order in Council of 1898, administered by a resident commissioner appointed by the Secretary of State and the British South Africa Company, whose charter of 1889 gave them wide administrative powers and remained in force until 1923. The Commissioner was helped by an executive council consisting of himself, the Company's administrators and at least 4 nominated members chosen with the approval of the Secretary of State. There was also a legislative council which sat for a three-year term; it had 3 official members, 5 Company nominees and 4 elected members. Ordinances passed by the Administrator and the Legislative Council took effect with the approval of the High Commissioner for British Southern Africa, but they might be disallowed by the Secretary of State within the year. The budget was drawn up by the Administrator and submitted to the Legislative Council.

In 1911 the North-Eastern and North-Western provinces were combined as Northern Rhodesia. It was given its own company administrator, appointed with the approval of the Secretary of State, who ruled with the help of an advisory council of 5 members chosen by European settlers.

In 1923 Southern Rhodesia was formally annexed as a self-governing colony, with internal autonomy except in legislation affecting the African population, Rhodesian railways and certain matters reserved to the Secretary of State. There was a governor, assisted by an executive council and a legislature; the latter was set up as a single chamber with power to create a legislative council in addition. With certain exceptions, the legislature might amend the constitution by a two-thirds majority vote. Its members were elected, the franchise being extended in 1928 to cover all British subjects (male) over 21 and all married women (subject to qualifications).

In 1924 Northern Rhodesia gained an executive council of 4 official members and a legislative council of 5 *ex officio* members, 4 nominated officials and 7 elected unofficial members. The territory was annexed by the Crown in 1924.

By 1940 the Legislative Council had 9 officials and 9 unofficials, and a European member nominated by the Governor to represent African interests. During the second world war 3 seats were added to the Executive Council for unofficial members and these had increased to 4 or 5 by 1948, by which date the governor was obliged to regard the unanimous advice of the unofficial members as the advice of the Executive, even if the officials disagreed. He must either accept it or refer his rejection to the Secretary of State. In 1949 two unofficial members held ministerial portfolios.

The Federation of Rhodesia and Nyasaland was formed in 1953. Britain retained ultimate responsibility for external affairs which, with defence, immigration, European education, European agriculture and health, was transferred to a new federal legislature. Territorial governments continued to administer African affairs, local government, housing, police, internal security, industrial relations, lands, mining and irrigation. Southern Rhodesia continued to have the status of a self-governing colony, Northern Rhodesia that of a protectorate. The Federation had a Governor General and a unicameral assembly elected on two common rolls with qualified franchise. In 1960 there were 44 seats for elected members of any race, 8 for Africans, 4 for specially elected Africans and 3 for Europeans responsible for African interests. The constitution provided for an African affairs board as a standing committee of the Assembly. It consisted of the 3 Europeans representing African interests and one specially elected African member from each territory. It had power to make representations to the Federal Assembly, assist a territorial government when asked to, and require any measure which it thought discriminatory to be reserved to the crown.

By 1960 Northern Rhodesia had a legislative council with an elected majority – 12 members elected by European constituencies, 6 by special African constituencies, 2 to seats reserved for Africans and 2 to seats reserved for Europeans. There was a franchise on a common roll with qualifications. Ministers were appointed to the Executive Council on the advice of the lower house.

The constitution of 1961 transferred to Southern Rhodesia some powers still vested in the British government and included the Declaration of Rights. It created the Governor's Council of Prime Minister and up to 11 ministers to replace the Executive Council. The constitution stated that certain of its basic provisions may not be altered without majority approval by each of the four main races voting separately in referendum *or* the approval of the British government, who could refuse to give a decision if it was thought that a referendum is desirable. The only reserved powers remaining related to the Sovereign and the Governor, international obligations and loans under Colonial Stock Acts. The Federal Legislature now had a majority returned by *A* roll voters in constituencies and a minority by *B* roll voters in electoral districts. Both franchises were qualified by property and educational standards.

The Federation came to an end in 1963.

Northern Rhodesia became the independent republic of Zambia in 1964, after 10 months of internal self-government. The constitution provided for a president, to be elected for the first term by the Legislative Assembly but thereafter by the electorate at each general election. There is a single chamber parliament, the National Assembly, with an elected majority; the government is led in the Assembly by a vice-president appointed by the President. Since 1972 Zambia has been a one-party state.

Southern Rhodesia reverted to the status of a self-governing colony but took on additional powers over matters previously transferred to the Federal government in 1953.

In 1965 the Prime Minister of Rhodesia declared a state of emergency, over-riding normal constitutional safegurads, and issued a unilateral declaration of independence. His government was dismissed by the Governor, but continued to carry on effective internal administration. The British Government reasserted its formal responsibility for Rhodesia and passed an enabling bill which gave it power to deal with the situation by Orders-in-Council. In 1970 the Rhodesian Prime Minister declared the country a republic under a new constitution, which the British government declared illegal. Attempts to reach an agreement (which would allow legal independence under agreed con-ditions) were made in 1966, 1968, 1970–2, 1974, 1975 and 1976.

PAPUA NEW GUINEA (TERRITORY OF PAPUA until 1949)

The territory was administered under a League of Nations mandate from 1920. The Australian government established a civil administration in 1921, and the territory was governed by an administrator. Civil government was disrupted by the Japanese occupation of 1942–5.

The Papua New Guinea Provisional Administration Act 1945 set up a single provisional administration. This was repealed by the Papua and New Guinea Act 1949 which placed the territory under international trusteeship and provided for an administrative union under one administrator. The act made provision for an executive council, to be appointed by the Governor General (of Australia). A legislative council was set up in 1951, consisting of the Administrator, 16 official members, 3 elected non-officials and 9 other non-officials representing various interests. Advisory councils and native councils could be set up by Ordinance.

In 1964 the Legislative Council was replaced by a house of assembly, and in 1968 an executive council was set up, consisting of 7 ministers (responsible for running their departments since 1970) and four other members. In the same year the House of Assembly became a mainly elected body; 69 members were returned from open electorates, 15 from electorates where an educational qualification is needed for the franchise; 10 were officials.

The territory became independent as Papua New Guinea in 1975. It had a single-chamber legislature with members elected on universal suffrage for a four-year term.

PITCAIRN ISLAND

Island affairs were conducted by an island council with a president (who acted as chief magistrate) and a vice-president (who acted as government secretary).

In 1952 responsibility for the island was transferred from the High Commissioner to the Governor of Fiji. He was assisted by the island council which now consisted of a chief magistrate, a secretary and chairman of an internal committee and 2 assessors. These officers were elected annually.

In 1964 a council of 10 members was established; 4 of them were elected, the Island Secretary served as an *ex officio* member and the others were nominated —3 by the elected members and 1 by the Governor. Members held office for a year except the presiding magistrate who was elected for a three-year term. The council was connected with the Governor through a commissioner at Suva, Fiji.

In 1970 Fiji became independent and the governorship of Pitcairn was transferred to the British High Commissioner in New Zealand, with liaison through a commissioner in Auckland.

SARAWAK

By an agreement of 1888 the territory was recognised as an independent state governed by a rajah under the protection of the United Kingdom. A British representative with limited powers was to be appointed in 1941, but this arrangement was made inoperative by the Japanese invasion. The Rajah ruled through two legislative bodies, the Supreme Council and the Council Negri; in 1941 he granted a constitution by which they were given powers corresponding to those of an executive council and a legislative council.

In 1946 the Rajah ceded Sarawak to the Crown.

A further constitution of 1956 provided for a legislative council of 24 elected (indirectly) unofficial members (21 elected by Sarawak and 3 by Kuching, Sibu and Miri), 14 *ex officio* members, 3 standing members and 4 nominated members. The Executive Council had 5 members elected from among the members of the Legislative Council, 3 *ex officio* members and 2 nominated. District and municipal councils, themselves elected, formed the electoral colleges for the Legislative Council.

Sarawak joined the Federation of Malaysia in 1963.

SEYCHELLES

The islands were ruled by an administrator after 1888; he was assisted by nominated executive and legislative councils. The Administrator was given the powers of Governor in 1897 and the rank of Governor in 1903. The Legislative Council had official and unofficial members; an unofficial member was added to the Executive Council in 1931. In 1948 the Legislative Council received 4 elected members.

In 1970 a new constitution provided for a legislative assembly of 15 elected members, 3 *ex officio* members and a speaker. Internal self-government was achieved in 1975 and independence in 1976.

SIERRA LEONE

Sierra Leone consisted of two territories, the Colony and the Protectorate. The Colony extended from the Scarcies River in the north to the border of Liberia in the south, and inland, for distances of 8–20 miles. It had a governor, with a nominated executive and legislative council. The Protectorate, which extended inland over an area of 27,000 square miles, was proclaimed in 1896. Its administration was ordered by an order in council of 1913, by which the Governor of the colony was also the Governor of the Protectorate, and the Colony's legislative council had authority over it. It was divided into three provinces, each with a European commissioner.

In 1923 the Legislative Council, still nominated by the Governor, increased its unofficial membership to 5.

In 1924 the Order in Council of 1913 was revoked and replaced by another, which made new arrangements combining the Colony and protectorate under the one legislative and executive authority. The Legislative Council now had 11 official members and 10 unofficials, of whom 3 were elected for a five-year term on a limited (male) franchise. The number of provinces in the protectorate had been reduced to two.

The Executive Council was increased by 2 unofficial members in 1943, and by one more in 1948. Under the constitution of 1951 the Executive Council had an unofficial majority and the Legislative Council a large elected majority, members being elected by the Protectorate for the first time. Seven members were elected from the Colony and 12 by the district councils of the Protectorate; two were elected by the Protectorate Assembly; two nominated by the Governor and 7 were *ex officio* members. The Governor had an executive council of 4 official members and 6 unofficials appointed from among the unofficial members of the Legislative Council. The Protectorate was administered by a chief commissioner responsible to the Governor, and although it was represented in the Legislative Council it had also the Protectorate Assembly previously mentioned. This consisted of representatives from each district council and 6 members nominated by the Governor to represent other interests; it met in an advisory capacity.

In 1952 departments of government were assigned as the special responsibility of certain members of the Executive. In 1953 a full ministerial system was introduced, the ministers all being elected members of the Legislative Council. A chief minister was appointed in 1954.

A new constitution in 1956 replaced the Legislative Council by a house of representatives which had a Speaker, 4 official members, 14 directly elected from the Colony and 25 directly elected from the Protectorate, 12 paramount chiefs elected by district councils in the Protectorate and 2 nominated members with no voting rights.

In 1958 the Executive was made collectively responsible to the legislature. The government consisted of at least 7 elected ministers appointed on the advice of the chief minister. The Governor retained his responsibility for 'peace and good government', external affairs, defence, internal security, police and public service. In 1960 he ceased to preside over the Executive and was replaced by the chief minister; he also transferred to the ministers his powers on police, defence and external affairs. The territory became fully independent in 1961.

Under the constitution of the independent state the Queen was represented by a Governor General appointed on the advice of the Prime Minister. There was a house of representatives of not less than 60 members elected from constituencies established by an electoral commission.

In March 1967 there were two successive military coups, the first of which overthrew the newly elected government and the second of which proclaimed the National Reformation Council; the Council consisted of 8 members. In April 1968 it was in turn overthrown by non-commissioned officers of the army and police force, who formed the Anti-Corruption Revolutionary Movement. This Movement appointed an interim council, and constitutional government was restored on 26 April.

In 1971 the state became a republic under the President as Head of State; he is also head of the cabinet.

SINGAPORE

Singapore became a separate colony in 1946, remained so until 1963 and was again separate as a republic in 1965.

The colony had an executive council nominated by the Governor and a partly elected legislative council; there were 6 members elected by territorial constituencies, 3 elected by chambers of commerce, 4 nominated unofficials, 5 nominated officials and 4 *ex officio*. In 1951 the number of elected members was increased to 12, 9 of them territorial representatives. The Executive Council members were the Governor, 4 *ex officio* members, 2 nominated officials, 4 nominated unofficial members and 2 members elected by the Legislative Council from among its own membership. The constitution of 1955 provided a legislative council with a Speaker and 32 members of whom 25 were elected; all adult citizens with residence qualification could vote. The Council of Ministers had 3 *ex officio* members and 6 from the Legislative Council, appointed by the Governor on the advice of the leader of the majority party.

The State of Singapore Act of 1958 provided a legislative assembly of 51 members elected in single-member constituencies; a cabinet of 9 ministers from the majority party; and an internal security council with power to vote decisions binding on the government. Powers on defence and external affairs were reserved to the United Kingdom government, although the government of Singapore had delegated authority to act with regard to other countries subject to safeguards over British international undertakings.

A president was appointed as Head of State when Singapore became a republic in 1965. In 1970 a presidential council was established to consider matters affecting any racial or religious community, as referred to it by Parliament or the Government, and to draw attention to any legislation which in its opinion is a differentiating measure.

SOLOMON ISLANDS (BRITISH SOLOMON ISLANDS until 1976)

The islands were administered by a resident commissioner at Tulagi, and were ruled as a protectorate. The Commissioner was assisted by a nominated council.

In 1960 a legislative council and an executive council were established, and direct elections introduced in 1967. In 1969 the legislative bodies were replaced by a single governing council with an elected majority of 17 members, 3 *ex officio* members and 6 public service members – the latter group being withdrawn in 1971. In 1974 a legislative assembly was established (the former Governing Council) and the elected members elected a chief minister on whose advice a council of ministers was appointed. The High Commissioner became the Governor. Full internal self-government followed in 1976.

THE SOMALI COAST PROTECTORATE

The area was administered from the Foreign Office from 1898 until 1905, when it was transferred to the Colonial Office as a protectorate. It was administered by a commissioner. Civil administration was disrupted by the Italian occupation of 1940–41; there followed a British military administration which lasted until 1948. Civil government was then resumed under a governor, who was the sole legislative and executive authority.

The Protectorate became independent in 1960 and merged with the former Italian Trusteeship Territory of Somalia to become the Somali Democratic Republic.

SOUTH AFRICA

The Union of South Africa was constituted in 1910 and comprised the formerly self-governing colonies of the Cape of Good Hope, Natal, the Transvaal and the Orange River. The Cape of Good Hope had been a colony with responsible government since 1872. It had an executive council of official members which, together with the Governor, held executive power. Parliament consisted of a house of assembly and a legislative council, electors to both houses having a property qualification.

Natal obtained responsible government in 1893 and had the same executive and legislative bodies as the Cape. Members of parliament were elected on a qualified franchise. The province annexed Zululand in 1897.

The Transvaal was annexed in 1900 and administered by a governor and lieutenant governor assisted by an executive and a legislative council. Responsible government was introduced in 1906.

The Orange Free State was annexed in 1900 as the Orange River Colony; Crown Colony government continued until 1906 when responsible government was introduced. The colony became a province of the new Union under its old name of Orange Free State.

The Union of South Africa was governed by a governor general appointed by the Crown and exercising executive power in conjunction with an executive council, its members being appointed by him. Members were heads of various departments of state. Legislative power was vested in a house of assembly and a senate which formed parliament together with the sovereign. The Senate could not be dissolved within 10 years of the Union, and Parliament as a whole was obliged to meet every year. The Senate had elected members in the majority and some nominated by the Governor General in Council. The senators were elected to represent their provinces by the members of the

111

provincial parliaments. The House of Assembly was elected on the same provincial franchises as were in force before the Union, and sat for a five-year term.

Money bills had to originate in the lower house; the Senate's powers to block them were restricted, as they could still be passed on recommendation from the Governor General. Each province after Union was administered by a provincial council elected for 3 years, each council having an executive committee presided over by an administrator appointed by the Governor General. The term was later extended to five years.

Members of the Union parliament had to be of European descent, but this did not apply to members of the provincial councils.

The franchise was broadened in 1930 when the vote was given to all white women over 21, and again in 1931 when all white men over 21 received it. The qualifications for coloured and African voters were not altered.

In 1936 provision was made for the election of 4 extra senators to represent Africans, and 3 members to be elected to the House of Assembly on the Cape Native Voters' Roll. An African representative council was also set up; it was abolished in 1951 and replaced by the Bantu authorities system of tribal, regional and territorial bodies.

A referendum was held in 1960 to decide whether the Union should become a republic; it was restricted to white voters. The republic came into being in 1961 with a president as head of state, elected by an electoral college for 7 years. The promotion of Bantu Self-Government Act was passed in 1959; it provided for 8 self-governing national territories.

South Africa left the Commonwealh in 1961.

SRI LANKA (CEYLON until 1948)

The constitution in force in 1900 provided for colonial government by an executive council of official members, assisting a governor, and a legislative council of official and unofficial members. The unofficials were chosen to represent different races and groups. By an order in council of 1920 the legislature was described as a Legislative Council, presided over by the Governor, with an unofficial majority of whom most were elected to represent territorial and special interest groups, and the rest nominated by the Governor to represent racial minorities. The Executive Council had an official majority and three nominated unofficials.

The constitution of 1931 replaced the Legislative Council with a state council having legislative and executive functions. It had 3 official members, up to 8 members nominated by the Governor and 50 members elected on universal adult suffrage. This council approved a new constitution in 1945, and that provided for two houses of parliament – a senate and a house of representatives, with a cabinet of responsible ministers and full internal autonomy. The Senate consisted of members half elected (by the House of Representatives) and half nominated by the Governor. It sat for a 6-year term, one-third of its members retiring every 2 years. In the case of disagreement between the two houses it could delay financial bills for one month and others for one year. Powers were still reserved to the Governor to prevent discrimination against minorities and Britain retained ultimate responsibility for defence and external affairs.

Ceylon became independent as a constitutional monarchy in 1948. The upper house of parliament was retained until 1971, the lower house continued to have a majority elected on universal suffrage and 6 nominated members.

In 1972 a new constitution came into force, setting up a republic with a president as head of state and the executive power vested in a council of ministers headed by a prime minister and responsible to a national assembly, elected by all over 18 years of age and combining legislative and executive functions. The Assembly sits for a six-year term. The President is appointed by the Prime Minister for a four-year term.

SWAZILAND

The territory was placed under the administration of the South African Republic (then the title of the Transvaal) in 1894 and transferred to the authority of the High Commissioner for British southern Africa in 1906; mineral and land concessions carrying privileges which made it difficult to impose crown authority were cancelled in return for compensation.

In 1921 an advisory council was set up, consisting of elected European members, to advise on European affairs. Native administration was in the hands of chiefs and their council; the Resident Commissioner was advised by the council through the paramount chief and by a special standing committee in his dealings with Swazi affairs.

In 1967 the country achieved internal self-government as a protected state with the paramount chief as king and head of state. The legislature was a house of assembly elected on universal adult franchise, with executive power vested in a cabinet and the King. There was a senate whose members were half elected by the lower house and half appointed by the King. The King assumed supreme power and repealed the the constitution in 1973.

TANGANYIKA (TANZANIA after 1964)

Tanganyika territory came under effective British control in 1919, to be administered under a League of Nations mandate by a governor with an executive council of nominated members, this council was appointed in 1920. The first legislative council was appointed in 1926, with 13 official and 10 unofficial members, presided over by the governor. From 1945 the number of official members was reduced to 7 and there were 8 *ex officio* and up to 14 unofficial members comprising a mixture of Africans, Europeans and Asians. The League of Nations agreement was replaced by a United Nations trusteeship in 1946.

In 1948 the Member system was introduced into the Executive Council — that is to say each department of government was the responsibility of one member of the council. A Speaker was appointed to the Legislative Council in 1953.

The constitution of 1955 provided for 31 official members and 30 unofficial in the Legislative Council, the latter being 10 Africans, 10 Asians and 10 Europeans, all nominated after consultation with the bodies they represented. The members of the Executive Council with responsibility for departments became ministers in 1957. The first elections to the Legislative Council were held in 1955–59; each constituency elected one African, one Asian and one European member. Voters were all over 21 with an educational or property qualification. Unofficials were appointed as ministers from 1959.

The constitution of 1960 provided an elected majority in the Legislative Council and ministers responsible to parliament. In 1961 internal self-government was introduced, with the withdrawal of official members from the Council of Ministers and a restriction of the powers of the Governor. The National Assembly had 71 members elected on a common roll and some nominated members. Full independence was attained in December 1961, when the trusteeship agreement with the UN came to an end. A republican constitution with a president as head of state was adopted in 1962.

An interim constitution for Tanzania was adopted in 1965. It provided for a national assembly of 107 elected members from Tanganyika, 10 appointed members, 15 members elected by the Assembly after nomination by various national interests, 20 regional commissioners, up to 32 members of the Zanzibar Revolutionary Council and up to 20 other Zanzibar members appointed by the President after consultation with the President of Zanzibar. The number of members elected from Tanganyika was later reduced to 96. There is only one political party.

TOKELAU ISLANDS

The group was transferred to New Zealand from the Gilbert and Ellice Islands in 1926. The islands were declared part of New Zealand in 1948 and are administered by the Governor General in Council (as legislative body) and the Secretary of Maori and Island Affairs (as Administrator, since 1972).

TONGA

Tonga is a monarchy whose King George Tupou I had granted a constitution in 1875. The main principles of this were retained under British protection from 1899. There was then a legislative assembly consisting half of hereditary nobles and half of representatives elected by every tax-paying adult male. Elections were held every three years, and the Assembly met annually. Seven ministers of the crown joined it as non-elected members. Britain retained responsibility for external relations until 1970, when Tonga became a full member of the Commonwealth with the constitution of King George Tupou I still essentially the same. There is a privy council of 8 members who attended the Legislative Assembly together with the nobles and the elected members, and there is a cabinet system of government. Women received the franchise in 1960.

TRINIDAD AND TOBAGO

Until 1924 the territory was a crown colony with a governor who was assisted by an executive and a legislative council, both composed of official and unofficial members who were all nominated. In 1924 elected members were introduced into the Legislative Council, returned on a limited franchise and not in the majority. Full adult suffrage was introduced in 1945.

The 1950 constitution provided for an elected majority in the Legislative Council and a ministerial system in the Executive Council. The post of Chief Minister was established in 1956, and a true cabinet in 1959, the Governor reserving some executive powers. The constitution of 1961 provided for internal self-government. There was a bicameral legislature with a nominated senate and an elected house of representatives. There were no executive powers reserved to the Governor and the cabinet no longer included officials.

Full independence followed in 1962, the constitution retaining a bicameral legislature; the Senate had 24 members appointed by the Governor General,

115

13 on the advice of the Prime Minister, 4 on the advice of the opposition leader and 7 from religious, social and economic bodies the Prime Minister considered should be represented.

Trinidad was a member of the West Indies Federation from 1957–62.

TURKS AND CAICOS ISLANDS

The territory was a dependency of Jamaica and governed by a commissioner with a legislative board of 5 members, all appointed by the Crown. The Governor of Jamaica had supervisory power. The membership of the Board was in time increased to 7. On the independence of Jamaica in 1962 the islands were administered by the Colonial Office. There was a state council which sat for a five-year term; it had a Speaker, 3 official members, 2–3 nominated members and 9 elected members.

The Governor of the Bahamas became Governor of the islands in 1965. On the independence of the Bahamas in 1973 the islands had their own Governor.

UGANDA

The territory became a British protectorate in 1894 and was administered by a governor. Native rulers with rights regulated by treaty had some powers over their subjects; the province of Buganda was recognized as a native kingdom under its Kabaka, who was assisted by a council of ministers and an assembly.

Exeeutive and legislative councils were introduced in 1921 to assist the Governor; the former had an entirely official membership and the latter an official majority. A constitution introduced in 1955 provided for ministers in the Executive Council. In 1958 the Legislative Council was given a majority elected on an extended franchise and the Executive Council became a council of ministers with a non-official majority. In 1961 internal self-government was introduced, with federal status for Buganda. There was a national assembly entirely elected on universal adult suffrage, and full responsible government. The Governor retained responsibility for external affairs, defence and security, pending full independence, which followed in 1962.

In 1963 the constitution was amended to provide Buganda with its own head of state; at the same time the Governor General was replaced by a president, elected by the National Assembly for a five-year term.

In 1967 Uganda became a republic, with executive authority vested in the President, assisted by a cabinet of ministers. Buganda became one of four administrative regions.

In 1971 President Obote was overthrown by General Amin, who set up a military government.

UNITED KINGDOM
See British Political Facts 1900–1975. David Butler and A. Sloman.

THE WEST INDIES FEDERATION

This was in existence from 1957–62, and included: Antigua, Barbados, Dominica, Grenada, Jamaica, Montserrat, St. Christopher and Nevis (including Anguilla), St. Lucia, St. Vincent, Trinidad and Tobago.

There was a federal parliament consisting of an appointed senate and a house of representatives elected on universal adult suffrage; the members could not also serve on the legislative or executive councils of member states. Both houses sat for a five-year term, money bills could only be introduced in the lower house and they could be passed to the Governor General for assent even if not passed by the Senate. On other bills the Senate had a delaying power of one year. Legislative powers were defined on an exclusive list (for the federal legislature alone), and a concurrent list (for territorial and federal legislatures). Laws could still be enacted by United Kingdom Order in Council on matters of defence, external affairs and financial stability. Executive power was exercised on the Queen's behalf by a governor general assisted by a council of state which consisted of a prime minister and other ministers appointed on his advice. There were also 3 official members appointed by the Governor General. It was laid down on the establishment of the federation that a council should be held not less than five years later to reconsider its constitution.

WEST PACIFIC HIGH COMMISSION TERRITORIES

The office of High Commissioner for the Western Pacific Islands was established in 1877. The High Commissioner was concurrently Governor of Fiji, with headquarters at Suva, until 1952 when the posts were separated and the High Commission headquarters moved to the British Solomon Islands. The Commission's jurisdiction extended over the Gilbert and Ellice Islands, the Solomon Islands, the New Hebrides Condominium (from 1922) and the Pitcairn Islands (between 1898 and 1952).

ZANZIBAR (TANZANIA after 1964)

Since 1891 Zanzibar had a government under a Sultan, with a British resident as first minister. In 1906 the United Kingdom extended its authority and in 1913 control of the protectorate was transferred from the Foreign Office to the Colonial Office. Under the Zanzibar Order-in-Council 1914, powers were defined for a high commissioner and a British Resident to administer the government; they were assisted by a council for the protectorate acting as an advisory and consultative body and consisting of the Sultan, the British Resident, three official and four unofficial members. Decrees of the Sultan were binding when countersigned by the Resident.

In 1926 a legislative council was established with 3 *ex officio* and 5 official members, and 6 unofficials appointed to represent various communities. An executive council was also set up.

In 1956 the membership of the Executive Council was altered to allow more Zanzibari representatives; the Legislative Council was expanded and 6 of its 12 unofficial members were to be elected.

A new constitution of 1960 opened the franchise to women on the same qualifications of property and education as applied to men. The Legislative Council now had 22 elected members, 3 *ex officio* and up to 5 nominated members. This was presided over by a Speaker. The Executive Council had 3 *ex officio* members and 5 unofficials, including a chief minister. In 1962 the Executive Council was replaced by a council of ministers, the franchise was widened by the removal of property and educational qualifications and the official members were removed from both the Executive and the Legislative Councils. Full ministerial government was introduced, as a preliminary to independent status in 1963, when the Legislative Council was replaced by a national assembly.

In 1964 the sultanate was abolished by a revolution and the People's Republic of Zanzibar established. Zanzibar joined with Tanganyika to form Tanzania, but retained its own executive and legislature. The first vice-president of the united republic is the head of the executive in Zanzibar under the title of President of Zanzibar.

4 MINISTERS

ANTIGUA

Date of taking office	Prime Minister
1 Oct 60	V. C. Bird
Feb 70	G. Walter
18 Feb 76	V. C. Bird

AUSTRALIA

Date of taking office	Prime Minister	Foreign Minister	Finance Minister
1 Jan 01	Sir E. Barton	Sir E. Barton	Sir G. Turner
24 Sep 03	A. Deakin	A. Deakin	
27 Apr 04	J. C. Watson	W. M. Hughes	J. C. Watson
18 Aug 04	G. H. Reid	G. H. Reid	Sir G. Turner
5 July 05	A. Deakin	A. Deakin	Sir J. Forrest
30 July 07			Sir W. Lyne
13 Nov 08	A. Fisher	E. L. Bachelor	A. Fisher
2 June 09	A. Deakin	L. E. Groom	Sir J. Forrest
29 Apr 10	A. Fisher	E. L. Bachelor	A. Fisher
14 Oct 11		J. Thomas	
24 June 13	J. Cook	P. McM. Glynn	Sir J. Forrest
17 Sep 14	A. Fisher	J. A. Arthur	A. Fisher
9 Dec 14		H. Mahon	
27 Oct 15	W. M. Hughes		W. C. Higgs
14 Nov 16			A. Poyton
17 Feb 17			Sir J. Forrest

(continued

AUSTRALIA (*continued*)

Date of taking office	Prime Minister	Foreign Minister	Finance Minister
27 Mar 18			W. A. Watt
28 July 20			Sir J. Cook
31 Dec 21		W. M. Hughes	S. M. Bruce
9 Feb 23	S. M. Bruce	S. M. Bruce	E. C. G. Page
22 Oct 29	J. Scullin	J. H. Scullin	E. G. Theodore
6 Jan 32	J. Lyons	J. G. Latham	J. A. Lyons
12 Oct 34		G. F. Pearce	
3 Oct 35			R. G. Casey
29 Nov 37		W. M. Hughes	
7 Apr 39	E. C. G. Page		
26 Apr 39		H. S. Gullet	R. G. Menzies
29 Apr 39	R. G. Menzies		
14 Mar 40		J. McEwen	P. C. Spender
28 Oct 40		F. H. Stewart	A. W. Fadden
29 Aug 41	A. W. Fadden		
7 Oct 41	J. Curtis	H. V. Evatt	J. B. Chifley
6 July 45	F. M. Forde		
13 July 45	J. B. Chifley		
19 Dec 49	R. G. Menzies	P. C. Spender	A. W. Fadden
26 Apr 51		R. G. Casey	
10 Dec 58			H. E. Holt
4 Feb 60		R. G. Menzies	
22 Dec 61		G. E. J. Berwick	
24 Apr 64		P. M. C. Haslock	
26 Jan 66	H. E. Holt		W. McMahon
18 Dec 67	J. McEwen		
10 Jan 68	J. G. Gurton		
10 Feb 69		G. Freeth	
11 Nov 69		W. McMahon	L. Bury
10 Mar 71	W. McMahon		
21 Mar 71		L. Bury	B. M. Snedden
1 Aug 71		N. Bowen	
5 Dec 72	G. Whitlam	G. Whitlam	G. Whitlam
19 Dec 72			F. Crean
9 Oct 73		D. Wiltesea	
21 Nov 74			J. Cairnes
5 Jun 75			W. Hayden
12 Nov 75	M. Fraser	A. S. Peacock	P. Lynch

COMMONWEALTH OF THE BAHAMAS

Date of taking office	Prime Minister
7 Jan 64	Sir R. Symonette
16 Jan 67	L. O. Pindling

BANGLADESH

Date of taking office	Prime Minister	Foreign Minister	Finance Minister
22 Dec 71	T. Ahmed	A. S. Azad	M. Ali
13 Jan 72	Sheikh Mujibur Rahman		T. Ahmed
15 Aug 75	Military coup.		

Since 1975 there has been Military government

BARBADOS

Date of taking office	Prime Minister
1 Feb 54	Sir G. Adams
10 Apr 58	G. Cummins
8 Dec 61	E. W. Barrow[1]
2 Sep 76	J. M. G. Adams

[1] Also Minister of Foreign Affairs from 30 Nov 1966.

121

BELIZE (formerly British Honduras)

Date of taking office	Prime Minister
7 Apr 61	G. C. Price

BOTSWANA (formerly Bechuanaland)

Date of taking office	Prime Minister	Foreign Minister	Finance Minister
3 Mar 65	Seretse Khama (became head of state, post abolished).		
30 Sep 66		Seretse Khama	Q. K. J. Masire
22 Oct 69			J. G. Haskins
June 70			Q. K. J. Masire
21 Oct 74		A. M. Mogwe	

CANADA

Date of taking office	Prime Minister	Foreign Minister	Finance Minister
1900	Sir W. Laurier	R. W. Scott	W. S. Fielding
9 Oct 08		C. Murphy	
9 Oct 11		W. J. Roche	
10 Oct 11	Sir R. L. Borden		Sir W. T. White
29 Oct 12		L. Coderre	
6 Oct 15		P. Blondin	
8 Jan 17		E. L. Patenaude	

122

(continued

CANADA (*continued*)

Date of taking office	Prime Minister	Foreign Minister	Finance Minister
12 Oct 17		M. Burrell	
2 Aug 19			Sir H. L. Drayton
31 Dec 19		A. L. Sifton	
10 July 20	A. Meighen	A. Meighen	
29 Dec 21	W. L. M. King	W. L. M. King	W. S. Fielding
5 Sep 25			J. A. Robb
28 June 26	A. Meighen	A. Meighen	
13 July 26			R. B. Bennett
25 Sep 26	W. L. M. King	W. L. M. King	J. A. Robb
26 Nov 29			C. A. Dunning
7 Aug 30	R. B. Bennett	R. B. Bennett	R. B. Bennett
23 Oct 30	W. L. M. King		
3 Feb 32			E. N. Rhodes
23 Oct 35		W. L. M. King	C. A. Dunning
6 Sep 39			J. L. Ralston
8 July 40			J. L. Ilsey
5 Sep 46		L. St Laurent	
10 Dec 46			D. C. Abbott
10 Sep 48		L. B. Pearson	
15 Nov 48	L. St Laurent		
1 July 54			W. E. Harris
21 June 57	J. Diefenbaker	J. Diefenbaker	
27 June 57			D. M. Fleming
12 Sep 57		S. E. Smith	
18 Mar 59		J. Diefenbaker	
4 June 59		H. C. Green	
9 Aug 62			G. C. Nowlan
22 Apr 63	L. Pearson	P. J. Martin	W. L. Gurdon
18 Dec 65			M. Sharp
20 Apr 68	P. E. Trudeau	M. Sharp	
22 Apr 68			E. J. Benson
28 Jan 72			J. N. Turner
8 Aug 74		A. J. MacEachen	
10 Sep 75			D. S. Macdonald
14 Sep 76		D. C. Jamieson	
16 Sep 77			J. Chrétian

CYPRUS

Date of taking office	Prime Minister	Foreign Minister	Finance Minister
5 Apr 59	Archbishop Makarios	Archbishop Makarios	R. Theocarous
16 Aug 60	None		
22 Aug 60		S. Kyprianou	
1 July 62			R. Solomides
15 June 68			A. Patsalides[1]
16 June 72		I. Khristofidhis[1]	

[1] Apart from a brief period of military government in 1974

DOMINICA

Date of taking office	Prime Minister
1 Jan 60	F. A. M. Baron
Jan 61	E. O. Le Blanc
1 July 67	P. R. John

FIJI

Date of taking office	Prime Minister
1 Sep 67	Ratu Sir K. Mara

THE GAMBIA

Date of taking office	Prime Minister	Foreign Minister	Finance Minister
22 Mar 61	P. N'jie		
4 June 62	Sir D. Jawara		Sharif Sisay
13 Mar 65		Sir D. Jawara	
30 Dec 67			Sharif Dibba
24 Apr 70	None		
9 Oct 72		A. B. N'Jie	I. G. Jahumpa
9 Apr 77		L. K. Jabang	L. B. M'Boya
13 June 77			A. M. Camera

GHANA

Date of taking office	Prime Minister	Foreign Affairs	Finance Minister
5 Mar 52	K. Nkrumah		
17 June 54			K. A. Gbedemah
6 Mar 57		K. Nkrumah	
17 Nov 58		K Botsio	
9 Apr 59		A. Adjei	
1 July 60	None		
8 May 61			F. K. D. Goka
3 Sep 62		K. Nkrumah	
17 Mar 63		K. Botsio	
19 Feb 64			K. Nkrumah
1 May 64			K. Amoaka-Atta
12 June 65		A. Quaison-Sackey	
24 Feb 66		None	None
19 June 66		General J. Ankrah	Brigadier A. A. Afrifa
13 Mar 67		J. W. K. Harlley	
14 Feb 69		P. Anin	

125

(continued

GHANA (continued)

Date of taking office	Prime Minister	Foreign Affairs	Finance Minister
9 Apr 69		V. Owusu	J. Mensah
15 Apr 69		P. Anin	
3 Sep 69	K. Busia		
7 Sep 69		V. Owusu	
28 Jan 71		W. Ofori-Atta	
29 Jan 72	Military coup		
	Since 1972 a military government		

GIBRALTAR

Date of taking office	Prime Minister
11 Aug 64	Sir J. Hassan
6 Aug 69	Major R. Peliza
23 June 73	Sir J. Hassan

GRENADA

Date of taking office	Prime Minister
1 Jan 60	H. A. Blaize
Mar 61	G. Clyne
Aug 61	E. Gairy
19 June 62	Constitution suspended
Sep 62	H. A. Blaize
Aug 67	E. Gairy

GUYANA (formerly British Guiana)

Date of taking office	Prime Minister
30 May 53	C. Jagan[1]
12 Dec 64	F. Burnham

[1] Constitution suspended 9 Oct 1953 to 5 Sept 1961.

INDIA

Date of taking office	Prime Minister	Foreign Minister	Finance Minister
1 Sep 46	J. Nehru	J. Nehru	J. Matthaei
26 Oct 46			L. Ali Khan

127

(continued

INDIA (*continued*)

Date of taking office	Prime Minister	Foreign Minister	Finance Minister
19 July 47			C. Rajagopalachari
15 Aug 47			S. Chatty
16 Aug 48			K. C. Neogy
22 Sep 48			J. Matthaei
25 May 50			Sir C. Desmukh
24 July 56			J. Nehru
1 Sep 56			T. T. Krishna-machari
13 Feb 58			J. Nehru
13 Mar 58			M. Desai
29 Aug 63			T. T. Krishna-machari
27 May 64	G. Nanda	vacant	
9 June 64	L. B. Shastri	L. B. Shastri	
20 July 64		S. S. Singh	
31 Dec 65			S. Chauduri
11 Jan 66	G. Nanda		
24 Jan 66	Mrs I. Gandhi		
13 Nov 66		M. C. Chagla	
13 Mar 67			M. Desai
5 Sep 67		Mrs I. Gandhi	
14 Feb 69		D. Singh	
16 July 69			Mrs I. Gandhi
27 June 70		S. S. Singh	Y. Chavan
10 Oct 74		Y. B. Chavan	C. Subramaniam
20 Mar 77	M. R. Desai	A. B. Vajpayee	H. M. Patel

JAMAICA

Date of taking office	Prime Minister
5 May 53	Sir A. Bustamente
2 Feb 55	N. Manley

128

(*continued*

JAMAICA (*continued*)

Date of taking office	Prime Minister
11 Apr 62	Sir A. Bustamente
22 Feb 67	Sir D. Sangster
11 Apr 67	H. L. Shearer
2 Mar 72	M. Manley

KENYA

Date of taking office	Prime Minister	Foreign Minister	Finance Minister
6 Apr 62	J. Kenyatta		J. Gichuru
1 June 63		J. Kenyatta	
12 Dec 64	post abolished		
5 Feb 69		M. Koinange	
22 Dec 69		N. Mungai	M. Kibaki
31 Oct 74		M. Waiyaki	

LESOTHO

Date of taking office	Prime Minister	Foreign Minister	Finance Minister
6 May 65	S. Maseribane		
11 May 65			B. Leseteli
7 July 65	Chief L. Jonathan		
4 Oct 66		Chief L. Jonathan	
8 July 67			P. Peete
31 Aug 71			E. R. Sekhonyana
July 72		P. Peete	
5 July 74		J. R. Kostsokoane	
5 June 75		C. D. Molapa	

MALAWI

Date of taking office	Prime Minister	Foreign Minister	Finance Minister
1 Feb 63	H. Banda (became head of state, post abolished)		H. E. I. Phillips
6 July 64		K. Chiume	J. Tembo
8 Sep 64		H. Banda	
1 Jan 69			A. Banda
4 Apr 72			D. Matenje

MALAYSIA

Date of taking office	Prime Minister	Foreign Minister	Finance Minister
4 Aug 55	T. A. Rahman		
31 Aug 57		T. A. Rahman	Sir H. H-S. Lee
9 Feb 59	D. A. R. B. Hussein	I. B. D. A. Rahman	
21 Aug 59	T. A. Rahman		
22 Aug 59			T. S. Sin
18 Aug 60		T. A. Rahman	
21 May 69			T. A. R. B. Hussein
22 Sep 70	T. A. R. B. Hussein		
23 Sep 70		T. A. R. B. Hussein	T. S. Sin
5 Sep 74			D. Hussein bin Onn
6 Aug 75	A. Razak	T. D. A. R. T. Ismail	
15 Jan 76	D. Hussein bin Onn		
5 Mar 76			T. T. S. R. Hamzah

MALTA

Date of taking office	Prime Minister	Foreign Minister	Finance Minister
4 Nov 47	P. Boffa		A. Colombo
17 Sep 50	E. Mizzi		
26 Sep 50			F. Azzopardi
20 Dec 50	B. Olivier		
10 Mar 55	D. Mintoff		D. Mintoff
30 Apr 58	constitution suspended		
5 Mar 62	B. Olivier		B. Olivier
21 Sep 64		B. Olivier	
21 June 71	D. Mintoff	D. Mintoff	J. Abela

MAURITIUS

Date of taking office	Prime Minister	Foreign Minister	Finance Minister
26 Sep 61	Sir S. Ramgoolam		Sir S. Ramgoolam
15 Aug 67			G. Forget
12 Mar 68		Sir S. Ramgoolam	V. Ringadoo
1 Dec 69		G. Duval	
17 Dec 73		Sir S. Ramgoolam	
1 June 76		Sir H. Walker	

MONTSERRAT

Date of taking office	Prime Minister
1 Jan 60	W. H. Bramble
Dec 70	P. A. Bramble

131

NEW ZEALAND

Date of taking office	Prime Minister	Foreign Secretary	Finance Minister
1 Jan 00			R. J. Seddon
10 June 06	W. Hall-Jones		W. Hall-Jones
6 Aug 06	Sir J. G. Ward		Sir J. G. Ward
28 Mar 12	T. Mackenzie		A. M. Myers
10 July 12	W. F. Massey		J. Allen
12 Aug 15			Sir J. G. Ward
1 Sep 19			Sir J. Allen
27 Nov 19		Sir J. Allen	
17 May 20		E. P. Lee	W. F. Massey
26 June 23		Sir F. Bell	
10 May 25	Sir F. Bell		
14 May 25			W. Nosworthy
30 May 25	J. G. Coates		
23 May 26		W. Nosworthy	W. D. Stewart
10 Dec 28	Sir J. G. Ward	Sir J. G. Ward	Sir J. G. Ward
28 May 30	G. W. Forbes	G. W. Forbes	G. W. Forbes
22 Sep 31			W. D. Stewart
20 Jan 33			J. G. Coates
6 Dec 35	M. J. Savage	M. J. Savage	W. Nash
4 Apr 40	P. Fraser		
30 Apr 40		F. Langstone (vacant 21 Dec 42)	
7 July 43		P. Fraser	
13 Dec 49	S. G. Holland	F. W. Doidge	S. G. Holland
Sep 51		T. C. Webb	
20 Nov 54			J. T. Watts
26 Nov 54		T. L. Macdonald	
20 Sep 57	K. Holyoake		
11 Dec 57	Sir W. Nash	Sir W. Nash	A. H. Nordmeyer
12 Dec 60	Sir K. Holyoake	Sir K. Holyoake	H. Lake
3 Mar 67			R. B. Muldoon
7 Feb 72	J. Marshall		
8 Dec 72	N. Kirk	N. Kirk	
18 Dec 72			W. Rowling
6 Sep 74	W. Rowling	W. Rowling	R. Tizard
12 Sep 75	R. D. Muldoon	B. E. Talboys	R. D. Muldoon

NIGERIA

Central Government

Date of taking office	Prime Minister	Foreign Affairs	Finance Minister
30 Aug 57	Sir A. T. Balewa		Sir A. T. Balewa
17 Sep 57			Chief P. Okotie-Eboh
1 Oct 60		Sir A. T. Balewa	
17 July 61		J. Wachuku	
7 Jan 65		Sir A. T. Balewa	
1 Dec 65		N. Bamali	
15 Jan 66	Military coup.		
	Since 1966 a military government.		

PAKISTAN

Date of taking office	Prime Minister	Foreign Minister	Finance Minister
19 July 47	L. A. Khan	L. A. Khan	L. A. Khan
18 Aug 47			G. Mohammed
28 Dec 47		Sir M. Z. Khan	
17 Oct 51	K. Nazim ud-Din		
27 Oct 51			C. M. Ali
17 Apr 53	M. Ali		
27 Oct 54		M. Ali	
12 Aug 55	C. M. Ali	C. M. Ali	
26 Sep 55		H. H. Chaudry	
17 Oct 55			S. A. Ali
12 Sep 56	H. S. Surawardi	M. F. K. Noon	
17 Oct 57	I. Chundrigar		

133

(continued

PAKISTAN (*continued*)

Date of taking office	Prime Minister	Foreign Minister	Finance Minister
24 Oct 57		M. Qadir	
16 Dec 57	M. F. K. Noon		
24 Oct 58	General M. A. Khan		M. Shoaib
27 Oct 58	post abolished		
30 Jan 62			A. Qadir
13 June 62		M. Ali	
14 Dec 62			M. Shoaib
24 Jan 63		Z. A. Bhutto	
18 June 66		Field Marshal M. A. Khan	
20 July 66		S. Pirzada	
25 Aug 66			N. Uqaili
24 Apr 68		A. Husain	
3 Mar 69		Y. Khan	None
4 Aug 69			N. M. A. Qizilbashi
4 Aug 70		H. Han	
21 Feb 71		None	None
7 Dec 71	N. Amin	Z. A. Bhutto	
24 Dec 71			M. Hasan

Pakistan left the Commonwealth in 1972.

ST KITTS

Date of taking office	Prime Minister
1 Jan 60	C. P. Southwell
July 66	R. Bradshaw

ST LUCIA

Date of taking office	Prime Minister
1 Jan 60	G. Charles
Apr 64	J. Compton

ST VINCENT

Date of taking office	Prime Minister
1 Jan 60	E. T. Joshua
May 67	R. M. Cato

SIERRA LEONE

Date of taking office	Prime Minister	Foreign Minister	Finance Minister
9 July 54	Sir M. Margai		
14 Aug 58			M. S. Mustapha
27 Apr 61		J. Karefa-Smart	
5 June 62			A. Margai
28 Apr 64	Sir A. Margai		
29 Apr 64		C. Rogers-Wright	R. G. J. King
23 Nov 65		M. Kallon	
21 Mar 67	S. P. Stevens		

135

(continued

SIERRA LEONE (continued)

Date of taking office	Prime Minister	Foreign Minister	Finance Minister
26 Mar 67	post abolished		
30 Mar 67		W. Leigh	Colonel A. Juxon-Smith
26 Apr 68	S. P. Stevens		M. S. Forna
11 Apr 69		C. Foray	
26 Apr 69		L. A. M. Brewah	
14 Sep 70			A. G. Sembu-Forna
21 Apr 71	S. I. Koroma	S. Pratt	C. A. Kamara-Taylor
16 May 73		D. F. Luke	
1 Apr 75		F. M. Minah	
July 75	C. A. Kamora-Taylor		S. I. Koroma
6 May 77		A. Conteh	A. B. Kamara

SINGAPORE

Date of taking office	Prime Minister	Foreign Minister	Finance Minister
6 Apr 55	D. Marshall		
8 June 56	Lim Yew Hock		
5 June 59	Lee Kuan Yew		Goh Keng-Swee
9 Aug 65		S. Rajaratnam	Lim Kin-San
17 Aug 67			Goh Keng-Swee
11 Aug 70			Hon Sui-Sen

SOUTH AFRICA

Date of taking office	Prime Minister	Foreign Minister	Finance Minister
31 May 10	General L. Botha		H. C. Hull
26 June 12			General J. C. Smuts

(continued

136

SOUTH AFRICA (*continued*)

Date of taking office	Prime Minister	Foreign Minister	Finance Minister
24 Feb 15			Sir D. de Villiers Graaf
1 Feb 16			H. Burton
4 Oct 17			T. Orr
3 Sep 19	General J. C. Smuts		
19 Mar 20			H. Burton
30 June 24	General J. B. M. Hertzog		N. C. Havenga
1 June 27		General J. B. M. Hertzog	
5 Sep 39	General J. C. Smuts		
6 Sep 39		General J. C. Smuts	J. H. Hofmeyer
15 Jan 48			F. Sturrock
4 June 48	D. F. Malan	D. F. Malan	N. C. Havenga
30 Nov 54	J. G. Strijdom	E. Louw	E. Louw
31 July 56			J. F. Naudé
2 Sep 58	H. F. Verwoerd		
20 Oct 58			T. E. Dönges

South Africa left the Commonwealth in 1961.

SOUTHERN RHODESIA

Date of taking office	Prime Minister	Foreign Minister	Finance Minister
1 Oct 23	Sir C. Coghlan		
11 Oct 23			P. Fynn
2 Sep 27	H. U. Moffat		
6 July 33	G. Mitchell		
12 Sep 33	Sir G. Huggins (later Lord Malvern)		J. H. Smit
26 Feb 42			M. Danziger
3 May 46			Colonel Sir E. L. Guest
23 Sep 46			Sir E. Whitehead

(*continued*

137

SOUTHERN RHODESIA (*continued*)

Date of taking office	Prime Minister	Foreign Minister	Finance Minister
7 Sep 53	G. Todd		D. MacIntyre
28 Jan 54			C. Hatty
14 Jan 58			A. E. Abrahamson
18 Feb 58	Sir E. Whitehead		C. Hatty
23 Sep 62			G. Ellman-Brown
17 Dec 62	W. Field		I. Smith
13 Apr 64	I. Smith		
14 Apr 64		I. Smith	J. J. Wrathall
19 Aug 64		C. W. Dupont	
13 Apr 70		J. Howman	
2 Aug 74		P. K. Van der Byl	
13 Jan 76			D. Smith

RHODESIAN FEDERATION

Date of taking office	Prime Minister	Foreign Minister	Finance Minister
7 Sep 53	Sir G. Huggins	Held by the Prime Minister	
17 Dec 53			Sir D. MacIntyre
1 Nov 56	Sir R. Welensky		
3 Sep 62			Sir J. Caldicott

SRI LANKA (formerly Ceylon)

Date of taking office	Prime Minister	Foreign Minister	Finance Minister
26 Sep 47	S. Senanayake	Held by the Prime Minister in each case	J. R. Jayawardene

138

(*continued*

SRI LANKA (*continued*)

Date of taking office	Prime Minister	Foreign Affairs	Finance Minister
26 Mar 52	D. Senanayake		
12 Oct 53	Sir J. Kotelawala		
13 Oct 53			Sir O. Goonetilleke
27 June 54			M. D. H. Jayawardene
12 Apr 56	S. Bandaranaike		S. de Zoysa
26 Sep 59	W. Dahanayake		
22 Nov 59			M. Mustafa
21 Mar 60	D. Senanayake		
21 July 60	Mrs S. Bandaranaike		F. D. Bandaranaike
27 Aug 62			C. P. de Silva
8 Nov 62			I. Kalugalla
29 May 63			T. Illangaratne
11 June 64			N. M. Perera
27 Mar 65			U. B. Wanninayake
31 May 70			N. M. Perera
17 Sep 75			F. R. D. Bandaranaike
21 July 77	J. R. Jayawardene	A. C. S. Hameed	R. de Mel

SWAZILAND

Date of taking office	Prime Minister	Foreign Minister	Finance Minister
25 Apr 67	Prince Mathesini Dhlamini		
16 May 67			L. Lovell
6 Sep 68		Prince Makhesini Dhlamini	
2 June 72		S. Matsebula	R. Stephens
Apr 73	Military coup.		
	Since 1973 a military government		

TANZANIA

Date of taking office	Prime Minister	Foreign Minister	Finance Minister
2 Sep 60	J. Nyerere		Sir E. Vasey
9 Dec 61		J. Nyerere	
22 Jan 62	R. Kawawa		P. Bomani
9 Dec 62	post abolished		
12 Mar 63		O. Kambona	
30 Sep 65		J. Nyerere	A. Jamal
5 Nov 70		I. Elinawings	
17 Feb 72	R. Kawawa	J. Malecela	C. Msuya
10 Nov 75		I. M. Kaduma	A. H. Jamal
13 Feb 77		B. Mkapa	E. Mlei

TONGA

Date of taking office	Ruler	Premier
1893	King George II	Jiosateki Toga[1]
Jan 1905		Jione Mateialona
30 Sep 12		Terita Tuivakano
5 Apr 18	Queen Salote Tupou III	
30 June 22		Prince Uiliami Tugi
July 40		Ata
12 Dec 49		Crown Prince Taufa'ahua Tungi
16 Dec 65	King Taufa'ahua Tupou IV	Prince Tu'ipelehake

[1] At 1 Jan 1900

140

TRINIDAD AND TOBAGO

Date of taking office	Prime Minister
28 Oct 56	Dr Eric Williams

UGANDA

Date of taking office	Prime Minister	Foreign Minister	Finance Minister
2 July 61	B. Kiwanuka		
1 Mar 62			L. Sebalu
30 Apr 62	A. Milton Obote	A. Milton Obote	A. K. Sempa
24 Aug 64		S. Odaka	
2 Oct 64			L. Kalule-Settaala
15 Apr 66	post abolished		
25 Jan 71	Military coup		
	Since 1971 military government		

UNITED KINGDOM

Date of taking office	Prime Minister	Colonial Secretary	Dominions Secretary
June 1885	Lord Salisbury		
1 Jan 1900		J. Chamberlain	
12 July 02	A. J. Balfour		
9 Oct 03		A. Lyttleton	

141

(continued

UNITED KINGDOM (*continued*)

Date of taking office	Prime Minister	Colonial Secretary	Dominions Secretary
5 Dec 05	Sir H. C. Bannerman		
11 Dec 05		Lord Elgin	
7 Apr 08	H. H. Asquith		
16 Apr 08		Lord Crewe	
7 Nov 10		L. Harcourt	
27 May 15		A. Bonar Law	
7 Dec 16	D. Lloyd George		
11 Dec 16		W. Long	
9 Jan 19		Lord Milner	
14 Feb 21		W. S. Churchill	
23 Oct 22	A. Bonar Law		
25 Oct 22		Duke of Devonshire	
22 May 23	S.Baldwin		
22 Jan 24	J. Ramsay MacDonald		
23 Jan 24		J. H. Thomas	
4 Nov 24	S. Baldwin		
7 Nov 24		L. S. Amery	L. S. Amery
5 June 29	J. Ramsay MacDonald		
8 June 29		S. Webb	S. Webb
13 June 30			J. H. Thomas
26 Aug 31		J. H. Thomas	
9 Nov 31		Sir P. Cuncliffe-Lister	
7 June 35	S. Baldwin	M. MacDonald	
27 Nov 35		J. H. Thomas	M. MacDonald
29 May 36		W. Ormsby Gore	
28 May 37	N. Chamberlain		
16 May 38		M. MacDonald	Lord Stanley
4 Nov 38			M. MacDonald
2 Feb 39			Lord Caldecote
4 Sep 39			A. Eden
11 May 40	W. S. Churchill		
15 May 40		Lord Lloyd	Lord Caldecote
4 Oct 40			Lord Cranborne
8 Feb 41		Lord Moyne	
18 Feb 42		Lord Cranborne	C. Attlee

(*continued*

UNITED KINGDOM (*continued*)

Date of taking office	Prime Minister	Colonial Secretary	Dominions Secretary
22 Nov 42		O. Stanley	
24 Sep 43			Lord Cranborne
			Secretary of State for Commonwealth Relations
26 July 45	C. Attlee	G. H. Hall	Lord Addison
7 Oct 47		A. Creech Jones	P. Noel-Baker
28 Feb 50		J. Griffiths	P. Gordon Walker
26 Oct 51	W. S. Churchill	O. Lyttleton	General Lord Ismay
12 Mar 52			Lord Salisbury
24 Nov 52			Lord Swinton
28 July 54		A. Lennox-Boyd	
6 Apr 55	A. Eden		
12 Apr 55			Lord Home
10 Jan 57	H. Macmillan		
14 Oct 59		I. Macleod	
27 July 60			D. Sandys
9 Oct 61		R. Maudling	
16 July 62		D. Sandys	
20 Oct 63	Sir Alec Douglas-Home[1]		
16 Oct 64	H. Wilson	A. Greenwood	A. Bottomley
22 Dec 65		Lord Longford	
5 Apr 66		F. Lee	
11 Aug 66			H. Bowden
7 Jan 67		(post abolished)	
28 Aug 67			G. Thomson
17 Oct 68			(merged with Foreign Office)
19 June 70	E. Heath		
4 Mar 74	H. Wilson		
5 Apr 76	J. Callaghan		

[1] Formerly Lord Home

WESTERN SAMOA

Date of taking office	Prime Minister
1 Jan 62	Fiame II Mata'afa Faumuina Mulinu'u
70	Tupua Tamasese Lealofi
73	Fiame II Mata'afa Faumuina Mulinu'u
75	Tupua Tamasese Lealofi
Mar 76	Tupuolo Efi

ZAMBIA (formerly Northern Rhodesia)

Date of taking office	Prime Minister	Foreign Minister	Finance Minister
23 Jan 64	K. Kaunda (became head of state, post abolished)		A. Wina
24 Sep 64		S. Kapwepwe	
7 Sep 67		R. Kamanga	E. Mudenda
23 Dec 68		E. Mudenda	S. Kapwepwe
25 Aug 69		K. Kaunda	E. Mudenda
2 Oct 70			J. Mwanakatwe
7 Oct 70		E. Mudenda	
13 Dec 73		V. J. Mwaanga	A. Chikwanda
27 May 75		R. Banda	
10 May 76		S. G. Mwale	

5 ELECTIONS

INTRODUCTORY NOTE

It is almost impossible to obtain accepted statistics of votes cast for each party in elections for certain countries of the Commonwealth. In the face of this, this chapter has attempted to give the dates when elections were held and the number of seats won by party. For precise figures of votes cast, reference should be made to Mackie, Thomas T., and Rose, Richard *The International Almanac of Electoral History* (Macmillan 1974). For the Commonwealth, this gives full information on Australia, Canada, Malta, New Zealand and the United Kingdom. Other useful books on these countries are Hughes, C. A. and Graham, B. D. *A Handbook of Australian Government and Politics* (Australian University Press, 1968); the *New Zealand Official Year Book*; Beck, J. M. *Pendulum of Power: Canada's Federal Elections* (McGraw-Hill, 1970). For Britain, see Butler, D. E. and Sloman, A. *British Political Facts, 1900–1974* (Macmillan, 1975). Basic data on dates and party representation can be found in *The Statesman's Year-Book*, *Keesing's Contemporary Archives*, as well as in official government year-books.

AUSTRALIA

1901 (30 Mar)	*Seats*
Australian Labor Party	14
Free Traders	28
Protectionists	31
Others	2
	75

1903 (16 Dec)	
Australian Labor Party	23
Free Traders	26

Seats

1903 (16 Dec) (continued)
Protectionists   25
Others   1
75

1906 (12 Dec)
Australian Labor Party   26
Protectionists   20
Anti-Socialists   27
Others   2
75

1910 (13 Apr)
Australian Labor Party   43
Liberal Party   31
Others   1
75

1913 (31 May)
Australian Labor Party   37
Liberal Party   38
75

1914 (5 Sep)
Australian Labor Party   42
Liberal Party   32
Others   1
75

1917 (5 May)
Australian Labor Party   22
Nationalist Party   53
75

1919 (13 Dec)
Australian Labor Party   26
Country Party   11
Nationalist Party   37
Others   1
75

	Seats
1922 (16 Dec)	
Australian Labor Party	29
Country Party	14
Nationalist Party	26
Liberals	5
Others	1
	75
1925 (14 Nov)	
Australian Labor Party	23
Nationalist Party	37
Country Party	14
Others	1
	75
1928 (17 Nov)	
Australian Labor Party	31
Nationalist Party	29
Country Party	13
Others	2
	75
1929 (12 Aug)	
Australian Labor Party	46
Nationalist Party	14
Country Party	10
Others	5
	75
1931 (19 Dec)	
United Australia Party	40
Australian Labor Party	14
Country Party	16
New South Wales Labor	4
Others	4
	75
1934 (15 Sep)	
United Australia Party	33
Australian Labor Party	18
New South Wales Labor	9

	Seats
1934 (15 Sep) (continued)	
Country Party	14
Others	1
	74

1937 (23 Oct)	
Australian Labor Party	29
United Australia Party	28
Country Party	16
Others	1
	74

1940 (21 Sep)	
Australian Labor Party	32
United Australia Party	23
Country Party	14
Non-Communist Labor	4
Others	1
	74

1943 (21 Aug)	
Australian Labor Party	49
United Australia Party	13
Country Party	7
Country National Party	3
Others	2
	74

1946 (28 Sep)	
Australian Labor Party	43
Australian Liberal Party	18
Country Party	11
Others	2
	74

1949 (10 Dec)	
Australian Labor Party	49
Australian Liberal Party	55
Country Party	19
	123

	Seats
1951 (28 Apr)	
Australian Labor Party	55
Australian Liberal Party	52
Country Party	16
	123

1954 (29 May)	
Australian Labor Party	59
Australian Liberal Party	47
Country Party	17
	123

1955 (10 Dec)	
Australian Labor Party	48
Australian Liberal Party	57
Country Party	18
	123

1958 (22 Nov)	
Australian Labor Party	47
Australian Liberal Party	58
Country Party	19
	124

1961 (9 Dec)	
Australian Labor Party	62
Australian Liberal Party	45
Country Party	17
	124

1963 (30 Nov)	
Australian Labor Party	52
Australian Liberal Party	52
Country Party	20
	124

Seats

1966 (26 Nov)

Australian Labor Party	41
Australian Liberal Party	61
Country Party	21
Others	1
	124

1969 (25 Oct)

Australian Labor Party	59
Australian Liberal Party	46
Country Party	20
	125

1972 (2 Dec)

Australian Labor Party	67
Australian Liberal Party	38
Country Party	20
	125

1974 (18 May)

Australian Labour Party		66
Australian Liberal Party	}	61
Country Party		
		127

1975 (13 Dec)

Australian Liberal Party	68
Australian Labour Party	36
National Country Party	23
	127

BAHAMAS

The first elections held under universal suffrage took place in Jan 1967. Since independence, the following elections have been held.

BAHAMAS (*continued*)

	Seats
1972 (19 Sep)	
Progressive Liberal Party	29
Free National Movement	9
	38
	—
1977 (19 July)	
Progressive Liberal Party	30
Bahamian Democratic Party	5
Free National Movement	2
	37 (1 vacant)

BANGLADESH

The only General Election since independence was held on 7 Mar 1973. The Awami League won 307 of the 315 seats.

BARBADOS

1966 (3 Nov)	
Democratic Labour Party (DLP)	14
Barbados Labour Party (BLP)	9
Barbados National Party (BNP)	1
	24
	—
1971 (Sep)	
Democratic Labour Party	18
Barbados Labour Party	6
	24
	—

BOTSWANA

	Seats
1965 (1 Mar)	
Botswana Democratic Party (BDP)	28
Botswana Peoples Party (BPP)	3
	31

1969 (18 Oct)	
Botswana Democratic Party	24
Botswana Peoples Party	3
Botswana National Front	3
Botswana Independence Party	1
	31

1974 (26 Oct)	
Botswana Democratic Party	27
Botswana Peoples Party	2
Botswana National Front	2
Botswana Independence Party	1
	32

CANADA

	Seats
1900 (7 Nov)	
Liberals	133
Conservatives	80
	213

1904 (3 Nov)	
Liberals	138
Conservatives	75
Others	1
	214

	Seats
1908 (26 Oct)	
Liberals	135
Conservatives	85
Others	1
	221
1911 (21 Sep)	
Conservatives	134
Liberals	87
	221
1917 (7 Dec)	
Conservatives	153
Liberals	82
	235
1921 (6 Dec)	
Liberals	116
Conservatives	50
National Progressive Party	64
Labor Party	2
Others	3
	235
1925 (29 Oct)	
Conservatives	116
Liberals	99
National Progressive Party	24
Labor Party	2
Others	4
	245
1926 (14 Sep)	
Liberals	128
Conservatives	91
National Progressive Party	20
Labor Party	3
Others	3
	245

	Seats
1930 (28 July)	
Conservatives	137
Liberals	91
National Progressive Party	12
Labor Party	2
Others	3
	245

1935 (14 Oct)	
Liberals	173
Conservatives	40
Co-operative Commonwealth Federation (CCF)	7
Reconstruction Party	1
Social Credit	17
Others	7
	245

1940 (26 Mar)	
Liberals	181
Conservatives	40
C.C.F.	8
Social Credit	10
Others	6
	245

1945 (11 June)	
Liberals	125
Conservatives	67
C.C.F.	28
Social Credit	13
Bloc Populaire	2
Others	10
	245

1949 (27 June)	
Liberals	193
Conservatives	41
C.C.F.	13

	Seats
1949 (27 June) (continued)	
Social Credit	10
Others	5
	262

1953 (10 Aug)	
Liberals	171
Conservatives	51
C.C.F.	23
Social Credit	15
Others	5
	265

1957 (10 June)	
Liberals	105
Conservatives	112
C.C.F.	25
Social Credit	19
Others	4
	265

1958 (31 Mar)	
Conservatives	208
Liberals	49
C.C.F..	8
	265

1962 (18 June)	
Conservatives	116
Liberals	100
New Democratic Party	19
Social Credit	30
	265

1963 (8 Apr)	
Liberals	129
Conservatives	95
New Democratic Party	17

	Seats
1963 (8 Apr) (continued)	
Social Credit	24
	265

1965 (18 Nov)	
Liberals	131
Conservatives	97
New Democratic Party	21
Ralliement des Créditistes	9
Social Credit	5
Others	2
	265

1968 (25 June)	
Liberals	155
Conservatives	72
New Democratic Party	22
Ralliement des Créditistes	14
Others	1
	264

1972 (30 Oct)	
Liberals	109
Conservatives	107
New Democratic Party	31
Social Credit	15
Others	2
	264

1974 (8 July)	
Liberals	141
Progressive Conservatives	95
Social Credit	11
New Democratic Party	16
Independents	1
	264

FIJI

Two elections have been held: in Apr 1972, when the Alliance Party won 33 seats, the National Federation Party 19; and in Mar 1977, when the Alliance Party won 24 seats, the National Federation Party 26, the Fijian Nationalist Party 1 and Independents 1.

THE GAMBIA

1972 (28–29 Mar)
Peoples Progressive Party	28
United Party	3
Independents	1
	32

1977 (5 Mar)
Peoples Progressive Party	27
Opposition Coalition	7
	34

GHANA

On 21 Feb 1964, Ghana became a one-party state (the Convention Peoples Party). In the June 1965 elections, all 198 CPP candidates were returned unopposed. Political parties were banned in Feb 1966. In 1969, a 140 member National Assembly was elected by universal suffrage from a slate of 480 candidates. The result was as follows:

1969 (29 Aug)
Progress Party	105
National Alliance of Liberals	29
Minority Parties	6
	140

GUYANA

1973 (16 July)
Peoples National Congress	37
Peoples Progressive Party	14
Liberator Party	2

INDIA

	Seats
1952	
Congress Party	362
Socialist Party	12
KMPP	9
Jan Sangh	3
CPI & allies	27
Others	39
Independents	37
	489

1957	
Congress Party	369
PSP	21
CPI	27
Jan Sangh	4
Independents & others	73
	494

1962 (Feb)	
Congress Party	361
Swatantra	18
Jan Sangh	14
DMK	7
Samyutka Socialists	6
Communists	29
Praja Socialists	12
Others	47
	494

	Seats
1967 (15–21 Feb)	
Congress Party	282
Communists	42
Swatantra	44
Jan Sangh	35
Praja Socialists	13
DMK	25
Samyutka Socialists	23
Others	54
	520

1971 (1–10 Mar)	
Congress Party	366
Communists	48
Swatantra	8
Jan Sangh	22
Telengana Praja Samiti	10
DMK	23
Samyutka Socialists	3
Others	38
	518

1977 (Mar)	
Janata Party	271
Congress Party	153
Congress for Democracy	28
Communists (Marxist)	22
DMK	19
Akali Dal	8
Communist Party of India	7
Others	32
	540

JAMAICA

	Seats
1967 (21 Feb)	
Jamaica Labour Party	33
Peoples National Party	20
1972 (29 Feb)	
Peoples National Party	37
Jamaica Labour Party	15
Independent	1
1976 (15 Dec)	
Peoples National Party	48
Jamaica Labour Party	12

KENYA

In Oct 1969 the sole opposition party, the KPU, was banned and Kenya became a one-party state (KANU). Elections contested only by KANU were held in December 1969 and Oct 1974. In this latter contest, 88 of the 158 MPs lost their seats.

LESOTHO

At the general election prior to Independence, on 30 Apr 1965, 31 members of the National Party were returned, 25 members of the Congress Party and 4 members of the Marematlou Freedom Party. On 30 Jan 1970 the Lesotho Independence Order of 1966 was suspended and the elections of 27 Jan 1970 declared invalid. An interim national assembly with a nominated membership was set up in Apr 1973.

160

MALAWI

Malawi is a one-party state. Elections, contested only by the Malawi
Congress Party were held in 1966, Apr 1971 and June 1976.

MALAYSIA

	Seats
1974 (24 Aug)	
National Front	135
Democratic Action Party	9
Sarawak National Party	9
Soual Justice Party (PEKEMAS)	1

MALTA

1966 (26–28 Mar)	
Nationalist Party	28
Labour Party	22
	50

1971 (12–14 June)	
Labour Party	28
Nationalist Party	27
	55

1976 (17–18 Sep)	
Labour Party	34
Nationalist Party	31
	65

MAURITIUS

1967 (7 Aug)	
Alliance Independence Party	43
Mauritian Social Democratic Party	27
	70

Seats

1976 (Dec)

MMM (Mouvement Militant Mauricien)	34
Independence Party	28
PMSD	8
	70
	—

NEW ZEALAND

Seats

1902 (25 Nov)

Liberals	47
Opposition	19
Others	10
	76

1905 (6 Dec)

Liberals	55
Opposition	15
Others	6
	76

1908 (24 Nov)

Liberals	47
Opposition	25
Labour	1
Others	3
	76
	—

1911 (14 Dec)

Liberals	30
Reform Party	36
Labour	4
Others	6
	76
	—

1914 (10 Dec)

Liberals	31

	Seats
1914 (10 Dec) (continued)	
Reform Party	39
Labour	6
	76

1919 (17 Dec)	
Reform Party	43
Liberal/United Party	17
Labour Party	8
Others	8
	76

1922 (7 Dec)	
Reform Party	35
Liberal/Labour	21
Labour Party	17
Others	3
	76

1925 (4 Nov)	
Reform Party	51
National Party	9
Labour Party	12
Others	4
	76

1928 (14 Nov)	
Reform Party	25
Liberal/United Party	25
Labour Party	19
Others	7
	76

1931 (2 Dec)	
Reform/United Party	42
Labour Party	24
Others	10
	76

	Seats
1935 (27 Nov)	
Reform/United Party	17
Labour Party	53
Others	6
	76
	—
1938 (15 Oct)	
National Party	24
Labour Party	50
Others	2
	76
	—
1943 (23 Sep)	
National Party	34
Labour Party	41
Others	1
	76
	—
1946 (27 Nov)	
Labour Party	42
National Party	38
	80
	—
1949 (30 Nov)	
Labour Party	34
National Party	46
	80
	—
1951 (1 Sep)	
Labour Party	30
National Party	50
	80
	—

	Seats
1954 (13 Nov)	
Labour Party	35
National Party	45
	80
	—
1957 (30 Nov)	
Labour Party	41
National Party	39
	80
	—
1960 (26 Nov)	
Labour Party	34
National Party	46
	80
	—
1963 (30 Nov)	
Labour Party	35
National Party	45
	80
	—
1966 (26 Nov)	
Labour Party	35
National Party	44
Social Credit	1
	80
	—
1969 (29 Nov)	
Labour Party	39
National Party	45
	84
	—
1972 (25 Nov)	
Labour Party	55
National Party	32
	87
	—

165

Seats

1975 (29 Nov)
National Party   55
Labour Party   32

NIGERIA

No elections have been taken place since 1965. The final results then were

NPC   162
NCNC   83
NNDP   36
AG   21
NPF   4
Inds   5

PAKISTAN

The elections of 7 Dec 1970 were the first ever held on the basis of one-man one-vote. Detailed electoral statistics are almost impossible to obtain. The following results, for 1970–1977 are only estimates. They were also the last ever held before the independence of Bangladesh. The results were Awami League 151, Pakistan Peoples Party 81, Qayyum Moslem League 9, Council Moslem League 7, Ahle Sunnat 7, Others 33.

The most recent election, on 7 Mar 1977, resulted in the ruling Pakistan Peoples Party winning 155 seats, the Pakistan National Alliance 36, the Qayyum Moslem league 1, Independents 8. The results were much disputed.

SEYCHELLES

1970 (Nov)
Seychelles Democratic Party   10
Seychelles Peoples United Party   5
                                    15
                                    ──

	Seats
1974	
Seychelles Democratic Party	13
Seychelles Peoples United Party	2
	15

SIERRA LEONE

1967 (17 Mar)
The elections were contested by the Sierra Leone Peoples Party and the All Peoples Congress. On 21 Mar before the final results were in, the country was placed under martial law.

1973 (11–15 May)
For this election, the Sierra Leone Peoples Party withdrew its nominations and the All Peoples Congress was returned unopposed.

1977 (Feb)	Seats
All Peoples Congress	62
Sierra Leone Peoples Party (SLPP)	15
Vacant	8

SINGAPORE

1972 (2 Sep)	Seats
Peoples Action Party (PAP)	65
Opposition Groups	nil

SRI LANKA

	Seats
1956 (April)	
M.E.P.	51
U.N.P.	8
N.L.S.S.P.	14

Seats

1956 (April) (continued)
Federal Party (FP)	10
Communists (CP)	3
Tamil Congress (TC)	1
Independents	8
	95

1960 (Mar)
U.N.P.	50
S.L.F.P.	46
L.S.S.P.	10
M.E.P.	10
C.P.	3
F.P.	15
T.C.	1
Independents & other parties	16
	151

1960 (July)
U.N.P.	30
S.L.F.P.	75
L.S.S.P.	12
M.E.P.	3
C.P.	4
F.P.	16
T.C.	1
Independents & other parties	10
	151

1965 (Mar)
U.N.P.	65
S.L.F.P.	41
L.S.S.P.	10
M.E.P.	1
C.P.	4
F.P.	14
T.C.	3
Independents & other parties	12
	151

168

	Seats
1970 (27 May)	
U.N.P.	17
S.L.F.P.	91
L.S.S.P.	19
C.P.	6
F.P.	13
T.C.	3
Indepentents & other parties	2
	151

SWAZILAND

	Seats
1972 (May)	
Imbokodvo National Movement	21
Ngwane National Liberatory	
Congress	3
	24

On 12 Apr 1973, King Sobhuza 11 repealed the 1968 Constitution. All political parties were dissolved and prohibited.

TANZANIA

The only political party is TANU (see page 186). In each electoral division, TANU puts forward two candidates chosen by TANU members. Subsequently, all adult citizens vote to decide which one shall represent that electoral division.

TRINIDAD

In the General Election held on 24 May 1971, the Peoples National Movement won all 36 seats.

UGANDA

On 2 Feb 1971, the national assembly was dissolved when General Amin took over all legislative, executive and military powers.

UNITED KINGDOM

	Seats
1900 (28 Sep—24 Oct)	
Conservative	402
Liberal	184
Labour	2
Irish Nationalist	82
	670

1906 (12 Jan—7 Feb)	
Conservative	157
Liberal	400
Labour	30
Irish Nationalist	83
	670

1910 (14 Jan—9 Feb)	
Conservative	273
Liberal	275
Labour	40
Irish Nationalist	82
	670

	Seats
1910 (2–19 Dec)	
Conservative	272
Liberal	272
Labour	42
Irish Nationalist	84
	670

1918 (14 Dec)	
Coalition Unionist	335
Coalition Liberal	133
Coalition Labour	10
(Coalition)	(478)
Conservative	23
Irish Unionist	25
Liberal	28
Labour	63
Irish Nationalist	7
Sinn Fein	73
Others	10
	707

1922 (15 Nov)	
Conservative	345
National Liberal	62
Liberal	54
Labour	142
Others	12
	615

1923 (6 Dec)	
Conservative	258
Liberal	159
Labour	191
Others	7
	615

1924 (29 Oct)	
Conservative	419
Liberal	40

	Seats
1924 (29 Oct) (continued)	
Labour	151
Communist	1
Others	4
	615
1929 (30 May)	
Conservative	260
Liberal	59
Labour	288
Others	8
	615
1931 (27 Oct)	
Conservative	473
National Labour	13
Liberal National	35
Liberal	33
(National Government)	(554)
Independent Liberal	4
Labour	52
Others	5
	615
1935 (14 Nov)	
Conservative	432
Liberal	21
Labour	154
Independent Labour Party	4
Communist	1
Others	4
	615
1945 (5 July)	
Conservative	213
Liberal	12
Labour	393
Communist	2

	Seats
1945 (5 July) (continued)	
Common Wealth	1
Others	19
	640
1950 (23 Feb)	
Conservative	298
Liberal	9
Labour	315
Others	3
	625
1951 (25 Oct)	
Conservative	321
Liberal	6
Labour	295
Others	3
	625
1955 (26 May)	
Conservative	344
Liberal	6
Labour	277
Others	3
	630
1959 (8 Oct)	
Conservative	365
Liberal	6
Labour	258
Others	1
	630
1964 (15 Oct)	
Conservative	304

Seats

1964 (15 Oct) (continued)
Liberal	9
Labour	317
	630

1966 (31 Mar)
Conservative	253
Liberal	12
Labour	363
Others	2
	630

1970 (18 June)
Conservative	330
Liberal	6
Labour	287
Scottish Nat. P.	1
Others	6
	630

1974 (28 Feb)
Conservative	297
Liberal	14
Labour	301
Plaid Cymru	2
Scottish Nat. P.	7
Others (G.B.)	2
Others (N.I.)	12
	635

1974 (10 Oct)
Conservative	277
Liberal	13
Labour	319
Plaid Cymru	3
Scottish Nat. P.	11
Others (N.I.)	12
	635

WESTERN SAMOA

General elections are held every three years. The last took place in 1976.

ZAMBIA

In Dec 1972, the 1964 Constitution was amended to provide for the introduction of a one-party state with UNIP (United National Independence Party) as the sole party. The first elections under this system were held in Dec 1973, with 125 UNIP candidates returned to Parliament and 10 members nominated by the President.

6 POLITICAL PARTIES

AUSTRALIA

Australian Labor Party
Founded in 1891. The oldest of Australia's present parties. Aims at democratic socialism with emphasis on improved social services. Closely linked with the trade unions.

Liberal Party of Australia
Founded by Sir Robert Menzies in 1945. The successor to the United Australia Party. A conservative, private enterprise party. Closely cooperates with the *Country Party* (qv). Anti-socialist and anti-communist.

Country Party
Founded in 1920. As its name implies, has a strongly rural and conservative approach on such issues as farm prices, rural transport etc. Historic ally of the United Australia Party and the Liberal Party.

More recent minor parties in Australia include the *Communist Party of Australia* (CPA). Founded in 1920, it has never secured a single seat in the Federal Parliament. The *Australian Democratic Labour Party*, founded in 1955, is a right wing, mainly Catholic, splinter from the Australian Labour Party. The *Australia Party*, founded in July 1969 by Senator Reginald Turnbull, is essentially the successor to the Australian Reform Movement.

BAHAMAS

Progressive Liberal Party
Governing party which has dominated Bahamas politics

Free National Movement
Opposition party. Amalgamation of the United Bahamian Party with dissident members of the Progressive Liberal Party

Peoples Democratic Party
Founded in 1974 and led by Lawrence McKinney.

BANGLADESH

Since independence, few political parties have had a long existence. The *Awami League* of Sheikh Mujib triumphed in the first general election on 7 Mar 1973. On 25 Jan 1975, Sheikh Mujib replaced the Awami League by a new party, *Baksal* (the Bangladesh Peasants Workers Peoples League). All other parties were banned. In August 1975 all political parties were disbanded by the new regime of President Mushtaq Ahmed.

BARBADOS

Democratic Labour Party
Founded in 1955 by breakaway members of Barbados Labour Party. Moderate socialist, similar to British Labour Party. The governing party, closely allied to the principal labour union.

Barbados Labour Party
Founded in 1938. Dominated Barbados politics in the 1950s under Sir Grantley Adams. Badly mauled in 1961 election. Similar policy to Democratic Labour Party.

Barbados National Party
Conservative, business party. Strongest support in Bridgetown.

BOTSWANA

Botswana Democratic Party
Ruling party of Sir Seretse Khama; easily strongest party in Botswana; favours close relations with South Africa and Western-style democracy.

Botswana Peoples Party
Until 1969 principal minority party; advocates Pan-Africanist policies and social democracy.

Botswana National Front
Left-wing pro-Communist party formed after the 1965 elections; polled second largest number of votes in 1969 and 1974 elections.

BRUNEI

Political parties were mainly disbanded after the failure of the 1962 rebellion. In 1966, all former political parties were amalgamated into the *Brunei People's Independence Front* (BAKAR)

CANADA

Liberal Party
One of Canada's two historic parties; formerly a traditional free trade and moderate social reform party, it has recently laid great emphasis on expanding social welfare meàsures, federal-provincial cooperation and a progressive foreign policy. Led by Pierre Trudeau.

Progressive Conservative Party
Canada's other historic party (founded 1854); although more nationalist and pro-Commonwealth than its Liberal rivals, its policies differ very little in practice; greater emphasis on free enterprise and individualism.

New Democratic Party
Founded 1961, a democratic socialist party favouring a planned economy and national social security. Achieved success in Manitoba in 1969 under Edward Schreyer.

Social Credit Party
Founded in Alberta in 1935, advocates monetary reform. Governing party of Alberta (1935–71) and British Columbia (1952–72)

Ralliement des Créditistes
Founded in Quebec in 1963, off-shoot of the Social Credit Party with emphasis on greater autonomy for Quebec and improvements in French Canadian Life.

Parti Québecois
Founded in Quebec in 1968; separatist party led by René Levesque.

CYPRUS

Political parties in Cyprus have been thrown into turmoil by recent events in the island. These parties have had a long history:

Unified Party (Enieon)
Founded 1960; essentially the Greek supporters of Archbishop Makarios.

Progressive Party of the Working People (AKEL)
Founded in 1941, the Cyprus Communist Party.

United Democratic Union of the Centre (EDEK)
Founded in 1969, the Socialist Party of Cyprus.

Democratic National Party (DEK)
Founded 1968, advocates Enosis (Union with Greece)

The two main Turkish-Cypriot parties are the *Republican Turkish Party* (founded 1970, left of centre social democrat) and the *National Unity Party*, largely modelled on Ataturk's reforms.

FIJI

Alliance Party
Multi-racial governing party: dominated the April 1972 elections.

National Federation Party
Founded in 1963, a fusion of the mainly Indian Federation Party and the purely Fijian National Democratic Party.

Nationalist Party
Founded 1974 to seek greater representation of Fijians in Parliament and improvements in Fijian welfare.

179

THE GAMBIA

Peoples Progressive Party
Founded in 1958, merged with Gambia Congress Party in 1968. The governing party: advocates closer economic and cultural links with Senegal. Opposition parties include the *United Party* (founded 1952) and the *National Convention Party* (founded 1975) and the *National Liberation Party* (founded 1975). The opposition parties combined for the April 1977 election.

GHANA

Under Nkrumah the *Congress Peoples's Party* dominated the political life of independent Ghana (on 21 Feb 1964 Ghana had officially become a one-party state). In Feb 1966, Ghana's new military rulers banned all political parties. This ban was lifted on 1 May 1969. The two major parties to emerge were the *Progress Party* (founded 1969 and led by Dr Kofi Busia) and the *Justice Party* (founded 1970, after a merger of the Nationalist Alliance of Liberals, the United Nationalist Party and the All-Peoples Republican Party. In January 1972, after the coup d'état, the ban on political parties was reimposed.

GUYANA

People's National Congress
The governing party, founded in 1955 (after a split with the people's Progressive Party), left-wing socialist led by Forbes Burnham.

People's Progressive Party
Founded in 1950. Gradually transformed into a Marxist-Leninist party under Dr Cheddi Jagan.

Other parties include *United Force*, which advocates rapid industrialisation through a partnership of private and state capital, and the *Liberator Party* (founded 1975) which includes former leaders of United Force.

INDIA

Janata Party
Founded in Jan 1977 by the four largest opposition parties. Subsequently merged with the Congress for Democracy. Won sweeping victory in 1977 elections.

Congress Party
Historic ruling party. Founded in 1885, it led the struggle for independence. Dominated Indian politics 1947–77. Now split by serious factions.

Swatantra Party
Founded 1959. Favours private enterprise.

Dravidian Forward Party (DMK)
Madras-based regional party, originally advocating independence for 'Dravida Nad'.

Among the myriad other parties operating in Indian politics are the pro-Russian *Communist Party of India* (formed in the 1920s), the pro-Chinese *Marxist Communist Party of India* (founded 1964), the Samyutka Socialists (founded 1964) and the Praja Socialist Party (founded 1952).

JAMAICA

People's National Party
Founded in 1938; its early moving spirit was Norman Manley. Swept to power in February 1972 elections. Draws support from National Worker's Union. Advocates social and economic change; foreign policy of non-alignment with strong third-world links.

Jamaica Labour Party
Founded in 1943 by Alexander Bustamente; more conservative, business-oriented than the Peoples National Party. Supports private enterprise.

KENYA

In October 1969, Kenya's sole opposition party, the *Kenya People's Union* (KPU) was banned. Kenya is now a one-party state under the *Kenya African National Union* (KANU). Founded in 1960, Jomo Kenyatta led this party to self-government and independence.

LESOTHO

The main political parties are the *Basotho National Party* (founded 1959 and led by Chief Leabua Jonathan). The *Congress Party* (founded 1952) and the *Marematlou Freedom Party* (founded 1962).

MALAWI

The *Malawi Congress Party* (MCP) is the only authorised political party. Founded in 1959, it succeeded the Nyasaland African Congress. Its life president is Dr. Hastings Banda. Its policy is strongly pro-western, multi-racial and with emphasis on internal development.

There is little organised opposition. Henry Chimpembere (a former Minister of Education) led an unsuccessful revolt in 1965.

MALAYSIA

National Front
The ruling multi-racial coalition of nine parties. It includes the United Malay National Organisation (UMNO, founded in 1946), the Malaysian Indian Congress (founded 1946) and the Pan-Malayan Islamic Party (founded 1951).

The three chief opposition parties are:
Democratic Action Party
Founded 1966; democratic socialist party advocating multi-racial Malaysia.

182

Social Justice Party (PEKEMAS)
Founded in 1971, the party has currently only 1 seat in the House of Representatives.

Sarawak National Party (SNAP): founded in 1961.

MALTA

Malta Labour Party
Governing party: founded in 1920. Democratic socialist party, favouring non-alignment; progressive and anti-colonialist, led by Dom Mintoff.

Nationalist Party
Catholic party, much more pro-western. Led by Borg Olivier. Favours Western styled democracy.

Progressive Constitutional Party
Founded 1953, favours association with the EEC; aims to establish a viable Maltese economy based on tourism and light industries.

National Democratic Party
Founded 1974 and led by Dr Arthur Colombo.

MAURITIUS

Mauritius Labour Party (MLP)
Governing party led by Sir Seewoosagur Ramgoolam. Strong urban trade union support, plus rural Hindu agricultural votes. Led the drive for independence.

Muslim Committee of Action (MCA)
Led by those Muslims who believe they can gain most by communal action. Part of the governing coalition.

Mauritian Social Democratic Party (PMSD)
Leading opposition party; strongly Francophile, gains support from the

Creole middle-class and Franco-Mauritian landowners; originally opposed independence.

Independent Forward Bloc
Founded 1958, a small party based on Hindu farm labourer support.

NEW ZEALAND

New Zealand National Party
Founded 1936; in office from 1949–57, from 1960–72 and again after 1975. Represents the Conservative and Liberal elements; encourages private enterprise and personal freedom.

Labour Party
Founded 1916; democratic socialist left-of-centre.

Other smaller parties include the *New Democratic Party* (founded May 1972, aiming to restore personal freedom). The *Social Credit League* (founded 1954, advocates a national credit authority) and the humanist *Values Party* (founded May 1972). On the left are the pro-Chinese *Communist Party of New Zealand* and the Marxist *Socialist Unity Party* (founded 1966).

NIGERIA

In May 1966, all existing political parties were banned following the military *coup d' état*. In October 1975 it was announced that political parties could operate again after October 1978.

SIERRA LEONE

All People's Congress
The governing party; all its candidates were returned unopposed in the May 1973 elections.

Sierra Leone People's Party
Main opposition party; the party withdrew all its nominations for the May 1973 elections.

SINGAPORE

People's Action Party
Founded 1954. Historic governing party. Formed the government in 1959, re-elected in 1963, 1968 and 1972. Led by Lee Kuan Yew.

United People's Front
Opposition group formed in late 1974 of seven former opposition parties, including the United National Front (formed 1970), the Singapore Justice Party and the Singapore Chinese Party.

Socialist Front (Barisan Sosialis Malaya)
Founded in 1961, left wing party of former members of the People's Action Party.

SRI LANKA

Sri Lanka Freedom Party (SLFP)
Governing party, founded in 1951 by Solomon Bandaranaike. A socialist party, aiming at nationalisation of key industries and a neutralist foreign policy.

United National Party (UNP)
Democratic socialist party aiming for a neutral foreign policy and with Sinhala as the official language.

Lanka Sama Samaja Party
Founded 1935, Trotskyist party dedicated to nationalisation of foreign owned companies; opposed to communalism.

Federal Party
Founded 1949, the principal Tamil party, and advocate of a federal constitution.

185

Other parties include the pro-Moscow *Communist Party* (founded 1943), the left wing, strongly Buddhist *People's United Front* (founded 1960) and the *Tamil Congress*, which draws its strength from northern and eastern Ceylon.

SWAZILAND

On 12 April 1973, all political parties were dissolved and prohibited by King Sobhuza II. Prior to that date, the four main parties were:

Imbokadvo National Movement
Founded 1964; moderate, sympathetic to white settlers; dominated Swazi elections.

Ngwane National Liberatory Congress
Founded 1962, opposed to the African feudalist alliance of the Imbokadvo Movement. In 1971, the Ngwane Congress split into two factions.

Swaziland Progressive Party
Founded in 1929, as Swazi Progressive Association.

Swaziland United Front
Founded 1962, an off-shoot of the Swaziland Progressive Party.

TANZANIA

Tanzania is a one-party state. The only permitted party is TANU (*Tanzania African National Union*).

TRINIDAD AND TOBAGO

The dominant political party is the main nationalist party, the *People's National Movement* (founded 1956), led by Dr Eric Williams. Opposition partis include the *United Progressive Party* (founded 1972), the Democratic

Action Congress (founded 1971), the *Tapia Group* and the *West Indian National Party*.

UNITED KINGDOM

Conservative Party
Dates back to 'Tories' of 18th century. Centre right party, represents business and agricultural interests particularly. With the *Labour Party* (q.v) one of the two traditional governing parties. In office 1951—64 and 1970—74. Currently led by Margaret Thatcher, the first woman to lead the party.

Labour Party
Founded 1900. A party representing the trade unions and working class. In office 1924, 1929—31, 1945—51, 1964—70, Feb 74-date. Its main leaders have been MacDonald, Attlee, Wilson and Callaghan.

Liberal Party
Heirs of the 18th century 'Whigs'. One of the two great governing parties of the 19th century, since 1924 it has been a weak third party. Witnessed important revivals in 1962—63 and 1972—74.

Scottish National Party
Formed 1928 as National Party of Scotland. Won its first General Election seat in 1970. In October 1974 polled 30% of Scottish vote.

Plaid Cymru
Welsh Nationalist Party, founded in 1925. First by-election victory at Carmarthen in 1966. Strongest in rural Welsh-speaking Wales.

Other smaller parties active in British politics, but not represented in Parliament, include the *Communist Party*, and the right-wing *National Front*.

ZAMBIA

In December 1972, Zambia was proclaimed a one-party state. Since then, the only legal party has been the *United National Independence Party* (UNIP), founded in 1959 and led by Dr Kenneth Kaunda. Prior to 1972, two other political parties existed – the African National Congress (founded 1944) and the United Progressive Party.

7 JUSTICE

AUSTRALIA

The judicial power of Australia is vested in the High Court of Australia (the federal Supreme Court), in the federal courts created by Parliament (the Federal Court of Bankruptcy and the Australian Industrial Court) and in the state courts invested by Parliament with federal jurisdiction.

High Court. The High Court consists of a chief justice and 6 other justices, appointed by the Governor General in Council. The Constitution confers on the High Court original jurisdiction, *inter alia*, in all matters arising under treaties or affecting consuls or other foreign representatives, matters between the states of the Commonwealth, matters to which the Commonwealth is a party and matters between residents of different states. Parliament may make laws conferring original jurisdiction on the High Court, *inter alia*, in matters arising under the constitution or under any laws made by Parliament. It has in fact conferred jurisdiction on the High Court in matters arising under the constitution and in matters arising under certain laws made by Parliament.

The High Court may hear and determine appeals from its own justices exercising original jurisdiction, from any other federal court, from a court exercising federal jurisdiction and from the supreme courts of the states. It also has jurisdiction to hear and determine appeals from the supreme courts of the territories. No appeal from the High Court to the Privy Council is permitted on questions as to the limits *inter se* of the constitutional powers of the states or the Commonwealth and the states except on the certificate of the High Court. No appeal to the Privy Council, whether special or otherwise, is permitted from a decision of federal courts (not being the High Court) or of the supreme court of a territory. Appeal from the High Court to the Privy Council by special leave of the Privy Council is possible only in a matter in which the decision of the High Court was a decision that: (*a*) was given on appeal from a decision of a supreme court of a state given otherwise than in the exercise of federal jurisdiction, and (*b*) did not involve the interpretation of the constitution, a law made by the Federal Parliament or an instrument (including an ordinance, rule, regulation or by-law) made under a law made by the Parliament.

Other federal courts. Two other federal courts, which have been created to exercise special jurisdiction, are the Australian Industrial Court (described later) and the Federal Court of Bankruptcy. The Federal Court of Bankruptcy consists of 2 judges appointed by the Governor General in Council. The state supreme courts have also been invested with federal jurisdiction in bankruptcy. Legislation was introduced in 1974 preparatory to the absorption of these two federal courts in a new federal superior court of wider jurisdiction. This legislation has not yet been enacted.

State courts. The general federal jurisdiction of the state courts extends, subject to certain restrictions and exceptions, to all matters in which the High Court has jurisdiction or in which jurisdiction may be conferred upon it. In matters of non-federal jurisdiction appeal is still possible, as a matter of law, from the state courts direct to the Privy Council.

Industrial tribunals. The chief industrial tribunals of Australia are at present the Australian Industrial Court, constituted by judges, and the Conciliation and Arbitration Commission, constituted by presidential members (with the status of judges) and commissioners. The Australian Industrial Court deals with questions of law, the judicial interpretation of awards, imposition of penalties, etc. The Commission's functions include settling industrial disputes, making awards, determining the standard hours of work, wage fixation, etc.

NEW SOUTH WALES

Legal processes may be carried on in lower or magistrates courts, or in the higher courts presided over by judges. There is also an appellate jurisdiction. Persons charged with more serious crimes must be tried before the higher courts.

Children's courts have been established with the object of removing children as far as possible from the atmosphere of a public court. There are also a number of tribunals exercising special jurisdiction, for example, the Industrial Commission and the Workers' Compensation Commission.

VICTORIA

There is a supreme court with a chief justice and 18 puisne judges. There are magistrates' courts, county courts, courts of mines, a court of licensing, and a bankruptcy court.

QUEENSLAND

Justice is administered by a supreme court, district courts, magistrates' courts and children's courts. The supreme court comprises a chief justice, a senior puisne judge and 12 puisne judges; the district court, 15 district court judges. Stipendiary magistrates preside over the lower courts, except in the small centres, where justices of the peace officiate. A parole board may recommend prisoners for release.

SOUTH AUSTRALIA

There is a supreme court, which incorporates admiralty, civil, criminal, matrimonial and testamentary jurisdiction; district criminal courts, which have jurisdiction in many indictable offences; local courts and courts of summary jurisdiction. Circuit courts are held at several places. Bankruptcy jurisdiction is administered by the state court of insolvency at Adelaide which is invested with jurisdiction by the Federal Bankruptcy Act.

WESTERN AUSTRALIA

In Western Australia justice is administered by a supreme court, consisting of a chief justice and 6 puisne judges at 31 Dec 1974, a district court comprising a chairman of judges and 5 district court judges at 31 Dec 1974, and magistrates' courts exercising both civil and criminal jurisdiction. The lower courts are presided over by justices of the peace, except in the more important centres, where the court is constituted by a stipendiary magistrate. There are special magistrates' courts for juvenile offenders.

TASMANIA

The Supreme Court of Tasmania, with civil, criminal, ecclesiastical, admiralty and matrimonial jurisdiction, established by Royal Charter on 13 Oct 1823, is a superior court of record, with both original and appellate jurisdiction, and consists of a chief justice and 4 puisne judges. There are also inferior civil courts with limited jurisdiction, licensing courts, mining courts, courts of petty sessions and coroners' courts.

COMMONWEALTH OF THE BAHAMAS

The supreme court has jurisdiction over civil matters. Appeals in all matters go to the court of appeal and certain cases go to the Privy Council. On New

Providence and Grand Bahama magistrates courts are presided over by qualified magistrates.

BANGLADESH

The judiciary comprises a supreme court with a high court and an appelate division. Subsidiary courts in addition to the supreme court have been established.

BARBADOS

Justice is administered by the supreme court and by magistrates' courts. All have both civil and criminal jurisdiction. There is a chief justice and 3 puisne judges of the supreme court and 8 magistrates.

BERMUDA

There are 4 magistrates' courts, a supreme court and a court of appeal.

BOTSWANA (formerly Bechuanaland)

The Botswana Court of Appeal succeeded the Court of Appeal of Basutoland, Bechuanaland and Swaziland, which was established in 1954. It has jurisdiction in respect of criminal and civil appeals emanating from the High Court of Botswana. Further appeal lies in certain circumstances to the judicial committee of the Privy Council.

The High Court of Botswana succeeded the High Court for Bechuanaland, which was established in 1938. It has jurisdiction in all criminal and civil causes and proceedings. Subordinate courts and African courts are in each of the 12 administrative districts.

BRUNEI

There is a supreme court consisting of the high court and the court of appeal. There are also magistrates' courts of first, second and third class.

CANADA

There is a supreme court in Ottawa, having general appellate jurisdiction in civil and criminal cases throughout Canada. There is an exchequer court, which is also a court of admiralty. There is a superior court in each province and county courts, with limited jurisdiction, in most of the provinces, all the judges in these courts being appointed by the Governor General. Police, magistrates and justices of the peace are appointed by the provincial governments.

CYPRUS

Under the constitution and other legislation in force the following judicial institutions are established: The supreme court of the Republic, the assize courts, district courts and communal and ecclesiastical courts.

The Supreme Court is composed of 5–7 judges, one of whom is the President. The Supreme Court adjudicates exclusively and finally: on all constitutional and administrative law matters, including any recourse that any law or decision of the House of Representatives or the budget is discriminatory against either of the two communities; on any conflict of competence between state organs, questions of unconstitutionality of any law or decisions on any question of interpretation of the Constitution in case of ambiguity, as well as recourses for annulment of administrative acts, decisions or omissions. The Supreme Court is the highest appellate court in the Republic and has jurisdiction to hear and determine all appeals from any court. It has exclusive jurisdiction to issue orders in the nature of *habeas corpus*, *mandamus*, prohibition, *quo warranto* and *certiorari* and in admiralty and matrimonial matters.

There are 6 assize courts and 6 district courts, one for each district. The assize courts have unlimited criminal jurisdiction and power to order compensation up to £800. The district courts exercise original civil and criminal jurisdiction, the extent of which varies with the composition of the Bench. In civil matters (other than those within the original jurisdiction of Supreme Court) a district court composed of not less than 2 and not more than 3 judges has unlimited jurisdiction. A president or a district judge sitting alone has jurisdiction up to £500, and is also empowered to deal with any action for the recovery of possession of any immovable property, and certain other specified matters. In criminal matters the jurisdiction of a district court is exercised by its members sitting singly and is of a summary character. A president or a district judge sitting alone has power to try any offence punishable with imprisonment up to 3 years, or with a fine up to £500 or with both, and may order compensation up to £500.

Civil disputes relating to personal status of members of the Turkish Community, including matrimonial cases and maintenance, are dealt with by 2 Turkish communal courts. There is a communal appellate court to which appeals may be made from the decision of the courts of first instance.

There is a Greek Orthodox Church tribunal with exclusive jurisdiction in matrimonial causes between members of the Greek Orthodox Church. There is an appellate tribunal of that Church.

GHANA

The judicial power of Ghana is vested in the judiciary with the Chief Justice as the Head. It has jurisdiction in all civil and criminal matters.

The Courts of Ghana are constituted as follows: *Superior Court of Judicature*, the Court of Appeal and the High Court of Justice. The Supreme Court of Ghana, created by the suspended Constitution in 1969, has been abolished and its functions taken over by the Court of Appeal.

The Court of Appeal. The Court of Appeal replaces the former Supreme Court of Ghana as the highest and final court of appeal in and for Ghana. It has all the power, authority and jurisdiction vested in any court established in the country. The Court of Appeal consists of the Chief Justice, as President, together with not less than 6 other justices of the appeal court and such other justices of superior courts as the Chief Justice may request. The court is duly constituted by 5 justices. A full Bench of the Court of Appeal has jurisdiction to review and determine, among other things, a decision of the Court of Appeal or any justice or division thereof upon a question of law, including matters relating to aspects of the Chieftaincy Act 1971. Divisions of the appeal court may be created, subject to the discretion of the Chief Justice.

The High Court of Justice. This court has jurisdiction in civil and criminal matters as well as those relating to industrial and labour disputes, including administrative complaints. It has supervisory jurisdiction over all inferior and traditional courts, but has no power in a trial for offences involving treason, to convict any person for any offence other than treason. The High Court consists of the Chief Justice, not less than 12 puisne judges and such other judges of the superior court as may be requested by the Chief Justice. It is constituted by between 1 justice (with or without a jury) to 3 justices for specific offences.

The country has been divided into 7 circuits, and there are 11 circuit judges sitting in these courts with original jurisdiction in all criminal cases, except offences where the maximum punishment is death. The original jurisdiction in civil matters is restricted to cases where the subject-matter of the suit is not more than N₵4,000 (or £2000). Dstrict Courts (Grade I and II) sit throughout the country in the magisterial districts. Juvenile Courts, dealing with persons under the age of 17, have been established in Accra, Cape Coast, Sekondi, Kumasi and Koforidua.

GIBRALTAR

The judicial system is based on the English system. There is a court of appeal, a supreme court, presided over by the Chief Justice, a court of first instance and a magistrates' court.

GUYANA

The law, both civil and criminal, is based on the common and statute law of England, save that the principles of the Roman-Dutch law have been retained in respect of the registration, conveyance and mortgaging of land.

The Supreme Court of Judicature consists of a court of appeal and a high court.

HONG KONG

There is a supreme court, having original, bankruptcy and companies winding-up, criminal, probate, divorce, admiralty and prize jurisdiction, and a court of appeal. There are also 3 district courts and 9 magistracies, most containing several courts. The district courts, apart from hearing civil cases where the claim does not amount to more than HK$10,000, also have jurisdiction over certain criminal matters. A tenancy tribunal hears cases covering disputes between landlord and tenant, etc.

INDIA

All courts form a single hierarchy, with the Supreme Court at the head, which constitutes the highest court of appeal. Immediately below it are the high courts and subordinate courts in each state. Every court in this chain, subject to the usual pecuniary and local limits, administers the whole law of the country, whether made by Parliament or by the state legislatures.

The Supreme Court of India is the highest court in respect of constitutional matters. The states of Andhra Pradesh, Assam (in common with Nagaland, Meghalaya, Manipur and Tripura and the Union Territories of Arunachal Pradesh and Mizoram), Bihar, Gujarat, Himachal Pradesh, Jammu and Kashmir, Karnataka, Kerala, Madhya Pradesh, Maharashtra, Orissa, Punjab (in common with the state of Haryana and the Union Territory of Chandigarh), Rajasthan, Tamil Nadu, Uttar Pradesh and West Bengal have each a high court. There is the Court of Judicial Commissioners which is in status equivalent to a high court, in the Union Territory of Goa. There is a separate high court for Delhi. For the Andaman and Nicobar Islands the Calcutta High Court, for Pondicherry the High Court of Madras, and for Lakshadweep the High Court of Kerala are the highest judicial authorities; in Dadra and Nagar Haveli the Appellate Court is the highest civil and criminal court. Below the high court each state is divided into a number of districts under the jurisdiction of district judges who preside over civil courts and courts of sessions. There are a number of judicial authorities subordinate to the district civil courts. On the criminal side magistrates of various classes act under the overall supervision of the high court.

The Code of Criminal Procedure, 1898, has been replaced by the Code of Criminal Procedure, 1973 (2 of 1974), which came into force with effect from 1 Apr 1974. The new code provides for complete separation of the judiciary from the executive throughout India.

ANDHRA PRADESH

The High Court of Judicature at Hyderabad has a chief justice and 17 puisne judges.

ASSAM

The seat of the High Court is Gauhati. It has a chief justice and 6 puisne judges.

BIHAR

There is a high court (constituted in 1916) at Patna with a chief justice, 17 puisne judges and 6 additional judges.

GUJARAT

The High Court of Judicature at Ahmedabad has a chief justice and 16 puisne judges.

HARYANA

Haryana shares the High Court of Punjab and Haryana at Chandigarh which had (1968) a chief justice and 16 puisne judges.

HIMACHAL PRADESH

The state has its own High Court at Simla.

JAMMU AND KASHMIR

The High Court, at Srinagar and Jammu, has a chief justice and 4 puisne judges. Its status was assimilated to that of the high courts of other states in 1959.

KARNATAKA

The seat of the High Court is at Bangalore. It has a chief justice and 16 puisne judges.

KERALA

The High Court at Ernakulam has a chief justice and 9 puisne judges and 4 additional judges.

MADHYA PRADESH

The High Court of Judicature at Jabalpur has a chief justice and 15 puisne judges.

MAHARASHTRA

The High Court has a chief justice and 26 judges. The seat of the High Court is Bombay, but it has a Bench at Nagpur.

MEGHALAYA

There is a high court at Shillong which is common to Assam, Meghalaya, Nagaland, Manipur, Tripura and the Union Territories of Mizoram and Arunachal Pradesh..

ORISSA

The High Court of Judicature at Cuttack has a chief justice and 6 puisne judges.

PUNJAB

The Punjab and Haryana High Court exercises jurisdiction over the states of Punjab and Haryana and the territory of Chandigarh. It is located in Chandigarh. It consists (1973) of a chief justice and 17 puisne judges.

RAJASTHAN

The seat of the High Court is at Jodhpur. There is a chief justice and 10 puisne judges.

SIKKIM

Each of the districts, north, south and west, have their own courts, and there is a high court at Gangtok.

TAMIL NADU

There is a high court at Madras with a chief justice and 18 judges.

UTTAR PRADESH

The High Court of Judicature at Allahabad (with a Bench at Lucknow) has a chief justice, 40 puisne judges including additional judges. There are 45 sessions divisions in the state.

WEST BENGAL

The High Court of Judicature at Calcutta has a chief justice and 38 puisne judges. The Andaman and Nicobar Islands come under its jurisdiction.

DADRA AND NAGAR HAVELI

The territory is under the jurisdiction of the Bombay (Maharashtra) High Court. There is a district and sessions court and one junior division civil court at Silvassa.

GOA, DAMAN AND DIU

The territory comes under the High Court of Bombay.

JAMAICA

The Judicature comprises a supreme court, a court of appeal, a revenue court, resident magistrates' courts, petty sessional courts, coroners' courts and a traffic court. The Chief Justice is head of the judiciary. All prosecutions are initiated by the Director of Public Prosecutions.

KENYA

The courts of justice comprise the High Court, established in 1921, with full jurisdiction both civil and criminal over all persons and all matters in Kenya, including admiralty jurisdiction arising on the high seas and elsewhere, and subordinate courts. The High Court has its headquarters at Nairobi and consists of the Chief Justice and 11 puisne judges; it sits continuously at Nairobi, Mombasa, Nakuru and Kisumu; civil and criminal sessions are held regularly at Eldoret, Nyeri, Meru, Kitale, Kisii and Kericho.

The subordinate courts are presided over by senior resident, resident or district magistrates and are established in the main centres of all districts. They sit throughout the year. There are also Moslem subordinate courts established in areas where the local population is predominantly Mohammedan; they are presided over by Kadhis and exercise limited jurisdiction in matters governed by Mohammedan law.

LESOTHO

An appeal court for Lesotho was established at Maseru on 4 Oct 1966.

MALAWI

Justice is administered in the High Court, the magistrates' courts and traditional courts. There are 23 magistrates' courts, 176 traditional courts and 23 local appeal courts.

Appeals from traditional courts are dealt with in the traditional appeal courts and in the High Court. Eventually, however, appeals from traditional courts will not go to the High Court, but will go to the national traditional appeal court. Appeals from magistrates' courts lie to the High Court, and appeals from the High Court to Malawi's Supreme Court of Appeal.

MALAYSIA

The judicial power of the Federation is vested in the high court in Peninsular Malaysia and the high court in East Malaysia and also in subordinate courts. Legally the two high courts are known as High Court and High Court Borneo. Above the high courts there also exists a federal court with its main registry in Kuala Lumpur, with exclusive jurisdiction to determine appeals from decisions of any high court.

The supreme head of the judiciary is the Lord President of the federal court, consisting of himself and 2 chief justices of the high courts and judges of the federal court. Every proceeding in the federal court is heard and disposed of by 3 judges or such greater uneven number of judges as the Lord President in any particular case may order. In his absence, the senior member of the court presides.

PENINSULAR MALAYSIA

The Courts Ordinance, 1948, established sessions courts, magistrates' courts and Penghulu's courts. There are also juvenile courts for offenders under the age of 17.

There are 17 penal institutions, including 4 Borstal establishments and 1 open prison camp.

SABAH

When Sabah attained independence on 16 Sep 1963 the Supreme Court of Sarawak, North Borneo and Brunei was replaced by the High Court in Borneo with 2 registries for Sarawak (at Kuching) and Sabah (at Kota Kinabalu).

There are native courts with jurisdiction in cases concerning local native customs. Appeals from native courts go to administrative officers, with a final appeal to the native court of appeal.

MALTA

The courts of Malta are the constitutional court, the court of appeal, the criminal court of appeal, commercial court, criminal court, courts of judicial police and a juvenile court.

NEW HEBRIDES CONDOMINIUM

There are Condominium and English and French national courts.

NEW ZEALAND

The judiciary consists of the Chief Justice, 3 judges of the Court of Appeal and 14 supreme court judges, 1 judge of the industrial court and 1 judge each for the courts of compensation and land valuation.

The death penalty for murder was replaced by life imprisonment in 1961.

The Criminal Injuries Act, 1963, which came into force on 1 Jan 1964, provided for the compensation of persons injured by certain criminal acts and of the dependants of persons killed by such acts.

NIGERIA

The highest court is the Federal Supreme Court, which consists of the Chief

Justice of the Federation, not less than 3 federal judges and the chief justice of each state. It has original jurisdiction in any dispute between the Federation and any state or between states; and to hear and determine appeals from any of the high courts and from any court or tribunal established by Parliament. It may be given powers of advisory jurisdiction by Parliament in respect of the exercise of the prerogative of mercy by the Heads of State of the Federation or the states.

High Courts, presided over by a chief justice, are established in most of the states. Magistrates' courts are established throughout the Federation, and customary law courts in Western, Eastern, South Eastern, East Central and Lagos States of Nigeria. In Northern States of Nigeria there are the Sharia Court of Appeal and the Court of Resolution. Moslem Law has been codified in a penal code and is applied through alkali courts.

The advisory judicial committee has powers of appointment and discipline.

The constitutional safeguard of fundamental rights was suspended 15 Feb 1966.

RHODESIA

The High Court consists of an appellate division and a general division. The appellate division consists of the Chief Justice, the Judge President and at least one other judge of appeal. The general division consists of the Chief Justice and 5 puisne judges. The appellate division considers appeals from the general division and the lower courts; the general division has full jurisdiction, civil and criminal, over all persons and matters within Rhodesia. The Chief Justice is the head of the judiciary of Rhodesia. The Judge President presides over the appellate division in the absence of the Chief Justice. The courts sit at Salisbury and Bulawayo, and sittings of the general division are held at 3 other principal towns three times a year.

Regional courts, established in Salisbury and Bulawayo, are intermediate in jurisdiction between the magistrates' courts and the High Court, but have no civil jurisdiction. There are 19 principal courts of magistrates and 64 periodical courts presided over by magistrates.

African courts have jurisdiction over African persons in civil matters which are decided in accordance with African law and custom.

202

SEYCHELLES

The courts consist of the court of appeal, the supreme court and magistrates' courts. In addition there is an industrial court.

SIERRA LEONE

The High Court has jurisdiction in civil and criminal matters. Subordinate courts are held by magistrates in the various districts. Native courts, headed by court chairmen, apply native law and custom under a criminal and civil jurisdiction. Appeals from the decisions of magistrates' courts are heard by the High Court. Appeals from the decisions of the High Court are heard by the Sierra Leone Court of Appeal. Appeal lies from the Sierra Leone Court of Appeal to the Supreme Court which is the highest court.

SINGAPORE

There is a supreme court in Singapore which consists of the High Court, the Court of Appeal and the Court of Criminal Appeal. The supreme court is composed of a chief justice and 6 judges. An appeal from the High Court lies to the Court of Appeal in civil matters and to the Court of Criminal Appeal in criminal matters. Further appeal can in certain cases be made to the judicial committee of the Privy Council. The High Court has original civil and criminal jurisdiction as well as appellate civil and criminal jurisdiction in respect of appeals from the subordinate courts. There are 7 district courts, 10 magistrates' courts, 1 juvenile court and 2 coroners' courts.

SRI LANKA

The sytems of law which obtain in Sri Lanka are the Roman-Dutch law, the English law, the Tesawalamai, the Moslem law and the Kandyan law.

The Kandyan law applies to the Kandyan Sinhalese in the Central, North-Central, Uva and Sabaragamuwa provinces in respect of all matters relating to inheritance, matrimonial rights and donations. The law of England is observed in most maritime and commercial matters. The law of Tesawalamai is applied to all Tamil inhabitants of Jaffna, in all matters relating to inheritance, marriages, gifts, donations, purchases and sales of land. The

203

Moslem law is applied to all Moslems in respect of succession, donations not involving *fidei commissa*, marriage, divorce and maintenance. These customary and religious laws have been modified in·many respects by local enactments.

District courts and courts of Requests administer justice on the civil side. The Supreme Court exercises only an appellate jurisdiction in civil matters. On the criminal side magistrates' courts, district courts and the Supreme Court exercise an original jurisdiction. The Supreme Court also exercises an appellate jurisdiction in cases decided by magistrates' courts and district courts. A court of criminal appeal exercises an appellate jurisdiction in cases tried by the Supreme Court in its original criminal jurisdiction. Rural courts exercise a criminal and civil jurisdiction in rural areas in respect of petty crimes and civil disputes where the subject matter is valued less than Rs 100. Conciliation Boards were established in 1958; the Minister of Justice may appoint conciliation boards in any area and he may appoint the panel of conciliators for them; 232 boards were functioning in Sep 1968. In 1971, appeals to the judicial committee of the Privy Council were replaced by appeals to a court of appeal which was inaugurated on 9 Mar 1971.

SWAZILAND

The judiciary is headed by the Chief Justice. A high court having full jurisdiction and subordinate courts presided over by magistrates and district officers are in existence.

There is a court of appeal with a president and 3 judges. It deals with appeals from the High Court.

There are 16 Swazi courts of first instance, 2 Swazi courts of appeal and a higher Swazi court of appeal. The channel of appeal lies from Swazi court of first instance to Swazi Court of Appeal, to Higher Swazi Court of Appeal, to the Judicial Commissioner and thence to the High Court of Swaziland.

TANZANIA

The judicial system consists of primary and district courts and the high court. The high court has jurisdiction in both criminal and civil cases subject only to appeal to the East African court of appeal. In Zanzibar since 1970 people's courts have been established with no right of appeal to the East African court.

TONGA

There is a court of appeal, a supreme court, a land court and magistrates' courts. Appeals from the supreme court are heard by the Privy Council.

Now that British extra-territorial jurisdiction has lapsed British and Foreign nationals are charged with an offence against the laws of Tonga, the enforcement of which is a responsibility of the Minister of Police, and are fully subject to the jurisdiction of the Tongan courts to which they are already subject in all civil matters.

TRINIDAD AND TOBAGO

The High Court consists of the Chief Justice and not fewer than 10 puisne judges. In criminal cases a judge of the High Court sits with a jury of 12 in cases of treason and murder, and with 9 jurors in other cases. The Court of Appeal consists of the Chief Justice and 3 justices of appeal; there is a limited right of appeal from it to the Privy Council. There are 10 high courts and 28 magistrates' courts.

UGANDA

The High Court of Uganda, presided over by the Chief Justice and 12 puisne judges, exercises original and appellate jurisdiction throughout Uganda. Subordinate courts, presided over by chief magistrates and magistrates of the first, second and third grade, are established in all areas; jurisdiction varies with the grade of magistrate. Chief and first-grade magistrates are professionally qualified; second- and third-grade magistrates are trained to diploma level at the Law School, Entebbe.

Chief magistrates exercise supervision over and hear appeals from second- and third-grade courts.

The Court of Appeal for Eastern Africa was re-established on 9 Dec 1962 as the Court of Appeal for Uganda; it hears appeals from the High Court.

A law school has been established at Entebbe to train magistrates in civil and criminal law. The African courts have been integrated with the central government courts so that a unified courts system has been established.

UNITED KINGDOM

The legal system of England and Wales, divided into civil and criminal courts, has at the head of the superior courts, as the ultimate court of appeal, the House of Lords. The High Court of Justiciary is the supreme criminal court in Scotland. The sheriff courts try both civil and criminal cases.

WEST INDIES

The British Caribbean Court of Appeal has replaced the West Indies Associated States Court of Appeal, serving the associated states. In each of the independent countries there is a Court of Appeal.

MONTSERRAT

There are 2 magistrates' courts, at Plymouth and Cudjoe Head.

ST LUCIA

The island is divided into 2 judicial districts, and there are 9 magistrates' courts. Appeals lie with the Court of Appeal of the Windward and Leeward Islands, subject to exceptions and conditions as may be enacted by the St Lucia legislature.

DOMINICA

There are 4 magistrates' courts. They dealt with 642 civil and 887 criminal cases in 1970.

ZAMBIA

The judiciary consists of the Supreme Court, the High Court and 4 classes of migistrates' courts; all have civil and criminal jurisdiction.

The Supreme Court hears and determines appeals from the High Court. Its seat is at Lusaka.

The High Court exercises the powers vested in the High Court in England, subject to the High Court ordinance of Zambia. Its sessions are held where occasion requires, mostly at Lusaka and Ndola. All criminal cases tried by subordinate courts are subject to revision by the High Court.

8 DEFENCE AND TREATIES

MILITARY EFFORT OF EMPIRE/COMMONWEALTH IN THE 1914–18 WAR

	Total Mobilized	Killed or died of wounds	Wounded	Missing and POWs[1]
Australia	412,953	58,460	152,100	164
Canada	628,964	56,119	149,733	306
India	1,440,437	47,746	65,126	871
New Zealand	128,525	16,132	40,749	5
South Africa	228,907	7,241	11,444	33
United Kingdom	5,704,416	662,083	1,644,786	140,312
Others	42,000	3,336	3,504	366
Total	8,586,202	851,117	2,067,442	142,057

[1] Prisoners repatriated not shown.

MILITARY EFFORT OF THE COMMONWEALTH IN THE 1939–45 WAR

	Total Mobilized	Killed	Wounded	Missing	Prisoners of War
Australia	992,545	31,395	65,000	2,475	22,885
Canada	1,086,343	42,042	54,414	2,866	9,051
India	2,394,000	24,338	64,354	11,754	79,489
New Zealand	214,700	11,625	15,749	2,129	7,218
South Africa	410,056	12,080	14,363	. .	15,044
United Kingdom	6,515,000	357,116	369,267	46,079	178,332
Others	504,250	7,716	7,386	14,393	8,265
Total	12,116,894	486,312	590,533	79,696	320,284

BATTLE CASUALTIES OF BRITISH AND
ASIA DEC 1941–

Hong Kong	8–25 Dec 41	British and Indian
		Canadian
		Local Forces
Malaya	8 Dec 41–15 Feb 42	British and Indian
		Australian
		Local Forces
Java and Sumatra	14 Feb 42–8 Mar 42	British
		Australian
Burma	25 Dec 41–12 May 42	British and Indian
		Burma Army
Burma	Oct 42–Aug 45	British, Indian and African

A further 524 British and Indian troops were killed, wounded or missing in the Borneo Campaign 24 Dec 41–9 Mar 42.

MAJOR CONFLICTS INVOLVING COMMONWEALTH
COUNTRIES 1945–76

PALESTINE 1945–8

A period of guerrilla warfare, waged by Jewish Zionists against British occupation forces and the Arab population, to achieve an independent Jewish nation. On 22 July 1946 the King David Hotel in Jerusalem, housing the British Headquarters, was blown up, with the loss of 91 lives. With the proclamation of the independence of Israel on 14 May 1948, Britain surrendered her mandate over Palestine and withdrew her armed forces.

INDIA-PAKISTAN CONFLICT IN KASHMIR 1947–9

The decision of the Hindu Raja of Kashmir that his state should join India led to a Moslem uprising on 26 Oct 1947. Indian troops were flown into Kashmir to crush the rebels on 27 Oct. In November Pakistani troops crossed the border to aid the rebels. An undeclared state of war between India and Pakistan continued until United Nations mediation brought about a ceasefire on 1 Jan 1949. India annexed Kashmir on 26 Jan 1957.

COMMONWEALTH LAND FORCES IN SOUTH-EAST
AUG 1945

Killed	Wounded	Missing and POWs
297	139	6,911
286	290	1,389
212	429	2,322
647	903	98,054
1,789	1,306	15,395
10	21	13,351
9	1	5,716
36	60	2,736
1,250	2,469	6,317
249	126	3,052
12,827	42,136	5,483

MALAYAN EMERGENCY 1948–60

The Federation of Malaya was proclaimed on 1 Feb 1948. Communist guerrilla activity began, and on 16 June a state of emergency was declared. In Apr 1950 General Sir Harold Briggs was appointed to coordinate anti-Communist operations by Commonwealth forces. He inaugurated the Briggs Plan for resettling Chinese squatters in New Villages to cut them off from the guerrillas. After the murder of the British High Commissioner, Sir Henry Gurney, on 6 Oct 1951, General Sir Gerald Templer was appointed High Commissioner and Director of Military Operations on 15 Jan 1952, and on 7 Feb a new offensive was launched. On 8 Feb 1954 British authorities announced that the Communist Party's High Command in Malaya had withdrawn to Sumatra. The emergency was officially ended on 31 July 1960. During the conflict Government forces suffered 2,384 killed and 2,400 wounded, against Communist losses of 6,705 killed, 1,286 wounded and 2,696 captured.

KOREAN WAR 1950–3

The invasion of South Korea by North Korea on 25 June 1950 led to

209

intervention by United Nations forces following an emergency session of the Security Council, which was being boycotted by the USSR. The advance of United Nations forces into North Korea on 1 Oct led to the entry of the Chinese into the war on 25 Nov. An armistice was signed at Panmunjon on 27 July 1953. Casualties suffered by Commonwealth army units between Aug 50 and July 53 were:

	Killed	Wounded	Missing
United Kingdom	686	2,498	1,102
Australia	261	1,034	37
Canada	294	1,202	47
New Zealand	22	79	1
South Africa	—	—	1
India (Medical units)	—	4	—

CYPRUS EMERGENCY 1952–9

Agitation for union with Greece by the Greek population of Cyprus led to terrorism and guerrilla warfare against British forces and the Turkish minority by EOKA, the militant wing of the Enosis movement. It was led by Colonel Grivas, and supported by Archbishop Makarios, who was deported to the Seychelles in Mar 1956. A cease-fire came into effect on 13 Mar 1959, prior to the establishment of the independent republic of Cyprus on 16 Aug 1960.

MAU MAU REVOLT 1952–60

Violence by the Mau Mau, an African secret society in Kenya, led to a British declaration of a state of emergency on 20 Oct 1952. Leading Kikuyu nationalists were arrested, and Jomo Kenyatta was given a seven-year prison sentence in Oct 1953. A separate East African command consisting of Kenya, Uganda and Tanganyika was set up under General Sir George Erskine. In campaigns in the first half of 1955 some 4,000 terrorists in the Mount Kenya and Aberdare regions were dispersed. Britain began to reduce her forces in Sep 1955; the state of emergency in Kenya ended on 12 Jan 1960.

SUEZ 1956

Following Egyptian nationalisation of the Suez Canal on 26 July 1956, Israel invaded Sinai on 29 Oct. When Egypt rejected a cease-fire ultimatum by France and Britain, their air forces began to attack Egyptian air bases on 31 Oct. On 5 Nov Franco-British forces invaded the Canal Zone, capturing Port Said. Hostilities ended at midnight on 6–7 Nov, following a cease-fire call by the United Nations. Allied losses were 33 killed and 129 wounded.

CHINA-INDIA WAR 1962

After a series of border incidents China attacked India on 20 Oct 1962, driving back the Indian forces on the north-east frontier and in the Ladakh region. India declared a state of emergency on 26 Oct. On 21 Nov the Chinese announced that from 22 Nov their troops would cease fire all along the border, and from 1 Dec would withdraw from some of the occupied territory. Indian casualties in the conflict were 1,383 killed, 1,696 missing and 3,968 captured.

'CONFRONTATION' BETWEEN INDONESIA AND MALAYSIA 1963–6

When the Federation of Malaysia was established on 16 Sep 1963, President Sukarno of Indonesia announced a policy of 'confrontation', on the grounds that it was 'neo-colonialist'. There followed a campaign of propaganda, sabotage and guerrilla raids into Sarawak and Sabah. An agreement ending 'confrontation' was signed in Bangkok on 1 June 1966 (ratified 11 Aug). In the conflict Commonwealth forces lost 114 killed and 181 wounded, and the Indonesians 590 killed, 222 wounded and 771 captured.

CONFLICT IN CYPRUS 1963–8

Fighting broke out between Greek and Turkish Cypriots in Nicosia on 21 Dec 1963. There was a cease-fire on 25 Dec, and a neutral zone was established in Nicosia on 30 Dec. A United Nations peace-keeping force was established in Cyprus on 27 Mar 1964. Turkish planes attacked Greek Cypriot positions on the north-west coast in retaliation for attacks on Turkish Cypriots on 7–9 Aug 1964, but the United Nations organised a cease-fire.

There was renewed fighting between the Turkish and Greek communities on 15 Nov 1967. Agreement was reached after mediation by the United Nations and the United States on 3 Dec, and 16 Jan 1968 saw the completion of the withdrawal of Greek troops from Cyprus and the demobilisation of Turkish forces held in readiness to invade Cyprus.

ADEN 1964–7

On 18 Jan 1963 Aden acceded to the South Arabian Federation. British troops were involved in frontier fighting with the Yemen, and in suppressing internal disorders in Aden. A large-scale security operation was launched in Jan 1964 in the Radfan region, north of Aden. On 26 Nov 1967 the People's Republic of South Yemen was proclaimed, and the British military withdrawal from Aden was completed on 29 Nov. In the period 1964–7 British security forces lost 57 killed and 651 wounded in Aden.

211

INDIA-PAKISTAN CONFLICT IN THE RANN OF KUTCH AND KASHMIR 1965

The dispute between India and Pakistan over the Rann of Kutch led to hostilities on 4 Apr 1965. A cease-fire was signed on 30 Apr, and a tribunal was established to settle the dispute; its decision was announced on 19 Feb 1968, and accepted by both sides.

Border clashes in Kashmir and the Punjab began on 5 Aug 1965. Pakistan retaliated against an Indian raid of 24 Aug by initiating a major invasion across the cease-fire line in Kashmir on 1 Sep. Indian forces in turn invaded West Pakistan on 6 Sep. A United Nations Security Council call for a cease-fire became effective on 27 Sep. Indian casualties were 2,212 killed, 7,636 wounded and 1,500 missing. On 10 Jan 1966 an agreement to renounce the use of force was signed by India and Pakistan at Tashkent.

VIETNAM 1965–71

Under the ANZUS Pact of 1951, Australia committed 1,000 troops to fight in Vietnam in May 1965, and New Zealand sent a small force of artillery. In Apr 1966 the Australian contingent was increased to 4,500, and reinforcements included the first group of conscript national service trainees. At the peak there were 8,000 Australians and 550 New Zealanders serving in Vietnam in 1968. On 18 Aug 1971 the Australian Prime Minister, Mr McMahon, announced that Australia and New Zealand would withdraw their forces from Vietnam over the next six months. Australia and New Zealand ended their combat role in Vietnam on 7 Nov 71. Casualties suffered by Australia were 492 killed and 2,900 wounded, and by New Zealand 35 killed and 197 wounded.

NIGERIAN CIVIL WAR 1967–70

On 30 May 1967 the military governor of Eastern Nigeria, Lt. Col. Ojukwu, declared the region an independent sovereign state under the name of the republic of Biafra. Troops of the Nigerian Federal Army attacked across the northern border of Biafra on 7 July. On 20 May 1968 they captured Port Harcourt, but the Ibos continued to resist tenaciously. In 1969 the Biafrans' loss of their temporary capital, Umuahia, on 22 Apr was offset by the recapture of Owerri on 24 Apr. On 22 May the Biafrans began air attacks on Federal territory, particularly oil installations. On 23 Dec Federal forces launched a four-pronged attack on Biafra, which led to the capture of Owerri on 11 Jan 1970, and the collapse of Biafran resistance. The formal surrender of secessionist officers took place on 15 Jan 1970.

NORTHERN IRELAND 1969–

As a result of a request by the government of Northern Ireland facing severe rioting, British troops moved into Londonderry on 14 Aug 1969 and into Belfast on 15 Aug. The first British soldier was killed by a sniper in Belfast on 6 Feb 1971. Internment without trial was introduced on 9 Aug 1971; it was ended on 7 Dec 1975. On 'Bloody Sunday', 30 Jan 1972, British troops opened fire on a Catholic civil rights march, and thirteen people were killed. Direct rule was imposed from 30 Mar 1972. At the peak in Aug 72 there were 21,500 British soldiers in Northern Ireland. Up to Aug 1976, 256 British soldiers, 86 police and RUC reservists and 60 members of the part-time Ulster Defence Regiment had been killed in Northern Ireland.

CREATION OF BANGLADESH 1971

26 Mar	Sheikh Mujibur Rahman, head of the Awami League, proclaimed East Pakistan an independent republic under the name Bangladesh. He was arrested, West Pakistan troops moved in to take control of Dacca and civil war began.
12 Apr	Pakistan army took the offensive throughout East Pakistan. Large-scale operations were ended by 10 May, but the Mukti Bahini began guerrilla warfare. Relations between India and Pakistan deteriorated, with growing border clashes and an influx of refugees from East Pakistan to India.
21 Nov	Guerrillas launched an offensive against Jessore.
23 Nov	President Yahya Khan declared a state of emergency in Pakistan.
28 Nov	India acknowledged that her troops had gone into Pakistan the previous day.
3 Dec	Pakistan airforce made surprise attacks on military airfields in western India.
4 Dec	Indian troops invaded East Pakistan.
5 Dec	Pakistan troops crossed the cease-fire line in Kashmir.
6 Dec	India recognised the provisional government of Bangladesh.
16 Dec	Pakistan forces in East Pakistan surrendered.
17 Dec	Cease-fire on the western front.

Pakistan left the Commonwealth on 30 Jan 1972. Indian troops were withdrawn from Bangladesh on 25 Mar 1972. In the war India lost 3,037 killed, 7,300 wounded and 1,561 captured and missing; Pakistan lost 7,982 killed, 9,547 wounded and 85,000 captured and missing, including 15,000 wounded.

TURKISH INVASION OF CYPRUS 1974

15 July	Archbishop Makarios, President of Cyprus, was deposed in a coup by the National Guard, and replaced by Nikos

213

Sampson, who had taken part in the EOKA campaign. Fighting broke out between Greek and Turkish Cypriots in Nicosia.

20 July   Turkey invaded northern Cyprus; Greece demanded the withdrawal of Turkish troops within forty-eight hours and mobilized her forces. The United Nations Security Council called for a cease-fire.

24 July   Konstantine Karamanlis returned to form a new civilian government in Greece. In Cyprus Sampson resigned, and was replaced by Glafkos Clerides, President of the House of Representatives.

25 July   Peace talks opened in Geneva between Britain, Greece and Turkey.

26 July   Renewed fighting in Cyprus.

30 July   British, Greek and Turkish foreign ministers signed Cyprus declaration in Geneva to establish a UN buffer zone between Turkish-occupied land and the rest of the island.

1 Aug   Fighting continued; the UN Security Council adopted a resolution to enlarge the role of the UN peace-keeping mission.

8 Aug   Second stage of the Geneva talks opened.

13 Aug   Geneva talks ended.

14 Aug   Turkish forces renewed their attacks. Greece withdrew from the military structure of NATO.

16 Aug   Turkey called for a cease-fire.

7 Dec   Archbishop Makarios returned to Cyprus to resume the Presidency.

ARMED FORCES OF COMMONWEALTH COUNTRIES

	Numbers in Armed Forces 1972–76					Armed Forces 1976				
	1972	1973	1974	1975	1976	Army	Navy	Air	Reservists (Estimate)	Para-Military Forces
Australia	88,100	73,300	68,900	69,100	69,400	31,600	16,200	21,600	26,700	–
Bangladesh	–	17,900	26,500	36,000	63,000	59,000	1,000	3,000	..	20,000
Canada	84,000	83,000	83,000	77,000	77,900	28,500	13,400	36,000	19,100	–
Ghana	18,600	18,900	17,700	15,450	17,600	15,000	1,200	1,400	..	3,000
Guyana	2,200	2,200	2,000	2,000	2,000	2,000[1]	–	–	..	2,250
India	960,000	948,000	956,000	956,000	1,055,500	913,000	42,500	100,000	240,000	180,000
Kenya	6,730	6,730	7,430	7,550	7,600	6,500	340	760	..	1,800
Malawi	–	–	1,600	1,600	2,300	2,300[1]	–	–	..	–
Malaysia	50,500	56,000	66,200	61,100	62,300	52,500	4,800	5,000	26,500	82,000
New Zealand	12,600	12,800	12,600	12,700	12,500	5,400	2,800	4,300	12,600	–
Nigeria	274,000	157,000	210,000	208,000	230,000	221,000	3,500	5,500	12,000	–
Rhodesia	4,700	4,700	4,700	5,700	9,200	7,900	–	1,300	13,000	44,000
Sierra Leone	–	–	1,650	2,125	2,145	2,145[1]	–	–	..	–
Singapore	17,100	20,600	21,700	30,000	31,000	25,000	3,000	3,000	45,000	37,500
Sri Lanka	12,500	12,500	13,600	13,600	13,600	8,900	2,400	2,300	13,100	16,300
Tanzania	11,100	11,600	14,600	14,600	14,600	13,000	600	1,000	..	35,000
Uganda	12,600	12,600	21,000	21,000	21,000	20,000	–	1,000	..	–
United Kingdom	372,300	361,500	354,600	345,000	344,200	177,600	76,400	90,200	237,300	–
Zambia	5,700	6,000	5,800	5,800	7,800	6,300	–	1,500	..	2,500

1 All forces form part of a single service

BRITAIN'S ROLE 'EAST OF SUEZ' 1947–76

Aug 47	Independence of India and Pakistan.
Jan 48	Independence of Burma.
May 48	British withdrawal from Palestine.
June 48	State of emergency in Malaya. Commonwealth forces suppressed communist insurgency, and state of emergency ended July 1960.
June 50	Outbreak of Korean War: forces from Britain, Canada, Australia, New Zealand and South Africa sent to support United Nations operations.
Sep 51	Pacific security agreement signed by USA, Australia and New Zealand (ANZUS Pact).
Oct 52	State of emergency in Kenya: violence by Mau Mau suppressed, and state of emergency ended Jan 1960.
July 54	Agreements reached on Indo-China at Geneva Conference chaired jointly by Britain and the USSR.
Sep 54	South-East Asia Collective Defence Treaty signed in Manila by Britain, USA, Australia, New Zealand, France, Pakistan and the Philippines.
Apr 55	Britain signed the Baghdad Pact with Turkey and Iraq; Pakistan and Iran joined in Sep and Nov.
July 55	Naval cooperation agreement between Britain and South Africa. The Simonstown base was transferred to South African control, but the Royal Navy could continue to enjoy its facilities; the British and South African navies would work under the Royal Naval Commander-in-Chief South Atlantic.
Oct 56	Suez Crisis: Britain and France attacked Egypt after the nationalisation of the Suez Canal and Israel's invasion of Sinai; a cease-fire call by the UN led to an end to hostilities 6–7 Nov.
Jan 57	Agreement between Britain and the Maldive Islands on establishment of airfield on island of Gan.
July 57	Sultan of Muscat and Oman requested British aid after his forces had been defeated by rebels. RAF began operations, and involvement of land forces on 6 Aug led to collapse of the rebellion.
Aug 57	Independence of Malaya: Britain committed herself to the defence of Malaya by a treaty signed 12 Oct.
Oct–Nov 57	Trincomalee naval base and Katunayake air force station transferred to Ceylon.
Nov 57	Decision announced to station an element of the strategic reserve in Kenya, available as reinforcement either for the

Arabian peninsula or the Far East.

July 58	British paratroopers sent to Jordan at the request of King Hussein.
June 59	Singapore became a self-governing state within the Commonwealth.
Mar 60	Decision announced to move amphibious warfare squadron to Aden.
June 61	Ruler of newly-independent Kuwait asked for British assistance in case of an Iraqi attack; the crisis passed and British troops were withdrawn in Sep.
May 62	After communist successes in Laos, SEATO forces from USA, Britain, Australia, New Zealand and the Philippines were sent to the support of Thailand.
July 62	Agreement reached on Laos at Geneva Conference chaired jointly by Britain and the USSR.
Dec 62	Brunei oil town, Seria, occupied by rebels; the rebellion collapsed after intervention by British troops.
Sep 63	Federation of Malaysia established: Commonwealth forces supported Malaysia against Indonesian policy of 'confrontation' until June 1966.
Jan 64	British troops called in by governments of Tanganyika, Uganda and Kenya to suppress army mutinies.
Dec 64	Last British troops left Kenya.
Aug 65	Singapore separated from Malaysia.
Feb 66	Defence Review undertaken by British Labour Government stated that Britain would not carry out major operations of war outside Europe without the cooperation of allies, or incur defence obligations unless the country in question was prepared to provide appropriate facilities; no defence facilities would be maintained in an independent country against its wishes. The base of Aden would be abandoned by the end of 1968, but there would be a small increase in forces in the Persian Gulf. The base at Singapore would be retained as long as possible, and there would be discussions about defence facilities in Australia. Britain's carrier force would be phased out in the 1970s.
Jan 67	Last British troops left Borneo; one battalion remained in Brunei.
Jan 67	Negotiations between Britain and the Republic of South Africa resulted in a new agreement on the Simonstown base. Britain withdrew the Commander-in-Chief South Atlantic and its remaining frigate from Simonstown, and defence of the Cape route became primarily the responsibility of the Republic of South Africa.

217

Apr 67	Agreement between Britain and USA on joint use of British Indian Ocean Territory for defence purposes.
July 67	British Supplementary Defence White Paper: British troops would be withdrawn from South Arabia and Aden by Jan 1968, though naval and air forces would remain in the area. Further cuts in Malaysia and Singapore would lead to complete withdrawal by the mid-1970s.
Nov 67	British withdrawal from Aden completed.
Jan 68	New cuts in British defence expenditure announced: all British bases outside Europe and the Mediterranean, except Hong Kong, would be closed by 1971. Britain would remain a member of SEATO, but cease to declare forces to any SEATO plans, and negotiations would take place regarding Britain's defence responsibilities towards Malaysia and Singapore. Britain's Far East amphibious force would be transferred to the Mediterranean. In the Persian Gulf the bases of Bahrain and Sharjah would be given up, and defence agreements with the Persian Gulf and Trucial States would be renegotiated.
Apr 68	Exchange of notes ending Anglo-Kuwaiti defence pact.
June 68	Conference at Kuala Lumpur between Britain, Australia, New Zealand, Malaysia and Singapore agreed to set up an integrated air defence system covering Malaysia and Singapore. Britain announced that it would continue to train and exercise forces in the area after 1971.
June 69	A joint programme for the defence of Malaysia and Singapore was outlined at talks in Canberra between Britain, Australia, New Zealand, Malaysia and Singapore. An Australian was given command of the group's integrated air force, and joint naval exercises were held in local waters.
July 70	At the SEATO Ministerial meeting in Manila Britain's new Conservative Government announced that it would consult its Commonwealth partners about maintaining a force in Malaysia and Singapore after 1971.
Oct 70	In a supplementary statement on defence policy the British Government outlined proposals for a continuing British presence 'East of Suez', including plans to contribute to five-power Commonwealth defence arrangements for Malaysia and Singapore, and to continue discussions with local leaders in the Gulf about a British presence there.
Dec 70	Agreement between Britain and USA to begin building a naval communications station on Indian Ocean island of Diego Garcia.
Jan 71	Talks between Britain, Australia, New Zealand, Malaysia and

Singapore in Singapore reached agreement on new five-power arrangements for the defence of Malaysia and Singapore. Britain, Australia and New Zealand would maintain land and naval forces in Singapore, and Australia would also station air forces in Malaysia and Singapore; the ANZUK forces took over on 1 Nov.

Apr 71   At five-power talks in London on the defence of Malaysia and Singapore it was agreed to set up a joint council for regular consultation.

Sep 71   Integrated air defence system under five-power agreement inaugurated at Butterworth, Malaysia.

Nov 71   Britain and Brunei signed a new defence agreement by which Britain would no longer assist in the event of internal, as well as external aggression.

Dec 71   British forces left the Persian Gulf, except for small rear parties.

Dec 73   Australia withdrew most of her land forces from the ANZUK force, but left her air forces as part of the integrated air defence system.

Dec 74   New cuts in British defence expenditure announced.

June 75   Simonstown agreement between Britain and Republic of South Africa ended.

Sep 75   SEATO Council agreed to disband the organisation, but not the treaty.

Mar 76   Britain withdrew her forces from Singapore, except for a small contribution to the integrated air defence system; New Zealand troops remained, along with Australian air forces in Malaysia.

DEFENCE AGREEMENTS AND ALLIANCES SIGNED BY COMMONWEALTH COUNTRIES SINCE 1939–45 WAR

NORTH ATLANTIC TREATY. *4 April 1949*

Signed in Washington by Belgium, Canada, Denmark, France, Iceland, Italy, Luxembourg, the Netherlands, Norway, Portugal, the UK and the USA to provide for the collective defence and security of the western world. The treaty came into force on 24 Aug 1949. Greece and Turkey joined on 18 Feb 1952, and the German Federal Republic on 5 May 1955.

SOUTH-EAST ASIA COLLECTIVE DEFENCE TREATY. *8 September 1954*

Signed in Manila by Australia, France, New Zealand, Pakistan, the Philippines, Thailand, the UK and the USA. The treaty came into force on 19 Feb 1955. Pakistan left SEATO on 7 Nov 1973. On 24 Sep 1975 the SEATO Council agreed to disband the organization, but not the treaty.

BAGHDAD PACT. *24 February 1955*

Pact signed by Turkey and Iraq on 24 Feb 1955. The UK joined on 4 Apr 1955. Pakistan joined on 23 Sep 1955, and Iran on 3 Nov 1955. Iraq withdrew from the Pact on 24 Mar 1959, and the name was changed to the Central Treaty Organisation (CENTO) on 21 Aug 1959. The USA signed bilateral defence agreements with Iran, Turkey and Pakistan on 5 Mar 1959.

ORGANISATION OF AMERICAN STATES.

The following Commonwealth countries are members of the OAS, which was founded at Bogota in 1948: Barbados, Grenada, Honduras, Jamaica and Trinidad and Tobago.

ORGANISATION OF AFRICAN UNITY.

The following Commonwealth countries are members of the OAU, which was founded at Addis Ababa in 1963: Botswana, Gambia, Ghana, Kenya, Lesotho, Malawi, Mauritius, Nigeria, Seychelles, Sierra Leone, Swaziland, Tanzania, Uganda and Zambia.

AUSTRALIA

13 May 47	Agreement with UK for construction of Woomera rocket-testing range.
1 Feb 51 and 20 Feb 51	Exchange of notes with USA concluding a mutual defence assistance agreement.
1 Sep 51	Pacific security treaty (ANZUS Pact) with USA and New Zealand.
8 Sep 51	Peace treaty with Japan.
13 Sep 53	Agreement to share with UK the cost of maintaining the Woomera range.
8 Sep 54	South-East Asia Collective Defence Treaty.
4 Apr 55	Agreement with UK on new atomic testing ground to be known as Maralinga.
23 Aug 60	Agreement with USA on a mutual weapons development programme.
9 May 63	Agreement on establishment of a USA naval communication station in Australia.

14–16 June 66	Australia joined the Asian and Pacific Council (ASPAC), established at a conference in Seoul.
28 Aug 69	Memorandum of understanding with New Zealand on joint defence planning and arms purchase.
7 June 70	Agreement with New Zealand to standardise defence equipment.
7–9 Jan 71	Talks with UK, New Zealand, Malaysia and Singapore in Singapore produced agreement on five-power arrangements for defence of Malaysia and Singapore.

BANGLADESH

19 Mar 72	25-year defence agreement with India.

CANADA

4 Apr 49	North Atlantic Treaty.
12 Apr 49	Agreement with USA to establish a joint industrial mobilization committee.
1 Aug 51	Agreement with USA on extension and co-ordination of the continental radar defence system.
8 Sep 51	Peace treaty with Japan.
25 May 52	Exchange of defence-science information with France.
30 Mar 53	Agreement with UK and Belgium on transit and stationing of Canadian forces in Belgium.
19 Apr 55	Agreement with France relating to Convention on Foreign Forces stationed in Germany of 1952 (further agreement 26 Jan 1956).
5 May 55	Establishment and operation with USA of a distant early warning system.
22 June 55	Agreement with NATO partners on atomic cooperation.
17 Sep 56	Agreement with Germany on training German aircrews in Canada (further agreement 10 Dec 1956).
12–13 Apr 57	Agreement with Netherlands on extension of NATO aircrew training programme.
17 Apr 57	Agreement with Denmark on aircrew training for NATO (renewed 25 Mar 1960; extended 30 June 1964).
12 May 58	Organisation and operation with USA of the North American Air Defense Command (NORAD) (extended 30 Mar 1968 and 12 May 1973).
20 June 58	Agreement on establishment, maintenance and operation by USA of aerial refuelling facilities in Canada.
29 Aug–2 Sep 58	Exchange of notes with USA providing for establishment of a Canadian-USA committee on joint defence.

221

1May 59   Agreement with USA on establishment, maintenance and operation of short-range tactical air navigation (TACAN) facilities in Canada.

13 July 59   Agreement with USA on establishment of a ballistic missile early warning system.

24 May 60   Exchange of information on defence with Norway.

12 June 61   Air defence cooperation and defence production sharing programme with USA.

27 Sep 61   Agreement with USA on extension and strengthening of the continental air defence system (CADIN).

17–18   Exchange of defence-science information with Greece.
July 62

23 July 62   Declaration on neutrality of Laos at Geneva.

16 Aug 63   Agreement with USA on availability of nuclear warheads for Canadian forces.

15 Nov 63   Agreement with USA establishing a joint Canadian-USA civil emergency planning committee.

30 June 64   Agreement with Norway on continuation of Canada's NATO air training programme.

19 May 71   Agreement with USSR for consultation on foreign affairs.

CYPRUS

19 Feb 59   Agreements on Cyprus between UK, Greece and Turkey and representatives of Greek and Turkish Cypriots; included was an alliance between Greece, Turkey and Cyprus (Cyprus unilaterally abrogated alliance with Turkey 14 Apr 1964).

17 July 60   Treaty with UK (*see* 'United Kingdom').

GHANA

18 Aug 61   Treaty of friendship with China.

GUYANA

26 May 66   On independence Guyana became a party to a territorial treaty signed by UK and Venezuela on 17 Feb 1966.

26 May 66   Agreement with USA on future use of Atkinson Field.

INDIA

8 Aug 49   Treaty of peace and friendship with Bhutan.

4 Jan 50   Treaty of peace and friendship with Afghanistan.

31 July 50   Treaty of peace and friendship with Nepal.

5 Dec 50   Treaty with Sikkim for her continuation as an internally

autonomous protectorate of India.

11 July 52	Treaty of peace and friendship with the Philippines.
29 Apr 54	Non-aggression treaty with China.
28 Feb 56	Five-year agreement with Indonesia on mutual aid between air forces.
3 Dec 58	Naval cooperation agreement with Indonesia.
3 June 60	Agreement with Indonesia for military cooperation and mutual assistance in developing armies.
19 Sep 60	Indus Waters Treaty with Pakistan, settling dispute over allocation of the waters of the Indus River System.
23 July 62	Declaration on neutrality of Laos at Geneva.
27 Nov 62	Agreement for supply of arms by UK only for defence against Chinese aggression.
13 Jan 65	Military assistance agreement with USA.
10 Jan 66	Declaration of conference with Pakistan at Tashkent on restoration of 'normal and peaceful relations'.
9 Aug 71	20-year treaty of peace, friendship and cooperation with USSR.
19 Mar 72	25-year defence agreement with Bangladesh.
3 July 72	Peace treaty with Pakistan signed at Simla.
11 Dec 72	Agreement with Pakistan defining 'line of control' in Kashmir area.

JAMAICA

6 June 63	Agreement with USA on providing Jamaica with defence articles and services.
31 Mar 65	Agreement with UK on training and development of Jamaican armed forces.

KENYA

6 Mar 64	Defence agreement with UK.
9 June 70	Treaty with Ethiopia delimiting border.

MALAYSIA

12 Oct 57	Treaty of defence and mutual assistance with UK.
17 Apr 59	Treaty of friendship with Indonesia.
31 July 61	Association of South-East Asia (ASA) formed with the Philippines and Thailand (dissolved 29 Aug 1967).
1 June 66	Agreement with Indonesia ending 'confrontation' signed at Bangkok.
14–16 June 66	Malaysia joined the Asian and Pacific Council (ASPAC), established at a conference in Seoul.

8 Aug 67	Association of South-East Asian Nations formed with the Philippines, Indonesia, Thailand and Singapore (further treaty of amity and cooperation 24 Feb 1976).
11 Nov 69	Agreement with Thailand to establish a joint command to combat insurgents on their border.
7 Mar 70	Agreement with Thailand for military cooperation against insurgents operating on their border.
17 Mar 70	Treaty of friendship with Indonesia.
7–9 Jan 71	Talks with UK, Australia, New Zealand and Singapore in Singapore produced agreement on five-power arrangements for defence of Malaysia and Singapore.
6 Apr 72	Agreement with Indonesia on closer anti-guerrilla cooperation in border areas.

MALTA

21 July 64	10-year defence agreement with UK (abrogated by Maltese Prime Minister, Mr Mintoff, 30 June 1971).
26 Mar 72	7-year agreement with UK and NATO on use of Maltese military facilities.

MAURITIUS

12 Mar 68	Defence agreement with UK.

NEW ZEALAND

28 Oct 48 and 12 Nov 48	Defence agreement with UK (acting on behalf of Fiji).
1 Sep 51	Pacific security treaty (ANZUS Pact) with USA and Australia.
8 Sep 51	Peace treaty with Japan.
19 June 52	Mutual defence assistance agreement with USA.
8 Sep 54	South-East Asia Collective Defence Treaty.
14–16 June 66	New Zealand joined the Asian and Pacific Council (ASPAC), established at a conference in Seoul.
28 Aug 69	Memorandum of understanding with Australia on joint defence planning and arms purchase.
7 June 70	Agreement with Australia to standardise defence equipment.
7–9 Jan 71	Talks with UK, Australia, Malaysia and Singapore in Singapore produced agreement on five-power arrangements for defence of Malaysia and Singapore.

224

NIGERIA

Nov 60	Defence agreement with UK (abrogated by joint decision 21 Jan 1962).
3 Mar 73	Treaty of cooperation and mutual assistance with Mali.

PAKISTAN

30 Aug 50	Treaty of friendship with Syria.
8 Sep 51	Peace treaty with Japan.
25 June 52	Treaty of peace and friendship with Burma.
2 Apr 54	Treaty of friendly cooperation with Turkey.
8 Sep 54	South-East Asia Collective Defence Treaty.
23 Sep 55	Pakistan joined the Baghdad Pact.
8 July 57	Treaty of friendship with Spain.
28 Aug 58	Treaty of friendship with Thailand.
5 Mar 59	Treaty of defence and cooperation with USA.
19 Sep 60	Indus Waters Treaty with India, settling dispute over allocation of the waters of the Indus River System.
2 Mar 63	Border treaty with China.
20–21 July 64	Regional cooperation for development formed with Iran and Turkey.
26 Mar 65	Border treaty with China.
10 Jan 66	Declaration of conference with India at Tashkent on restoration of 'normal and peaceful relations'.
3 July 72	Peace treaty with India signed at Simla.
11 Dec 72	Agreement with India defining 'line of control' in Kashmir area.

SIERRA LEONE

26 Mar 71	Treaty of mutual defence with Guinea.

SINGAPORE

8 Aug 67	Association of South-East Asian Nations formed with Malaysia, Indonesia, Thailand and the Philippines (further treaty of amity and cooperation 24 Feb 1976).
7–9 Jan 71	Talks with UK, Australia, New Zealand and Malaysia in Singapore produced agreement on five-power arrangements for defence of Malaysia and Singapore.

SOUTH AFRICA

8 Sep 51	Peace treaty with Japan

9 Nov 51	Mutual defence assistance agreement with USA.
4 July 55	Simonstown naval cooperation agreement with UK (revised 25–27 Jan 1967; ended 16 June 1975).

SRI LANKA

11 Nov 47	Defence agreement with UK.
8 Sep 51	Peace treaty with Japan.

TANZANIA

20 Feb 65	Treaty of friendship with China
15 Nov 69	Agreement with Zambia and China on building Tan-Zam Railway.
6 May 70	Agreement with China on building naval base at Dar-es-Salaam.
5 Oct 72	Peace treaty with Uganda.

TONGA

25 Aug 58	Treaty of friendship with UK.

TRINIDAD AND TOBAGO

19 Nov 53	Exchange of letters with USA on military bases (further agreements 19 July 1954, 10 Feb 1961 and 2 and 5 Dec 1964).

UGANDA

3 Mar 64	Defence agreement with UK.
28 June 72	Mutual defence and trade agreements with Sudan.
5 Oct 72	Peace treaty with Tanzania.

UNITED KINGDOM

22 Mar 46	Treaty with Jordan (replaced by treaty of 15 Mar 1948).
10 Feb 47	Peace treaties with Italy, Bulgaria, Finland, Hungary and Romania.
4 Mar 47	Treaty of Dunkirk—50-year alliance with France.
13 May 47	Agreement with Australia for construction of Woomera rocket-testing range.
29 Aug 47	Defence agreement with Burma (ended by Burma 3 Jan 1953).
27 Oct 47	Agreement with Chile regarding military services (ended 29 Sep 1959).

9 Nov 47	Agreement with Nepal on employment of Gurkha troops in British army.
11 Nov 47	Defence agreement with Ceylon.
15 Mar 48	20-year mutual defence treaty with Jordan (ended 14 Mar 1957).
17 Mar 48	Treaty of Brussels with Belgium, France, Luxembourg and the Netherlands for collective military aid and economic and social cooperation (amended and expanded by Paris agreements of 23 Oct 1954—Brussels Treaty Organization renamed Western European Union).
19 Apr 48	Agreements with France regarding military facilities and air transit.
28 Oct 48 and 12 Nov 48	Defence agreement between UK (acting on behalf of Fiji) and New Zealand.
4 Apr 49	North Atlantic Treaty.
21 Dec 49	Military service agreement with France.
27 Jan 50	Mutual defence assistance agreement with USA.
21 July 50	Agreement with USA on long-range proving ground for guided missiles in the Bahamas.
23 Oct 50	Agreement with USA, France and Germany on defence materials.
30 Oct 50	Treaty of peace and friendship with Nepal.
8 Sep 51	Peace treaty with Japan.
15 Jan 52	Agreement with USA extending Bahamas long-range proving ground by additional sites in the Turks and Caicos Islands.
6 Mar 52	Military service agreement with France.
26 May 52	Convention on relations between UK, USA and France, and Germany.
1 and 3 July 52	Exchange of notes with Ethiopia on provision of facilities for military aircraft.
9 Sep 52	Agreement with Germany on British bases (further agreements 15 and 18 Oct 1954 and 22 and 31 May 1957).
12 Nov 52	Agreement with Belgium on establishment of a military base at Campine.
1 Jan 53	Agreement with Maldive Islands by which UK retained right to establish and maintain defence facilities.
11 and 13 Mar 53	Exchange of notes with Ethiopia on provision of facilities at Asmara for UK military aircraft.
30 Mar 53	Agreement with Canada and Belgium on transit and stationing of Canadian forces in Belgium.
27 July 53	Korean War armistice signed.
29 July 53	Treaty of friendship and alliance with Libya (in 1967 Libya

	requested the withdrawal of all British forces and liquidation of bases).
13 Sep 53	UK to share with Australia the cost of maintaining the Woomera range.
8 June 54	Agreement with USA on a special programme of facilities assistance for mutual defence purposes.
20 July 54	Geneva Conventions on Indo-China.
31 July 54	Military service agreement with Chile.
8 Sep 54	South-East Asia Collective Defence Treaty.
20 Jan 55	Military service agreement with Denmark.
4 Apr 55	UK joined the Baghdad Pact.
4 Apr 55	Agreement with Australia on new atomic testing ground to be known as Maralinga.
5 Apr 55	Military services agreement with Brazil.
15 May 55	Austrian State Treaty signed with USA, USSR, France and Austria.
15 June 55	Agreement with USA on cooperation regarding atomic information for mutual defence purposes (further agreement regarding atomic cooperation with NATO countries 22 June 1955).
4 July 55	Simonstown naval cooperation agreement with South Africa (revised 25–27 Jan 1967; ended 16 June 1975).
25 June 56	Agreements with USA extending Bahamas long-range proving ground by additional sites in St Lucia and Ascension Island (further agreements 25 Aug 1959, 7 July 1965 and 17 July 1967).
6 Dec 56 and 4 Jan 57	Exchange of notes with USA on civil aviation and long-range proving grounds for guided missiles in the West Indies.
3 Jan 57	Agreement with Maldive Islands on reestablishment of wartime airfield on island of Gan.
1 Apr 57	Exchange of notes with USA extending Bahamas long-range proving ground to include island of Great Exuma.
11 Apr 57	Agreement with Germany relating to Convention on Foreign Forces stationed in Germany of 1952.
7 June 57	Agreement with Germany on maintenance cost of British forces stationed in Germany (further agreements 3 Oct 1958 and 28 Apr 1967).
11 June 57 and 13 June 57	Agreement with the Netherlands relating to Convention on Foreign Forces stationed in Germany of 1952
12 Oct 57	Treaty of defence and mutual assistance with Malaysia.
22 Feb 58	Agreement with USA on supply of intermediate range ballistic missiles.

228

3 July 58	Agreement with USA on cooperation on uses of atomic energy for mutual defence purposes.
25 July 58	Agreement with Muscat and Oman for military and economic assistance.
25 Aug 58	Treaty of friendship with Tonga.
11 Feb 59	Treaty of friendship and protection with Federation of Arab Emirates of the South.
19 Feb 59	Agreements on Cyprus with Greece and Turkey and representatives of Greek and Turkish Cypriots.
7 May 59	Agreement with USA enabling UK to purchase component parts of US atomic weapons and weapons systems, other than warheads, and allowing mutual transfer of nuclear materials.
14 Feb 60	Agreement with Maldive Islands granting Britain use of Gan airfield for 30 years retrospectively from Dec 1956 (confirmed under independence agreement of 26 July 1965).
15 Feb 60	Agreement with USA on establishment and operation of a ballistic early warning station at Fylingdales Moor.
24 June 60	Agreement with USA on establishment in the Bahama Islands of a long-range aid to navigation station.
7 July 60	Treaty with Cyprus, which defined areas of two UK bases, Akrotiri and Dhekelia, and gave UK the right to use 31 defence sites and installations, and 10 training areas and ranges in other parts of the island.
1 Nov 60	Agreement with USA to provide facilities for US Polaris nuclear submarines at floating base in Holy Loch on the Clyde.
Nov 60	Defence agreement with Nigeria (abrogated by joint decision 21 Jan 1962).
19 June 61	Defence agreement with Kuwait (ended 13 Apr 1968).
18 July 61	Agreement with USA setting up a missile defence alarm system in UK.
29 June 62	Agreement with USA on a weapons production programme.
23 July 62	Declaration on neutrality of Laos at Geneva.
27 Nov 62	Agreement with India for supply of arms to be used against China only.
6 Apr 63	Agreement with USA on terms of sale of up to 100 Polaris missiles to Britain.
3 Mar 64	Defence agreement with Uganda.
6 Mar 64	Defence agreement with Kenya.
21 Sep 64	10-year defence agreement with Malta (abrogated by Maltese Prime Minister, Mr Mintoff, 30 June 1971).

31 Mar 65	Agreement with Jamaica on training and development of her armed forces.
17 Feb 66	Settlement of territorial dispute with Venezuela.
30 Dec 66	Agreement with USA on availability of certain Indian Ocean islands for defence purposes.
1 Apr 67	Agreement with USA on joint use of British Indian Ocean Territory for defence purposes.
12 Mar 68	Defence agreement with Mauritius.
15 Dec 70	Agreement with USA to start work in 1971 on naval communications station on Indian Ocean island of Diego Garcia.
7–9 Jan 71	Talks with Australia, New Zealand, Malaysia and Singapore in Singapore produced agreement on five-power arrangements for defence of Malaysia and Singapore.
18 Mar 71	Agreement with Germany on troop support costs.
15 Aug 71	Treaty of friendship with Bahrain.
3 Sep 71	Agreement with USA, USSR and France on Berlin.
3 Sep 71	Treaty of friendship with Qatar.
23 Nov 71	Defence agreement with Brunei.
2 Dec 71	Treaty of friendship with Union of Arab Emirates.
26 Mar 72	7-year agreement with Malta and NATO on use of Maltese military facilities.
5 Feb 74	Agreement with USA to expand military facilities at Indian Ocean base of Diego Garcia.

ZAMBIA

15 Nov 69	Agreement with Tanzania and China on building Tan-Zam Railway.

PARTICIPATION OF COMMONWEALTH FORCES IN UNITED NATIONS PEACE-KEEPING OPERATIONS 1945–75

Operation	Australia	Canada	Ghana	India	Malaya	New Zealand	Nigeria	Pakistan	Sierra Leone	Sri Lanka	United Kingdom
Special Commission in the Balkans (UNSCOB) 1947–54	×					×					×
Truce Supervision Organisation (UNTSO) Palestine/Israel 1948–75	×	×				×					×
Military Observer Group India/Pakistan (UNMOGIP) 1948–75		×				×					
Commission for Indonesia (UNCI) 1949–51	×										
Emergency Force (UNEF) Egypt-Israel border 1956–67		×		×		×				×	
Observer Group in Lebanon (UNOGIL) 1958		×		×		×				×	
Congo Operation (UNCO) 1960–64		×	×	×	×		×		×	×	
Temporary Executive Authority/Security Force (UNTEA-UNSF) West Irian 1962–63		×		×			×	×			
Yemen Observation Group (UNYOM) 1963–64		×	×	×				×			
Force in Cyprus (UNFICYP) 1964–75	×	×					×			×	×
India and Pakistan Observer Mission (UNIPOM) 1965–66	×	×				×		×			
Emergency Force (UNEF) Egypt-Israel border 1973–75		×	×	×							
Disengagement Observer Force (UNDOF) Syria-Israel border 1974–75		×									

231

ADHERENCE OF COMMONWEALTH COUNTRIES TO

	Antarctic Treaty		Partial Test Ban Treaty		Outer Space Treaty	
	A^2	B^3	A^2	B^3	A^2	B^3
Australia	1959	1961	1963	1963	1967	1967
Bahamas	–	–	–	–	–	–
Barbados	–	–	–	–	–	1968
Botswana	–	–	–	1968	1967	–
Canada	–	–	1963	1964	1967	1967
Cyprus	–	–	1963	1965	1967	1972
Fiji	–	–	–	1972	–	1972
Gambia	–	–	–	1965	1967	–
Ghana	–	–	1963	1963	1967	–
Grenada	–	–	–	–	–	–
Guyana	–	–	–	–	1967	–
India	–	–	1963	1963	1967	–
Jamaica	–	–.	1963	–	1967	1970
Kenya	–	–	–	1965	–	–
Lesotho	–	–	–	–	1967	–
Malawi	–	–	–	1964	–	–
Malaysia	–	–	1963	1964	1967	–
Malta	–	–	–	1964	–	–
Mauritius	–	–	–	1969	–	1969
New Zealand	1959	1960	1963	1963	1967	1968
Nigeria	–	–	1963	1967	–	1967
Pakistan[4]	–	–	1963	–	1967	1968
Sierra Leone	–	–	1963	1964	1967	1967
Singapore	–	–	–	1968	–	–
Sri Lanka	–	–	1963	1964	1967	–
Swaziland	–	–	–	1969	–	–
Tanzania	–	–	1963	1964	–	–
Tonga	–	–	–	1971	–	1971
Trinidad and Tobago	–	–	1963	1964	1967	–
Uganda	–	–	1963	1964	–	1968
United Kingdom	1959	1960	1963	1963	1967	1967
Western Samoa	–	–	1963	1965	–	–
Zambia	–	–	–	1965	–	1973

[1] Treaty for prohibition of nuclear weapons in Latin America.
[2] Date of signature.
[3] Date of ratification, accession or succession.
[4] Pakistan left the Commonwealth in 1972.
[5] Additional Protocols I and II to the Treaty of Tlatelolco.

MULTILATERAL AGREEMENTS ON DISARMAMENT

Treaty of Tlatelolco[1]		Non-Proliferation Treaty		Sea-Bed Treaty		Convention on Bacteriological and Toxin Weapons	
A[2]	B[3]	A[2]	B[3]	A[2]	B[3]	A[2]	B[3]
—	—	1970	1973	1971	1973	1972	—
—	—	—	1973	—	—	—	—
1968	1969	1968	—	—	—	1973	1973
—	—	1968	1969	1971	1972	1972	—
—	—	1968	1969	1971	1972	1972	1972
—	—	1968	1970	1971	1971	1972	1973
—	—	—	1972	—	—	1973	1973
—	—	1968	1975	1971	—	1972	—
—	—	1968	1970	1971	1972	1972	1975
—	1975	—	1975	—	—	—	—
—	—	—	—	—	—	1973	—
—	—	—	—	—	1973	1973	1974
1967	1969	1969	1970	1971	—	—	1975
—	—	1968	1970	—	—	—	1976
—	—	1968	1970	1971	1973	1972	—
—	—	—	—	—	—	1972	—
—	—	1968	1970	1971	1972	1972	—
—	—	1969	1970	1971	1971	1972	1975
—	—	1968	1969	1971	1971	1972	1972
—	—	1968	1969	1971	1972	1972	1973
—	—	1968	1968	—	—	1972	1974
—	—	—	—	—	—	1972	—
—	—	—	1975	1971	—	1972	—
—	—	1970	—	1971	—	1972	1975
—	—	1968	—	—	—	1972	—
—	—	1969	1969	1971	1971	—	—
—	—	—	—	1971	—	1971	—
—	—	—	1971	—	—	—	—
1967	1970	1968	—	—	—	—	—
—	—	—	—	—	—	—	—
1967[5]	1969	1968	1968	1971	1972	1972	1975
—	—	—	1975	—	—	—	—
—	—	—	—	—	1972	—	—

9 POPULATION*

ADEN, PERIM, SOKOTRA AND THE KURIA MURIA ISLANDS

		Aden
1901C	55,974	43,974
1911C	58,165	46,165
1921C	66,923	54,923
1931C	60,338	48,338

1946C   The Colony 80,876 including 9,456 Indians
1946E   The Protectorate 600,000
1949E   Kamaran included as administered by Aden 2,000.
1955C   The Colony 138,441
1955E   The Protectorate 1,000,000

The territory, excluding Perim and the Kuria Muria Islands, joined the Federation of South Arabia in 1963.

ANGLO-EGYPTIAN SUDAN (1920–1955)

		Khartoum	*Omdurman*
1922E	5,850,000	30,600	78,000
1932E	5,600,000	50,463	103,669
1942E	6,342,477	44,950	116,196
1951E	8,764,000	82,700	125,300

* C = Census, E = Estimate.

ASCENSION ISLAND

1901C	430
1912C	180
1918C	250
1931C	188
1951C	174
1961C	336
1971C	1,231[1]

[1] Including 674 immigrants from St Helena.

AUSTRALIA

		Aborigines (Estimate)	*Sydney*	*Melbourne*	*Canberra*[1]
1901C	3,771,715	20,760	496,990	496,079	
1911C	4,455,005	37,633	636,353	600,160	
1921C	5,436,794	60,000			2,572
1933C	6,677,839	48,000			8,947
1947C	7,591,358				16,905
1961C	10,508,186				58,828
1971C	12,755,678	106,288			144,063

[1] Canberra was taken from New South Wales in 1911.

BAHAMAS

1901C	53,735
1911C	55,944
1921C	53,031
1931C	59,828
1948E	80,639
1961E	106,677
1970C	168,812

235

BANGLADESH

1961C[1]	50,840,000
1972E	75,000,000

[1] When part of Pakistan.

BARBADOS

		births	*deaths*
1901C	195,588		
1911C	171,982	6,106	4,561
1921C	156,312	5,082	6,746
1931E	173,674	4,853	4,488
1946C	192,841		
1951E	215,169	6,793	3,000
1961E	241,706	6,754	3,410
1973E	247,506	5,084	2,287

BELIZE (formerly British Honduras)

		birthrate	*deathrate*
1901C	37,479	39·55	28·39
1911C	40,458	42·40	24.80
1921C	45,317	35·48	24·00
1931C	51,347	36·78	36·72
1946C	59,220	34·30	16·90
1951E	70,741	41·07	11·32
1960C	90,343	44·69	7·83
1970C	119,934	39·00[1]	5·30[1]

[1] 1972.

BERMUDA

		Hamilton	birthrate	deathrate
1901C	17,535	2,246		
1911C	18,994	2,627		
1921C	20,127	2,578	33·0	18·4
1931C	27,789	3,259	26·9	13·3
1951C	38,044	2,800	27·4	11·4
1961C	45,491	2,800[1]	26·0	6·8
			births	deaths
1971C	53,000	3,000	1,138	438

[1] Estimate.

BORNEO, BRUNEI AND SARAWAK

1900E	North Borneo	200,000
	Brunei	45,000
	Sarawak	600,000
1911C	North Borneo	108,183 including estimated – 88,000 Dusuns 26,000 Chinese
1911E	Brunei	30,000
1911E	Sarawak	500,000
1921C	Brunei	25,454 including – 23,938 Malays and Borneans
1921E	Sarawak	600,000
1931C	North Borneo	270,223 including – 97,862 Dusuns 47,799 Chinese
1931C	Brunei	30,135 including – 26,972 Malays and Borneans
1931E	Sarawak	475,000
1946	Labuan was included as part of North Borneo.	
1947C	Brunei	40,657 including– 31,161 Malays and Borneans
1947C	Sarawak	546,385 including – 145,158 Chinese 97,469 Malays

237

BORNEO, BRUNEI AND SARAWAK (*continued*)

1960C	North Borneo	454,421 including
		306,498 Borneans, mainly Dusuns
		104,542 Chinese
1961E	Sarawak	769,034 including –
		240,709 Chinese
		134,624 Malays
1962E	Brunei	86,500
1963	North Borneo and Sarawak became part of Malaysia.
1973E	Brunei	145,170

BOTSWANA (Bechuanaland until 1966)

1901E	200,000	
1911C	125,350	35,000[1]
1921C	152,983	35,000[1][2]
1936C	265 656	101,481[1]
1946C	296,883	100,987[1]
1956C	320,675	109,080[1]
1971C	630,379	216,058[1]

[1] Bamangwato included in total.
[2] Estimate.

BURMA 1937–1948

1937   (Indian government census 1931): 14,667,146, of whom 9m. were Burmese. Rangoon, 400,415.

CAMEROON (mandate 1916–1961)

1932E	774,585
1951C	1,084,000

CANADA

		Immigrants
1901C	5,371,315	49,149
1911C	7,204,838	311,084
1921C	8,788,483	89,999
1931C	10,376,787	88,223
1941C	11,420,084	9,329
1949	Newfoundland and Labrador joined Canada.	
1951C	14,009,429	194,391
1961C	18,238,247	71,689
1971C	21,568,311	121,900

CAYMAN ISLANDS (separated from Jamaica in 1962)

1960C	7,616
1970C	10,249

CYPRUS

		Greek	Nicosia
1901C	237,022	182,739	14,752
1911C	274,108	214,480	16,052
1921C	310,715	E 249,000	18,461
1931C	347,959	E 283,000	23,677
1946C	450,114	361,199	38,669
1960C	577,615	442,521	95,500
1973E	631,778	498,511	115,718

FALKLAND ISLANDS

		South Georgia[1]	Stanley
1901C	2,043		916
1911C	3,275		800

[1] Not included in census total.

239

(continued

FALKLAND ISLANDS (*continued*)

1920E	2,271	1,000	900
1931C	2,393	562	1,213
1951C	2,280	360	1,270
1962C	2,172	521	1,074
1973C	1,874	22	*c.* 1,000

FIJI

1901C	117,870
1911C	139,541
1921C	157,266
1931E	185,573
1951E	301,959
1961C	413,872
1966C	476,727

THE GAMBIA

	Colony	*Protectorate*
1901C	13,456	76,948
1911C	7,700	138,400
1921C	9,000	200,000
1931C	14,370	185,150
1951C	27,297	252,389
1963C	315,486[1]	
1973E	494,279[1]	

Bathurst: 1901C, 8,807; 1963C, 27,809; as Banjul 1973E, 39,476.

[1] Colony and Protectorate.

GHANA (formerly Gold Coast)

		Accra
1901C	1,486,433	14,842
1911C	1,502,899	19,585

(*continued*

GHANA (*continued*)

1921C	2,078,043	38,000
1931C	3,121,214	59,895
1948C	4,111,680	135,926

1957   Ghana combined the Gold Coast and Togoland.

Accra

1960C	6,726,000	337,770
1970C	8,545,561	663,880

GIBRALTAR

		birthrate	*deathrate*	*Garrison*
1901C	27,460	31·31	21·35	5,349[1]
1911C	25,367	24·30	16·00	5,340[1]
1921C	20,638	22·41	17·53	2,932[1]
1931C	21,372	21·23	17·32	3,218[1]
		births	*deaths*	
1951C	23,232	396	280	..
1961C	24,075	560	241	..
1970C	26,833	577	215	..

[1] Included in total but not in vital statistics.

GILBERT AND ELLICE GROUP

Formed in 1915. Total population 1947C 36,000.

Gilbert Islands		Ellice Islands		Ocean Islands	
1921E	29,897	1919E	3,500	1921E	1,030
1930E	24,800	1930E	3,969	1951E	2,307
1950E	28,830	1951E	4,671	1961E	2,564
1961E	36,168	1961E	5,120	1973E	2,314
1973E	57,816	1973E	5,817 (as Tuvalu)		

Phoenix Islands		Line Islands	
1951E	1,186	1927E	540
1961E	926	1950E	668
1971	Uninhabited	1961E	1,355
		1973E	1,472

GUYANA (formerly British Guiana)

		Indians	birthrate	deathrate	Georgetown
1911C	296,000	133,000			54,000
1921C	307,391[1]	124,900	34·5	30 ·9	55,490
1931C	318,312[2]	131,919	31·4	21·8	62,690
1951E	437,022	197,696	42·0	13·4	87,279
1961C	590,140	289,790	42·7	9·2	148,451
1971E	740,000	..	34·3	6·6	167,068

[1] Aborigines 9,700.   [2] Aborigines 7,379.

HONG KONG

		Chinese
1901C	283,905	274,543
1911C	366,145	354,187
1921C	625,166	612,310
1931C	840,473	821,104
1950E	2,360,000	
1961C	3,133,131	
1971C	3,948,179	

INDIA

		Hindus	Moslem	Bombay	Calcutta	Delhi
1901C	294,361,056	207,000,000	62,000,000	776,006	1,125,400	208,575
1911C	315,156,396	217,500,000	66,600,000	979,445	1,222,313	232,837
1921C	318,942,480	216,000,000	68,000,000	1,175,914	1,327,547	304,420
1931C	352,837,778	239,000,000	77,000,000	1,161,383	1,485,582	447,442
1951C	361,129,622	303,000,000	35,000,000	2,839,270	2,548,677	1,191,104
1961C	439,072,893	366,500,000	46,900,000	4,152,056	2,927,289	2,061,758
1971C	546,955,945	453,200,000	61,400,000	5,900,000	7,000,000	3,600,000

IRAQ (mandate 1920—1927)

1920C   2,849,282, of whom, 2,640,700 Moslem

87,488 Jewish

78,792 Christian

JAMAICA

		births	*deaths*	*Kingston*
1902E	770,242	31,268	16,756	46,542[1]
1911C	831,383	32,750	18,383	57,379[2]
1921C	858,188	30,064	24,383	62,707
		birthrate	*deathrate*	
1931E	1,050,667	34·81	18·65	
1943C	1,237,063			109,056
		births	*deaths*	
1960C	1,613,148	66,305	14,237	
1970C	1,861,300	66,219	13,970	

[1] 1891 census.
[2] Being rebuilt after being destroyed by earthquake and fire, 1907.

KENYA (East African Protectorate until 1920)

1902   Addition of Naivasha and Kisumu provinces, bringing population to (estimate) 4m. of whom 25,450 were non-African. Mombasa, 27,000.

				Estimate	
				Asian	*European*
1912E	4,038,000	Mombasa	30,000	25,000	2,000
		Nairobi	14,000		
1921E	2,376,000	Mombasa	32,000	22,822	9,651
		Nairobi	24,000		
1931E	3,040,940	Mombasa	57,000	39,500	16,800
		Nairobi	85,722		
1951C	5,700,000	Mombasa	. .	154,000	42,000
		Nairobi	. .		
1961E	7,290,000	Mombasa	. .	(289,000 non-African)	
		Nairobi	297,000		
1969C	10,942,708	Mombasa	. .	139,037	40,593
		Nairobi	. .		

243

LABUAN (incorporated in Singapore in 1907)

1901C   8,411   Victoria (town) 1,500

LAGOS, COLONY AND PROTECTORATE

1901E   1,500,000   Lagos Town 41,847

LEEWARD ISLANDS (including Dominica until 1940)

1901C	127,536	
1911C	127,193	
1921C	122,242	
1931C	127,829	
1949C	108,847	
1960C	St Kitts-Nevis-Anguilla	56,644
	Montserrat	12,157
1961C	Antigua	63,190
	British Virgin Islands	7,338
1963C	Antigua	61,664
1970C	St Kitts-Nevis-Anguilla	51,457
	British Virgin Islands	2,183
1973C	Montserrat	12,230

LESOTHO (Basutoland until 1966)

1904C	348,626	895[1]
1911C	405,903	1,396[1]
1921C	498,781	1,603[1]
1936C	562,411	1,434[1]
1946C[2]	563,854	1,689[1]
1956C	641,674	1,926[1]
1966C	969,634	

[1] Europeans included in total.
[2] An estimated 110,000 African labourers were out of the country at the census.

MALAWI (formerly Central African Protectorate)

	African	European	Indian	Blantyre
1901C	900,000	450	250	6,100
1907	Renamed Nyasaland.			
	African	European	Asian	
1912E	1,000,000	773	463	
1921C	1,199,934	1,486	563	
1931C	1,498,836	1,910	1,537	
1952C	2,392,031	4,073	5,248	
1961E	2,900,000	8,900	12,200[1]	
1964	Independent as Malawi			
1966C	4,020,724	7,395	11,299	

[1] Including Colonials.

FEDERATED MALAY STATES

PERAK, SELANGOR, NEGRI SEMBILAN AND PAHANG

	Total	Malays	Chinese	Indians	Kuala Lumpur
1901	678,595	312,486	299,739	58,211	77,234
1911	1,036,999	420,840	433,244	172,465	47,000
1921	1,324,890	510,820	494,548	305,219	80,000
1931	1,713,096	443,618	711,540	379,996	111,738

	Total	Perak	Selangor	Negri Sembilan	Pahang
1901	678,595	329,665	168,789	96,028	84,113
1911	1,036,999	494,057	294,035	130,199	118,708
1921	1,324,890	599,055	401,009	178,642	146,064
1931	1,713,096	765,989	533,197	233,799	180,111

MALAY STATES (Outside the Federation)

	Kelantan	Trengganu	Kedah	Perlis	Johore
1909	286,750	154,073	245,986	32,746	180,142
1921	309,293	153,092	338,554	40,091	282,244
1931	362,517	179,664	429,645	49,297	505,309

245

All nine states joined the Malayan Union in 1946 which was replaced by the Federation of Malaya in 1948. Population 4,908,086 of which 2,427,834 were Malays, 1,884,534 Chinese and 530,638 Indian.

	Total	Malays	Chinese	Indians
1961E	7,136,804	3,576,889	2,633,516	796,880

MALAYSIA (from 1963, including Sabah and Sarawak)

			Malays	Chinese	Indians
1970C	Malaya	8,809,557	4,671,874	3,131,320	936,341
	Sabah	653,604			
	Sarawak	976,269			

MALTA

		births	deaths	Valletta
1901C	188,141			. .
1911C	228,534			. .
1921C	213,024	7,813	4,584	. .
1931C	241,621	7,804	5,564	. .
1951E	312,646	9,511	3,476	23,138[1][2]
1957C	319,620	8,794	2,955	18,190[1]
1967C	314,216	5,309	2,985	15,279

[1] Estimate
[2] 1952

MAURITIUS AND DEPENDENCIES

		Indian	birthrate	deathrate
1901E	378,195	206,131	34·7	40·3
1911E	377,083	258,251	35·6	31·4
1921E	385,074	165,884	39·7	42·6
1931E	393,418		36·9	33·3
1944E	419,185			
1951E	494,519		47·5	14·9
1962E	680,305		39·8	9·9
1972E	826,199		22·7	7·8

246

NAURU (Mandate from 1920)

1922C	2,129
1932C	2,316
1951C	3,434
1962C	4,849
1972C	6,768

NEWFOUNDLAND AND LABRADOR

		Labrador
1901C	220,984	3,947
1911C	242,619	3,949
1921C	261,979	3,621
1931C	281,549	4,264

Newfoundland and Labrador joined Canada in 1949.

NEW GUINEA
(mandate 1920–1949, from which date it has been administered by Australia)

1920E	Bismarck Archipelago	188,000
	German Solomon Islands	15,000
	New Guinea	110,000–350,000
1932E		394,360

NEW HEBRIDES

1906E	70,000
1919E	60,000
1930C	51,201
1950C	48,716
1960C	60,374
1967C	77,988
1970E	85,000
1976E	97,468

NEW ZEALAND

		birthrate	deathrate
1901C	815,862 of whom Maori, 43, 143	26·34	9·81
	North Island 390,571		
	South Island 381,661		
1911C	1,058,312 of whom Maori, 49,844		
	North Island 563,729		
	South Island 444,152		
1921C	1,218,913 of whom Maori, 52,750E	23·34	8·73
	North Island 741,255		
	South Island 477,658		
1932E	1,455,167 of whom Maori, 69,890E	18·42	8·34
	North Island 984,277		
	South Island 540,644		
1951C	1,939,472 of whom Maori, 115,676	24·39	9·56
	Cook Islands and Niue 19,632		
	Tokelau (Union) Islands 1,580		
	Trust Territory of		
	Western Samoa 83,565		
1961C	2,414,984 of whom Maori, 167,086	26·97	8·97
	Cook Islands and Niue 23,242		
	Tokelau Islands 1,938		
1971C	2,862,631 of whom Maori, 227,414	22·59	8·49
	Cook Islands and		
	Niue 21,227		
	Tokelau Islands 1,587		

Wellington (Capital)

1901	43,638
1911	70,729
1931	143,000
1951	133,414
1961[1]	150,537
1971[2]	552,640

[1] Urban area
[2] Statistical area

NIGERIA

1901E   25,000,000
1906   Lagos incorporated together with Eastern and Central Provinces, as Southern Nigeria.

	Northern	Southern	East	West	Colony	Lagos
1911E	9,269,000	7,857,400				
1921E	10,500,000	8,000,000				
1931C	11,434,924	8,168,227			325,020	
1941C	12,238,350		4,778,978	3,691,848	331,544	
1962E[1]	20,000,000		10,000,000	9,000,000		450,000
1963C	55,670,052					665,246
1973C[1]	79,800,000					

[1] Census declared void.

PAKISTAN (from partition, 1947, until leaving the Commonwealth in 1972)

		Karachi	Lahore
1951C	75,842,165	1,126,417	849,476
1961C	93,720,613	1,912,598	1,296,477
1972C	104,890,000	3,469,000	2,148,000

PALESTINE (mandate 1920–1948)

		Moslem	Jewish	Christian	Jerusalem
1922C	757,182	590,890	83,794	73,024	62,578
1931C	1,035,154	759,952	175,006	90,607	90,407
1942E	1,605,816	987,985	478,449	126,344	141,100

PAPUA NEW GUINEA
(Papua Australian controlled from 1905, New Guinea from 1949)

1901E   350,000
1911C   272,057
1922E   276,884
1932E   276,144

249   (continued

PAPUA NEW GUINEA (*continued*)

	Papua	New Guinea
1950E	372,939	
1951E		1,102,970
1961C	523,442	1,448,919
1971E	671,384	1,795,602

PHOENIX ISLANDS
(included in the Gilbert and Ellice Group in 1937)

1914C	59

PITCAIRN

1901E	126
1911E	145
1914E	140
1941E	193
1951E	134
1961E	126
1973E	74

RHODESIA

	Northern	Southern
1904C		577,623
1911C		767,222
1911E	1,001,434	
1921C	931,500	806,620
1931C	1,386,081	1,109,012
1941C	1,381,829	1,448,000
1951C	1,930,842	2,146,324
1961C	2,480,000	3,849,000

The Federation of Rhodesia and Nyasaland was established in 1953 and dissolved in 1963.
Northern Rhodesia became independent as Zambia in 1964. (*see* p. 5)
Southern Rhodesia declared unilateral declaration of independence in 1965.

ST HELENA

		births	*deaths*
1901C	9,850[1]	116	165
1911C	3,520	95	39
1921C	3,747	93	24
1933C	3,995		
1951C	4,748	131	48
1961C	4,648	112	39
1973C	5,159	117	60

[1] Including 1,532 garrison and 4,655 Boer POWs.

SEYCHELLES

		births	*deaths*
1901C	19,237		
1911C	26,000		
1921C	24,811		
1931C	27,444		
1952E	36,613	1,036	456
1962C	43,750	1,775	574
1971C	52,650	1,832	462

SIERRA LEONE

		Colony	*Protectorate*
1901C		76,655	
1911C		75,572	1,327,560
1921C		85,163	1,456,148
1934E		100,579	
1951E	2,005,000[1]		
1963C	2,183,000[1]		

[1] Colony and Protectorate

251

SOLOMON ISLANDS

1901E	600
1912E	150,000
1931C	94,105
1950C	98,571
1959C	124,320
1971C	152,000

SOMALILAND PROTECTORATE

1911C 300,000 estimated as the size of a nomad population.
Main towns in the trading season:

	Berbera	30,000
	Zeyla and Bulhar	*c.* 7,000 each

1921C 300,000 estimated as the size of a nomad population.
Main town in the trading season:

	Berbera	30,000
	Zeyla and Bulhar	*c.* 7,000 each

1931C 344,700 estimated as the size of a nomad population.
Main towns in the trading season:

	Berbera	30,000
	Zeyla	5,000

1951C 700,000

UNION OF SOUTH AFRICA

CAPE COLONY

1904C 2,405,552 Cape Town 77,183 African and Asian 1,825,172

NATAL

1901C 925,118 Durban 57,000 African 786,912

In Jan 1903 7,000 sq. miles of territory and an estimated 58,000 people were transferred from Transvaal to Natal administration.

TRANSVAAL

1904C   1,268,716   Johannesburg   158,580   African   945,498

ORANGE RIVER COLONY

1904C   385,045   Bloemfontein   33,890   African and Asian   241,626
Cape Colony, Natal, Transvaal and the Orange River Colony
combined in 1910 as the Union of South Africa.

	Total	African	European	Pretoria
1911C	5,973,394	4,019,006	1,276,242	29,618[1]
1921C	6,928,580	4,697,813	1,519,488	45,361[1]
1936C	9,589,898	6,596,689	2,003,857	76,954[1]
1946C	11,418,349		2,372,690	145,220[1]
1951C	12,646,375	8,535,341	2,643,187	151,100[1]

The Union left the Commonwealth in 1961.

[1] Europeans.

SOUTH WEST AFRICA/NAMIBIA (mandate 1920–1961)

	African	European
1921E	208,000	19,432
1930E	237,647	31,586
1936C	233,516	30,677
1951C	368,219	49,549

SRI LANKA (formerly Ceylon)

		Sinhalese	Tamil	Colombo
1901C	3,578,333	2,300,000	953,535	158,228
1911C	4,105,535	2,670,000	599,771	213,396
1921C	4,504,549	3,000,000	1,119,699	244,000
1931C	5,306,863		692,540	284,155

253

(continued

SRI LANKA (*continued*)

1946C	6,657,339	4,620,000	462,000	362,000
1953C	8,098,095	5,600,000	1,850,000	424,816
1960C	9,896,000	6,900,000	2,000,000	426,127
1971C	12,711,143	9,000,000	2,500,000	562,160

STRAITS SETTLEMENTS

	Singapore[1]	Penang	Malacca	Total
1901C	228,555	248,207	95,487	572,249
1911C	311,985	278,003	124,081	714,069
1921C	423,768	304,572	153,599	881,939
1931C	567,363	359,851	186,351	1,146,984
1952E	1,079,794[2]			
1961C	1,712,600			
1970C	2,074,507			

	Chinese	Malay	Births	Deaths
1901C	281,933	215,058	14,568	22,876
1911C	369,843	240,206	18,069	33,075
1921C			28,772	28,000
1931C			41,361	27,369
1952E				
1961C	1,287,700			
1970C	1,579,866			

[1] Singapore until 1946 included Penang, Malacca and Christmas Islands; Cocos Islands were included from 1903, and Labuan from 1907–1946.
[2] Excluding Penang and Malacca which joined Malaya in 1946, but including Christmas Islands (1,639) which transferred to Australia in 1958 and Cocos Island (1,000) which transferred to Australia in 1955.

SWAZILAND

		Europeans
1911C	99,959	1,083
1921C	112,951	2,200
1936C	156,715	2,740
1946C	185,215	3,201
1956C	237,041	5,919
1966C	374,571	—

TANZANIA, including Zanzibar and Pemba, from 1964 (formerly Tanganyika)

		Non-African	Dar-es-Salaam
1921C	4,124,447	17,447	15,000
1931C	5,063,544	10,904	33,147
1952E	7,500,000	87,409	99,140
1962E	9,399,100	113,500	128,742
1967E	11,876,982	..	372,515

TOGOLAND (mandate 1914–1957)

1921C	188,265	British Zone
1931C	275,925	
1950E	404,000	

TONGA

		Tongans
1900	18,959	18,300
1911C	23,737	23,011
1919E	23,562	22,689
1931C	28,574	27,700
1951E	45,587	44,460
1956C	56,838	55,156
1966C	77,429	76,121

TRINIDAD AND TOBAGO

		births	deaths
1901C	273,898	9,513	6,892
1911C	330,074	11,674	7,870
1921C	365,913	11,627	8,824
1931C	412,783	12,366	8,264
1946C	557,970	22,342[1]	7,828[1]
1960C	827,957	32,858	6,608
1970C	931,071	28,496	6,955

[1] 1947.

255

TRISTAN DA CUNHA

1932C	163
1950C	267
1960C	281

Immigration to the United Kingdom 1961–63 but most returned.

1969C	271

TURKS AND CAICOS ISLANDS
(separated from Jamaica in 1962)

1960C	5,716
1970C	5,675

UGANDA

		African	Baganda
1901E	4,000,000	–	1,000,000
1911C	2,843,325	2,840,469	650,000
1921E	3,066,327	3,059,583	640,000
1931C	3,553,534	3,536,267	874,000
1948C	4,958,520	4,917,555	850,000
1959C	6,523,628	6,436,570	1,044,000
1970E	9,760,000 of whom Asians 88,000, Europeans 9,000.		

UNION ISLANDS
(transferred to New Zealand in 1926)

1901E	1,050
1911E	914
1915E	1,000

UNITED KINGDOM

	England & Wales	Scotland	Northern Ireland
1901C	36,070,492	4,472,103	4,456,546[1]
1931C	39,952,377	4,842,980	1,256,561[2]
1971C	48,749,000	5,229,963	1,536,065

[1] Ireland.
[2] 1926.

WEIHAIWEI

1901	The city had about 2,000 people
1911C	147,177
1921C	154,416

It was transferred to China in 1930.

WESTERN SAMOA (mandate from 1920)

1922C	37,791
1931C	46,023
1951C	83,023
1961C	114,427
1971C	146,635

WINDWARD ISLANDS (including Dominica from 1940)

	Grenada	St Vincent	St Lucia	Dominica
1901C	64,288	47,548	50,237	
1911C	66,750	41,877	48,637	
1921C	66,302	44,925	52,250	
1931C	78,662	47,961	59,676	
1951E	80,056	70,128	88,711	55,914
1960C	88,677	80,042	94,718	59,124
1965E			10,000	
1970C				70,302
1972C		100,000		
1973E	106,219			

ZAMBIA (formerly Northern Rhodesia)

Lusaka

1964E	3,545,200	
1969E	4,057,000	347,000[1]
1974E	4,751,000	415,000

[1] 1972E.

ZANZIBAR PROTECTORATE

	Zanzibar	*Zanzibar Town*	*Pemba*	*Total*
1901E	150,000	50,000	50,000	200,000
1911C	115,477	35,000	83,437	198,914
1921C		35,000		197,000
1931C	137,741	45,276	97,687	235,428
1948C	149,575	45,284	114,587	264,162
1958C	165,253	57,923	133,858	299,111
1964	United with Tanganyika as Tanzania.			

10 TRADE UNIONS

ADEN (now Yemen People's Democratic Republic)

The first union in Aden was the Harbour Pilots' Association, formed in 1951, ten years after the Trade Union and Trade Disputes Ordinance gave workers the right to organise. The Aden Trades Union Congress was established in 1956 and was an affiliate of the International Confederation of Free Trade Unions and the International Confederation of Arab Trade Unions. In 1963 the Congress claimed 22,000 members in nine unions, amounting to 95 per cent of the Colony's organised workers. At that time, it campaigned for independence and eventual merger into the Yemen. A rival organisation, the Free Workers' Trade Union Congress, had a very small membership. After independence, trade unions were centred in the General Federation of Trade Unions.

ANTIGUA

The major trade unions, of which six are registered, include two 'blanket' unions, each tied to a political movement. The Antigua Trades and Labour Union was registered in 1939, and claims 7,000 members. It is affiliated to the International Confederation of Free Trade Unions (ICFTU) and the Caribbean Congress of Labour. The Antigua Workers' Union was registered in 1967, and claims 8,426 members. There is also the Antigua Public Services Association which claims 400 members.

AUSTRALIA

Trade unions formed by convicts early in the nineteenth century were suppressed, and the first effective union was the Sydney Shipwrights' United Friendly Society of 1830. By 1850 there were craft unions in most trades, and the Melbourne Trades Hall Committee of 1856 was the basis for the state-wide Victoria Trades and Labour Council. In Dec 1975 there were 280 trade unions with a reported membership of 2,814,000; that is, 58 percent of wage and salary earners. The ten largest unions embraced 1,120,800 of these members. The Australian Council of Trade Unions (ACTU) was formed in 1927; it is a loose federation of federal, state and local unions. It is the most important federation of trade unions, with 1.4m. members in over 150 affiliated unions. The six state federations, known as Trades and Labour Councils, are ACTU branches, although they are in fact much older than ACTU. In recent years, the number of unions affiliated to ACTU has increased rapidly. In 1966, the main independent union until then—the Australian Workers' Union, which was formed in 1886—joined ACTU. Although ACTU is not itself tied to the Australian Labour Party, it has some formal connections with it, as have the state trades and labour councils. Many unions within ACTU are not affiliated to the ALP, but unionism is seen as part of the socialist movement. Three federations of non-manual workers exist: the Australian Council of Salaried and Professional Associations, the Council of Commonwealth Public Service Organisations, and the Council of Professional Associations; overlapping with ACTU is frequent. There are also other federations of unions in a particular industry or occupation. ACTU has been an ICFTU member since 1951, and individual unions take an active role in the International Trade Secretariats.

BAHAMAS

Trade union organisations developed after World War II with the formation of the Bahamas Musicians' Union, the Bahamas Hotel and Catering Workers' Union, the United Brotherhood of Longshoremen, the Construction Workers' Union and the Taxi Cab Union. In 1955 these unions formed the Bahamas Federation of Labour. Many of the unions are very small, but the principal affiliates include the Bahamas Transport, Agricultural, Distributive and Allied Workers' Trade Union (1,362 members).

Among non-affiliated unions are the Bahamas Public Services Union (2,000 members), and the Bahamas Workers' Council International.

BAHRAIN

There were no trade unions in Bahrain during the period of British protection.

BANGLADESH

Trade unions of textile workers date from before Indian independence, and the Bangladesh trade unions were linked successively to the Indian and Pakistani labour movements. In August 1975 trade union national organisations were dissolved, but trade unions continued to function at local level. The Jatio Shramik League was the ICFTU affiliated trade union centre in Bangladesh, with a membership of 1.2m. The Bangladesh Trade Union Kendra also existed. (*see* Pakistan.)

BARBADOS

Trade unions are registered under the Act of 1964. In 1976 there was only one functioning union in the private sector; this union is also one of the two accredited bargaining agents for public service employees. About 50 per cent of the island's labour force is either organised or effectively covered by collective agreements. The 'blanket' union is the Barbados Workers' Union. This was registered in 1941, and claims 30,000 members among the island's 95,000 strong workforce. It is an ICFTU affiliate. The union has over one hundred divisions or branches at firm level, and there are groupings of branches involved in the same industry.

The National Union of Public Workers (founded 1944) operates in the public sector, and it claims 5,000 members. A separate union for secondary teachers also exists.

BELIZE (formerly British Honduras)

The General Workers' Development Union was formed in 1960 from a merger of the General Workers' Union and the British Honduras Development Union. It is an ICFTU affiliate and a member of the International Transport Workers' Federation. The central body, with its two branch unions, claims just 3,000 members. The Christian Workers Union (1962), now called the National Federation of Workers, and the Public Officers' Union (1922) are the other principal labour organisations. The NFW claims 2,000 members and it is affiliated to the World Confederation of Labour. A National Teachers Union and the Democratic Independent Union also operate.

BERMUDA

The main union is the Bermuda Industrial Union. It is a general union catering for members in all industries, including certain government departments. Formed in 1946, the BIU is an ICFTU affiliate with 6,000 members. It is composed of numerous divisions for the main industries and services. Smaller separate unions exist for government service employees, teachers, musicians and the police force.

BOTSWANA (formerly Bechuanaland)

A large proportion of the country's economically active population finds work in the Republic of South Africa. Trade unions were formed in pre-independence days, but they are not highly developed. The following labour organisations exist: Botswana General Workers' Organisation; Botswana Teachers' Union; Botswana Trades Union Congress, Botswana Workers' Union and the Francistown African Employees' Union. In 1974 the four competing general unions were all based in Francistown where the opposition Botswana People's Party had its main strength. These four unions have some 1,400 members.

BRUNEI

Unionisation is not well developed. The few trade unions are small and concentrated in the sectors of government service and the oil industry. The Brunei Government Workers' Union, registered in 1962, claimed 2,689 members in 1974, and the Brunei Oilfield Workers' Union (1962) had 733 members. The other three registered unions cover health service workers, clerks and customs officers.

BURMA

The Trades Union Congress of Burma, the union arm of the Socialist Party and the Anti-Fascist People's Freedom League, was formed in 1945. Other labour organisations also existed, namely the Union of Burma Labour Organisation and the Burma Trades Union Congress, which was affiliated to the World Federation of Trade Unions.

CANADA

Trade unions date from the War of 1812, when craftsmen in New Brunswick formed self help organisations. Craft unions spread to the rest of Canada. Outside Quebec, early links with the British labour movement were replaced by a close relationship with United States trade unions. Membership of labour organisations active in Canada totalled approximately 2,610,000 at the beginning of 1973. Of the total civilian labour force, 29.4 per cent were union members. In 1975, 2,043,484 of the members were in unions affiliated with the Canadian Labour Congress (CLC); 225,000 were affiliates of the Confederation of National Trade Unions (CNTU). Small numbers were affiliated with the Centrale des Syndicats Démocratiques (CSD); and the Confederation of Canadian Unions (CCU). The remaining members belonged to unaffiliated national and international unions and independent local organisations. The CLC was formed in 1956, in a merger between the Trades and Labour Congress of Canada and the Canadian Congress of Labour. There are about 110 international, national and provincial affiliates. Established in 1921, the CNTU was formerly known as the Canadian and Catholic Confederation of Labour, and it is affiliated to the World Confederation of Labour. Membership is concentrated in Quebec, where there are over 1,000 union branches.

Of the total union members, 55.3 per cent belonged to international unions, that is unions based in the United States. National unions accounted for 44.7 per cent of union membership in Canada.

Twenty-one unions reported a membership of 30,000 or more in the 1973 survey. The five largest unions are the United Steelworkers of America (173,700); the Canadian Union of Public Employees (167,500); the Public Service Alliance of Canada (133,500); the International Union, United Automobile, Aerospace and Agricultural Implement Workers of America (107,300); and the Quebec Teachers' Corporation (87,500).

CYPRUS

In 1972, there were 105 unions with 254 branches and eight trade union federations and five confederations with ten branches. There was a total membership of 87,655. The Pancyprian Federation of Labour (the 'old' trade unions), was founded in 1946, and previously it was known as the Pancyprian Trade Union Committee. It claims sixteen unions and 225 branches with a total membership of 43,701. It is a WFTU affiliate. The Cyprus Workers' Confederation was founded in 1944. It claims seven federations, five labour centres, forty-one unions, thirteen branches and a membership of 30,168. It is affiliated to the Greek Confederation of Labour and to the ICFTU. The Cyprus Turkish Trade Unions Federation is also affiliated to the ICFTU, and to the Federation of Trade Unions of Turkey. Founded in 1954, it claims fourteen unions and 8,000 members. The Pancyprian Federation of Independent Trade Unions, founded in 1956, claims seven unions and 1,008 members. The Cyprus Democratic Labour Federation, founded in 1962, claims four unions and 3,500 members. The Cyprus Civil Servants' Trade Union, founded in 1949, represents workers in the government's civil employment. It has six branches and 9,000 members.

DOMINICA

There are five registered trade unions with a total affiliation of some 9,000 workers. These organisations act independently of each other and have no affiliation with political parties. The Dominica Trade Union was formed in 1945. It has 900 members and is an ICFTU affiliate. Of greater strength are the Dominica Amalgamated Workers' Union (4,000), the Waterfront and Allied Workers' Union (3,800), the Civil Service Association (1,300) and the Managers' and Supervisors' Union.

EGYPT

In 1890, the 'Patenta Laws' gave to all Egyptians the right of free choice of work. This undermined the traditional guild system. The first trade union, the Cigarette Workers' Union, was formed in 1899, and the Union of Employees of International Trade Firms appeared in 1903. By 1911, Egypt had eleven unions with 7,000 members. After World War I, the Egyptian labour movement joined in the struggle against the British presence. In 1921, a General Federation of Labour was founded at Alexandria, but this was short lived. Official recognition of trade unions came in 1942, when 200 unions representing 80,000 workers were registered. By 1950 there were about 500 unions claiming 149,424 members. These were grouped in various trade federations, for example petroleum workers and transport workers. Then in 1956, the Egyptian General Federation of Labour was established for all existing labour unions, and in 1959, a new labour code consolidated laws affecting the wide field of labour management relations. Trade unions were reorganised at this time, resulting in a structure of 608 trade union (works) committees, 261 local trade unions and fifty-nine national trade unions, with a total membership of about 1m. Trade unions played a major role in Arab Socialism as laid down in laws of 1961–2.

FALKLAND ISLANDS

The trade union centre is the General Employees' Union which claimed 450 members in 1976. The union was formed in 1943, and membership is open to all employees.

FIJI

Trade unions were first organised in the 1940s, and were governed by the Industrial Associations Ordinance of 1942. Only five out of nineteen pioneer unions have survived. Unions are now registered under the Trade Union Ordinance of 1964. The Fiji Trades Union Congress of 1966 superceded the Fiji Industrial Workers' Congress (1952) and the Fiji Federation of Labour. The Congress has twenty-four affiliated unions and it is a member of the ICFTU. There are over 20,000 members. The largest unions are the Fiji Waterside Workers' and Seamens' Union, the Fiji Sugar and General Workers' Union (1944) and the Public Employees' Union (1946). Several small organisations remain outside the Fiji TUC, making a total registration of thirty-seven trade unions in 1972.

THE GAMBIA

There are two national centres, the Gambia Labour Union and the Gambia Workers' Union. There are four large unions and ten small ones. The GLU was formed in 1935 and claims 7,800 members. It was an affiliate of the ICFTU from 1949 to 1962, and later it was affiliated to the International Federation of Christian Trade Unions. It was then aligned to the communist World Federation of Trade Unions. The Gambia Workers' Union, the other national centre, was formed in 1958 and claims 6,474 members. It is an affiliate of the ICFTU and the Organisation of African Trade Union Unity. The GWU is also affiliated with the International Federation of Petroleum and Chemical Workers. The World Confederation of Labour's regional organisation, the Pan African Workers' Congress, had offices in Banjul. Other unions in existence include the Gambia Trades and

Dealers Union (founded in 1960), the National Farmers and General Workers' Union (1962), the Taxi Drivers and Mechanics' Union (1962), and the Gambia Teachers' Union (1937).

GHANA (formerly Gold Coast)

Trade unions were first formed in the 1920s. Before independence, there was a proliferation of small, ineffective and badly organised unions, but under the 1958 Industrial Relations Act the Ghana TUC was reformed with twenty-four constituent member unions covering the whole of the labour force without competition or overlapping. By 1965, there were only ten unions covering all workers.

The Ghana Trades Union Congress, the country's single trade union centre, was formed in 1945 as the Gold Coast TUC and in 1973 it had a total membership of 379,196, roughly 75 per cent of the estimated number of wage and salary earners. After the military coup d'état of 1966, the GTUC was reorganised, as were all the constituent unions. Major amendments were made to the Congress constitution which gave liberal autonomy to the national unions. Previously the GTUC had had a close relationship with the Convention People's Party, and the GTUC had played a leading role in the formation of the All African Trade Union Federation. In 1971, the TUC as then constituted was dissolved by parliament but following the revolution of January 1972 it was re-formed and industrial relations law restored and considered as never having been amended.

The Congress is composed of seventeen unions: Construction and Building Trade Union (40,000), General Agricultural Workers' Union (66,149), General Transport, Petroleum and Chemical Workers' Union (4,500), Ghana Private Road Transport Union (20,000), Health Services Workers' Union (7,795), Industrial and Commercial Workers' Union (80,000), Local Government Workers' Union (38,000), Maritime and Dockworkers' Union (18,660), Mine Workers' Union (23,074), National Union of Seamen (7,000), Posts and Telecommunications Workers' Union (7,422), Public Services Workers' Union (15,600), Public Utility Workers' Union (12,000), Railway Enginemen's Union (816), Railway and Port Workers' Union (10,180), Teachers' and Educational Workers' Union (14,000), Timber and Woodworkers' Union (14,000). Many of the unions are affiliated to relevant International Trade Secretariats. The Organisation of African Trade Unity is based in Accra.

GIBRALTAR

The Gibraltar Trades Council covers unions representing 90 per cent of the work force. Many United Kingdom unions have branches in Gibraltar. These are mainly for public employees and include AUEW, ASTMS, CPSA, IPCS and SCS. The Transport and General Workers' Union is the largest organisation, with 4,561 members. This branch was formed in 1924. A local Gibraltar Workers' Union formed in 1974, has 2,294 members. Other local unions exist for taxi drivers, clerks, teachers and security police.

GILBERT ISLANDS (formerly Gilbert and Ellice Islands)

There are six registered trade unions, namely: Designated Contract Officers' Association (1971); the Te Botaki ni Karikirakean Aroia Tani Makuri (1972) for both the private and public sector; the Gilbert and Ellice Islands Overseas Seamen Trade Union (1972); the Line Islands International Union (1973); the Public Employees Association (1974) and the Gilbert Islands Development Authority, Senior Local Staff Association (1976).

GRENADA

Most trade unions tend to be general unions having support more in the undertaking than the industry. In agriculture, one union dominates the scene, and in commerce very few workers are organised. There were at the beginning of 1972, fourteen employees' organisations. One of these is the Trade Union Council, to which five unions are affiliated. Most of the registered unions have affiliations with international unions. The Grenada Trade Union Council was formed in 1955 and claims about 5,000 members. It is affiliated to the Caribbean Congress of Labour and to the ICFTU. Member unions participate in International Trade Secretariats. The affiliates are the Commercial and Industrial Workers' Union, the Grenada Union of Teachers, the Manual and Metal Workers' Union, the Seamen and Waterfront Workers' Union and the Technical and Allied Workers' Union.

GUYANA (formerly British Guiana)

Trade unions, which date from the Guyana Labour Union of 1919, are safeguarded in law and are organised into industrial unions, general unions, public service unions and commercial unions. Of fifty-nine registered trade unions in 1973, only twenty-two are affiliated to the National Trades Union Congress, the body recognised by government as the workers' mouthpiece. Many unaffiliated unions are too small or lacking in the membership requirements of the TUC. The Guyana TUC was formed in 1940 and claims 50,000 members. It is a member of ICFTU and the Caribbean Congress of Labour. Its affiliates include the powerful Manpower Citizens' Association (1936), active mainly in agriculture, which has been rivalled by the unaffiliated Guyana Agricultural Workers' Union, backed by the Peoples' Progressive Party.

The Guyana Agricultural Workers' Union which was founded in 1953 represented about 90 per cent of the sugar industry's labour force, but until 1975 it was unrecognised by British colonial authorities or by post independence Peoples' National Congress government. That party supported the Guyana National Confederation of Workers and Peasants in 1976; the National Confederation of Plantation Workers has separate status. Six public service unions form the Federation of Unions of Government Employees.

HONG KONG

Trade unions date from 1909, and many early unions were linked to the All China General Union and the nationalist movement. In 1974 there were 291 trade unions in Hong Kong, with a declared membership of 296,481. The Hong Kong and Kowloon Trades Union Council was founded in 1949. It claims 125,000 members in 103 affiliated unions, mostly in the catering, building, textiles and craft trades. The Council is a founder member of the ICFTU and it is strongly anti-communist. It maintains close links with the Chinese Federation of Labour on Taiwan. The Hong Kong Federation of Trade Unions was founded in 1948. It has sixty-six affiliated unions. Membership figures are not available, but the main strength is in the sectors of shipyards, seafaring, textile mills and public utilities. There are also a further twenty-six associate members of the Federation, which supports the Chinese Peoples' Republic and its policies. A large number of other unions are not affiliated to a national centre.

INDIA

Trade unions date from the nineteenth century, and the Trade Union Act of

1926 gave them recognition and legal status. In 1971, there were 847 registered central unions and 19,865 registered state unions. Membership is estimated at 5 million.

The Indian National Trades Union Congress, is the largest of all Indian workers' organisations. Founded in 1947, it is linked to the Congress Party and it is an ICFTU affiliate. It claims 2,426,936 members in 2,416 unions. Within INTUC, there are a number of industrial federations for particular sectors. The Hind Mazdoor Sabha is also an ICFTU affiliate. Founded in 1948, it was close to the Lohia and Praja Socialist Parties. It claims 1,144,164 members in 525 affiliated unions.

The WFTU has the All India Trades Union Congress as its affiliate. Founded in 1920, it claims 2,070,504 members in 3,712 affiliated unions. There are eighteen regional branches. A Trotskyite grouping, the United Trades Union Congress was founded in 1948. There are many other trade union groupings and many independent unions. A Confederation of Central Government Employees' Unions covers some 700,000 members, and the National Federation of Indian Railwaymen is a strong sectional organisation. The National Front of Indian Trade Unions represents the WCL's foothold in India. Other labour federations are: the Bharatiya Mazdoor Sangh; National Front of Indian Trade Unions; National Labour Organisation; and the Centre of Indian Trade Unions, linked to the Communist Party of India (Marxist).

IRELAND

Trade unionism first emerged in the larger cities (Dublin, Belfast and Cork) during the eighteenth century, despite legislation against combinations of workers. This development continued in the nineteenth century, and a number of British unions also established branches in Ireland.

The first association of trade unions, representing thirty crafts and industries, was formed in 1863, and in 1894 the Irish Trades Union Congress, representing most Irish and a number of British unions, was established. Ninety-one unions comprising Irish and foreign-based unions, representing 550,000 workers, are affiliated to the all-Ireland Irish Congress of Trade Unions. This body, set up in 1959, is the sole coordinating body for Irish unions, and includes a committee for unions in Northern Ireland.

The Irish Transport and General Workers' Union, is the largest trade union with 159,000 members. Other large unions include the Amalgamated Transport and General Workers' Union (26,000) and the Workers' Union of Ireland (36,000).

JAMAICA

The Longshoremen Workers' Union, formed in 1918, was the first trade union. In 1972 there were 115 trade unions registered by the Ministry of Labour. In the public sector, the Jamaica Civil Service Association and the Jamaica Association of Local Government Officers are the recognised trade unions. The 'blanket' type trade unions are politically aligned. The Bustamente Industrial Trade Union was founded in 1938 and claims 100,459 members. It is the trade union arm of the Jamaica Labour Party and it is an ICFTU affiliate. The National Workers' Union of Jamica is aligned to the Peoples' National Party. Founded in 1952, when the Trades Union Congress split up, it claims 149,569 members. Its international affiliation is also to ICFTU, ORIT and CCL. A third national centre is the Trades Union Congress of Jamaica, which claims 20,000 members. The Jamaica Congress of Labour was formed in 1966, and in 1968 this joined with five other unions in the Independent Trade Union Action Council. This is affiliated to the Central Latinamericana de Trabajadores and the World Confederation of Labour.

KENYA

The Kenya Federation of Labour was formed in 1952. A previous organisation, the East African Trade Union Congress, was linked to the World Federation of Trade Unions. In 1964, a new Kenya Federation of Progressive Trade Unions was formed and this was affiliated to the All African Trade Union Federation.

The Central Organisation of Trade Unions was formed in 1965, as a successor to the Kenya Federation of Labour and the Kenya African Workers' Congress, which were dissolved by the government. The COTU is the country's only trade union centre and in 1966 had some 215,000 members, 36 per cent of all wage and salary earners. A number of small unions remain outside the COTU, but the centre has some twenty-eight affiliated unions. The principal affiliates are the Amalgamated Union of Kenya Metalworkers; Chemical Workers' Union; Civil Servants' Union; Dockworkers' Union; External Telecommunications Workers' Union; Kenya African Custom Workers' Union; Kenya Engineering Workers' Union; Kenya Game and Hunting Workers' Union; Kenya Management Staff Association; Kenya Petroleum and Oil Workers' Union; National Union of Journalists; National Union of Musicians; National Union of Seamen; Plantation and Agricultural Workers' Union; Printing and Kindred Workers' Union; Quarry and Mineworkers' Union; Shoe Leather Workers' Union; Timber Workers'

Union; Union of Sugar Plantations. The main independent unions are the East African Railways and Harbour Asian Union (Kenya), the Kenya National Union of Teachers, and the Senior Civil Servants' Association of Kenya. Many of the unions are members of appropriate International Trade Secretariats.

LESOTHO (formerly Basutoland)

Trade unions were established before independence, but the Basutoland Congress of Trade Unions, formed in 1961, was shortlived. Lesotho can provide work for only 5 per cent of its labour force, and most workers migrate to the Republic of South Africa for employment. These workers have formed the Lesotho Mineworkers' Union.

The following unions are in existence; membership figures are not available: Basutoland Federation of Labour; Lesotho Council of Workers; Lesotho General Workers' Union, formed in 1954; Lesotho Industrial Commercial and Allied Workers' Union, formed in 1952; Lesotho Labour Organisation, formed in 1962; Lesotho Transport and Telecommunications Workers' Union, formed in 1959; Lesotho Union of Printing, Bookbinding and Allied Workers, formed in 1963; National Council of Construction and Allied Workers, formed in 1967; Union of Shop, Distributive and Allied Workers, formed in 1966.

MALAWI (formerly Nyasaland)

Unions have tended to be small, numerous and weak. Trade union membership is about 10,000, only 5 per cent of employed persons. The Trades Union Congress of Malawi was formed in 1964, as a successor to the Nyasaland TUC (formed in 1956). It is affiliated to the ICFTU. Several of the International Trade Secretariats have affiliates in Malawi. The Trades Union Congress claims 6,500 members in seven unions, the main ones being the Building, Construction, Civil Engineering and Allied Workers' Union and the Malawi Railway Workers' Union. Outside the Congress, the principal unions are the Teachers' Union of Malawi, with 3,000 members, and the Malawi Government Employees' Association. In 1974, all the country's industrial disputes were unofficial, involving no trade unions.

MALAYSIA
(Peninsular Malaysia, Sarawak and Sabah)

Trade unions date from before World War II, but development was interrupted by Japanese occupation and subsequent civil strife. The communist General Labour Union and its successors, the Pan-Malayan Federation of Trade Unions and the Singapore Federation of Trade Unions, were opposed by the authorities. The largest union, the National Union of Plantation Workers was formed in 1954 from several older bodies. The Asian Officers' Union was formed in 1949.

In June 1976, there were 361 registered trade unions, of which 273 were in the peninsula, sixty-two in Sarawak and twenty-six in Sabah. There were 513,000 accredited members. The largest union, the National Union of Plantation Workers, claims 165,000 members. A Registry controls all trade unions, and undertakes periodic inspections of accounts and statutory provisions. The Registry maintains liaison between trade union officials and the staff of the Department of Labour and Industrial Relations. The Malaysian Trades Union Congress, formerly known as the Malayan Trades Union Council, is the main trade union centre. It claims 321,000 members. Founded in 1949 and a member of the ICFTU, the Congress is politically independent, and has 103 member unions. Affiliated unions with a membership over 10,000 include the National Mining Workers' Union of Malaya, the National Union of Plantation Workers in Malaya and the Railwaymen's Union of Malaya. The Congress of Unions of Employees in the Public and Civil Services was founded in 1957. It draws together sixty unions with a total membership of 90,000. Other labour federations covering workers in the white collar, professional and government sectors, include the Malayan Federation of Clerical and Administrative Staff Unions, the Amalgamated Union of Employees in Government Clerical and Allied Services, the All Malayan Federation of Government Medical Employees' Trade Unions, the Federation of Government Medical Services Unions and the Federation of Indian School Teachers' Unions. The unions in Sabah and Sarawak are numerous and small. They cater mainly for wharf labourers in the river ports, but the largest organisation is the Sarawak Government Asian Officers' Union.

MALTA

In 1972, there were fifty-six registered trade unions with a total membership of 41,211. The General Workers' Union was founded in the dockyards in 1943. It is affiliated to the ICFTU, and in 1976 it claimed 27,167 members, who are organised in sections formed on an industrial basis; each section seeks to cover industrial workers in a particular industry, and there is a section for white collar employees. The Confederation of Malta Trade Unions is affiliated to the WCL. It was founded in 1958 and claims 10,000 members in twenty-four unions. The independent Malta Union of Teachers claimed 2,384 members in 1965. Other unions are very small.

MAURITIUS

Unions date from the years after World War I. Following large scale strikes and public disorder in 1937 and the passing of the Industrial Associations Ordinance, based on South African laws, some forty unions were formed in three years.

In 1971, there were 115 trade unions, including fourteen employers' unions, with a total membership of 36,000. There are three national centres for trade unions, of which the largest is the Mauritius Labour Congress. In 1973 this claimed 32,194 members. It was formed in 1963 by a merger of the Confederation of Free Trade Unions of Mauritius and a faction of the Mauritius Trades Union Congress. The Mauritius Federation of Trade Unions, was formed in 1960 and is affiliated to the OATUU. The Mauritius Trades Union Congress, formed in 1946, is affiliated to the World Confederation of Labour. A number of independent unions remain outside the national centres. The Federation of Civil Service and Primary Aided School Teachers' Unions coordinates the activities of a number of organisations.

MONTSERRAT

The Trades and Labour Union, formed in 1948, was admitted to the ICFTU in 1955. The present general union, the Montserrat Allied Workers' Union, was founded in 1973. Its membership, however, is only 500. Separate small unions exist for teachers, sea and waterfront workers.

NAURU

The Nauruan Workers' Organisation was founded in 1953 to improve the welfare and wellbeing of Nauruan workers, and to provide a medium of cooperation between them and the government.

273

NEW ZEALAND

The Benevolent Society of Carpenters and Joiners was formed in Wellington before 1842, and craft unions were later established in most sectors first at local level and later on a national scale. The Trades and Labour Councils' Federation, the Alliance of Labour and the New Zealand Workers' Union were important bodies. In December 1974 there was a total of 199 registered trade unions in the private sector with a combined membership of 420,741 or 47 per cent of estimated non-government wage and salary earners. The top ten unions account for nearly 40 per cent of total membership, and there is a proliferation of small craft-oriented district unions. There have been many recent moves towards amalgamation. Among the largest unions are the New Zealand Meat Processors, Packers, Preservers, Freezing Workers and Related Trades Union; the New Zealand Clerical and Office Staff, Employees' Association; the New Zealand Engineering, Coachbuilding, Aircraft, Motor and Related Trades Industrial Union of Workers, and the New Zealand Hotel, Hospital and Restaurant Industrial Association of Workers. In Dec 1974 there were thirty-two registered industrial associations covering 158 unions. The New Zealand Federation of Labour is the trade union centre, an unregistered organisation formed in 1937 with a total affiliated membership of 396,805 (1975) in 180 organisations, covering 225 unions or societies (1974). It is an ICFTU affiliate and many constituent unions play an active part in the International Trade Secretariats. At regional level, there are twenty trades or district councils and one trade union committee.

In the public sector, twenty-one unions belong to the Combined State Services Organisation. Membership totals 166,287 and includes civil servants, railway workers, teachers, post office employees, and health service workers. Unlike the private sector, state services unions are industry based.

NIGERIA

The first central organisation was the Nigerian Trades Union Congress, formed in 1943. Subsequent attempts to bring trade union unity came in 1948, with the appearance of the Nigerian National Federation of Labour, affiliated to the World Federation of Trade Unions; then in 1953 the All Nigerian Trade Unions Federation was formed and when this split, the National Council of Trade Unions of Nigeria emerged. In March 1959 a congress of reunification led to the formation of the Trades Union Congress of Nigeria. This was challenged by a new Nigerian Trades Union Congress, and later by the Labour Unity Front. These clashed with each other over the question of international affiliation. In the early 1970s there were an estimated 2,000 trade unions representing more than 1m. workers. The Nigerian Labour Congress was formed in 1975 in an attempt by the unions themselves to bring trade union unity, but the government then aimed to establish its own single national trade union centre.

PAKISTAN

The Pakistan Federation of Labour and the All-Pakistan Trade Union Federation, which were active in West and East Pakistan respectively, merged in 1950 to form the All Pakistan Confederation of Labour, which had western and eastern federations. The Pakistan Trade Union Federation changed its name in 1951 to the Pakistan Mazdoor Federation. In the 1970s there were more than six national trade union centres and thousands of independent and local trade unions.

PALESTINE

A highly developed trade union movement was built up by Zionist endeavour during the British mandate period. Histadrut, the General Federation of Labour, founded in 1920, has engaged in large scale entrepreneurial operations in agriculture, industry, trade and finance, and in the field of social and cultural services and cooperatives, in addition to performing normal trade union functions. Histadrut joined the ICFTU in 1953, and in 1976 claimed 1,456,000 members in forty unions. This figure includes a sizeable minority of Arab and Druse workers. The Herut National Labour Federation in Israel, founded in 1934, is close to the conservative Herut party.

The League of Palestinian Workers was formed in 1925 for Palestinian Arabs. The Palestine Trade Union Federation, based in Damascus, represents the trade union arm of the Palestine Liberation Organisation.

PAPUA NEW GUINEA

A number of small local trade unions exist. The largest unions include the Australian Staffing Assistance (PNG) Association, the Papua New Guinea Teachers' Association (10,000 members), the Police Association of Papua New Guinea, and the Public Service Association (15,560 members). In 1965, efforts began to form a Federation of Workers' Associations of Papua New

Guinea, and the Papua New Guinea Trades Union Congress (1970) is affiliated to the ICFTU.

RHODESIA

Trade union organisation covers both African and European labour, in four national centres. The Zimbabwe African Congress of Unions is the trade union centre for the African liberation movement. The African Trades Union Congress was formed in 1962, as the Southern Rhodesia African Trades Union Congress. The present name was adopted after absorption of the old Southern Rhodesia TUC in 1963. It was affiliated to the African Trade Union Confederation. The organisation claims a total membership of 29,198, about 36 per cent of all trade union members, in nine affiliated unions. The main affiliates are the Commercial and Allied Workers' Union, the Engineering and Metal Workers' Union and the Railway Associated Workers' Union.

The rival national centre for African workers is the National African Federation of Unions, formed in 1965 by affiliates of the banned Zimbabwe African Congress of Unions which had close ties with the freedom fighting ZANU party. It was affiliated to the All African Trade Union Federation, and its member unions comprised 14,669 members. The main affiliated unions are the Agricultural and Plantation Workers' Union, the Building and Woodworkers' Union and the Municipal Workers' Union.

European workers have their own Trades Union Congress of Rhodesia, which claims 16,359 members. It was established in 1964 as successor to the TUC of the Federation of Rhodesia and Nyasaland, and it supports the Rhodesian Front policies. The main affiliated unions include the Associated Mine Workers of Rhodesia and the Rhodesian Railway Workers' Union. The Congress has no international affiliation. The National Association of Local Government Officers and Employees is the registered trade union federation (1966) for the public sector.

Several unions remain independent of the national centres. These include the Amalgamated Engineering Union, the Tailors and Garment Workers' Union, and the Rhodesia African Teachers' Association. A number of International Trade Secretariats have affiliates in Rhodesia.

ST CHRISTOPHER (ST KITTS)-NEVIS-ANGUILLA

Trade unions are registered under the 1940 Trade Union Act. There are five registered and active trade unions, of which the largest is the St Kitts-Nevis

276

Trades and Labour Union. Registered in 1940, it claims 5,700 members and it is affiliated to the ICFTU and the Caribbean Congress of Labour. It is also closely linked to the St Kitts-Nevis Labour Party. The Working People's Union, a second smaller general union, is associated with the Peoples' Action Movement. Other unions are the St Christopher Sugar Producers' Association, the St Kitts-Nevis Civil Service Association and the St Kitts Managers and Overseas Association. There is no trades union congress.

ST HELENA

The St Helena General Workers' Union claims 941 members and is an ICFTU affiliate. It was founded in 1958.

ST LUCIA

A Trade Union Council was established in the 1970s to promote unity among trade unions. The main unions are the St Lucia Workers' Union (1939), which claims 2,000 members, the Civil Service Association, the National Workers' Union (5,500), and the St Lucia Seamen and Waterfront Workers' Trade Union. There are ten other unions.

ST VINCENT

There is no national centre for trade unions. Among the registered unions, the Federated Industrial and Agricultural Workers' Union is the largest general body, claiming 3,000 members and affiliated to the ICFTU and the Caribbean Congress of Labour. Other unions are the Commercial Technical and Allied Workers' Union, the Civil Service Association and two teachers' unions.

SEYCHELLES

A Seychelles Trade Union Congress is in existence. The fourteen registered unions at the end of 1974 included the Christian Workers' Union (part of WCL); the Teachers' Union (1949); the Civil Servants' Union; the Seychelles Building, Construction and Civil Engineering Workers' Union; the Artisans',

Engineers', Constructors' and Builders' Union; the Government Workers' Union; the Postal Workers' Union; the Seamen's Union; the Agricultural, Domestic and Shopworkers' Union; and the Stevedores, Winchmen and Dockworkers' Union. Registered membership was 3,513. The Hotels and Allied Employees' Union had its registration cancelled in 1974.

SIERRA LEONE

In 1975, there were twenty-two registered trade unions for workers. Following the Trade Union Ordinance of 1939, there were eleven registered trade unions in 1942. The Sierra Leone TUC was formed, but it split and the Sierra Leone Federation of Labour and the dissident Sierra Leone Council of Labour were superceded in 1966 by the Sierra Leone Labour Congress. It claims some 18,000 members, and it is affiliated to the ICFTU. Many of its member unions are attached to the International Trade Secretariats. The principal unions include the Clerical, Mercantile and General Workers' Union; the Sierra Leone Dockworkers' Union; the Sierra Leone Teachers' Union; the Sierra Leone Transport, Agricultural and General Workers' Union and the United Mineworkers' Union. In 1976 the Congress merged with the other trade union national centre, the Sierra Leone Labour Council. The Artisans', Ministry of Works Employees' and General Workers' Union was formed in 1946 and claims 5,600 members.

SINGAPORE

Trade unionism dated from 1946 when the first union was registered. By the end of June 1976, membership of employee unions reached 213,521, about 31 per cent of Singapore's employee workforce. Out of ninety-one unions, fifty unions with a total membership of 198,892 are affiliated to the National Trades Union Congress. This is the only national centre, and it is attached to the ruling People's Action Party. Formed in 1961 and an ICFTU affiliate, the Congress emerged after a split in the former Singapore Trades Union Congress. The short lived Singapore Association of Trade Unions, attached to the opposition Barsian Socialist Party, was formed at that time. The unions are generally organised along industrial lines.

SOLOMON ISLANDS

In 1976, there were four trade unions. These are the Solomon Islands Public Servants' Association, founded in 1974; the Solomon Islands General Workers' Unions, founded in 1975; the Guadalcanal Plains General Workers' Union, founded in 1975; and the Solomon Islands Nurses' Association, founded in 1975. There is no national centre for trade unions. The SIGWU claimed 10,000 members.

SOMALILAND

The Somali Federation of Labour, formed in 1960, operated in the area of the former British protectorate. In 1965 it affiliated to the main trade union centre, the Confederazione Somalia dei Lavoratori. The Skilled and General Workers' Union, formed in 1956 as the Labour Society, was also active in the Hargeisa area.

SOUTH AFRICA

Trade unions were first established among white craftsmen at the Cape in 1881, and a union for the mining industry appeared at Kimberley in 1884. The white Federation of Trade Unions won government recognition in 1911, and from 1914 the South African Industrial Federation fought to protect the interests of white skilled labour and to uphold the colour bar.

The Industrial Conciliation Act of 1956 as amended, which excludes Africans from its coverage, specifies no legal prohibition of trade unions for African workers, but African unions are denied the legal recognition which, among other things, provides for the right to organise collective bargaining. Since 1956, all unions have been organised in accordance with apartheid policy.

The Trade Union Council of South Africa, formed in 1954, includes non-white unions among its affiliates and it is the largest trade union national centre. The other two national centres for whites are the Co-ordinating Council of South African Trade Unions, formed in 1948 and a supporter of the government's labour policies and the South African Federation of Trade Unions, formed in 1951. These two national centres, together with the Federal Consultative Council of South African Railway and Harbours Staff Associations, cooperate within the South African Confederation of Labour, which is a coordinating body which supports apartheid. Many unions are grouped together in federations for particular industries, for example mining, engineering and transport.

Political conditions have not favoured the growth of African trade unions, but there are many well established labour organisations for 'coloured' workers. The first black unions appeared early in the century, when the Industrial and Commercial Workers' Union was formed in 1918 for workers in Cape harbours. In 1925, the ICU which had spread to the Transvaal claimed 100,000 members and supporters. This organisation was short lived, however, and in 1951 the Industrial Legislation Committee reported that the 199 registered trade unions in South Africa included thirty-six unions for black workers and sixty-three multi-racial unions but with a total African membership of only 8,870. More recently, bodies such as the African National Union of Clothing Workers have won considerable support. The Federation of Free African Trade Unions of South Africa was active for some time, but the main body of African trade unionists has been the South African Congress of Trade Unions (SACTU) aligned with the African National Congress. This has operated from headquarters in Zambia.

At the end of 1970 there were 182 trade unions in the Republic with a total membership of 405,032 whites and 182,210 coloureds and Asians. Figures for African trade union membership were not available.

SOUTH WEST AFRICA (Namibia)

The Union of South West Africa Workers in Exile was formed in Dar-es-Salaam in 1962. No other trade unions were known to exist by 1966, apart from branches of South African unions. The South West Africa People's Organisation (SWAPO) maintains a workers' section to promote trade unionism.

SRI LANKA (formerly Ceylon)

Unions were first established at the end of the nineteenth century. In December 1973, there were 1,644 registered unions, of which 590 employees unions reported a membership of 1,216,252. The 'blanket' type union is common. The unions are mainly closely aligned to political parties, and there are numerous rural and splinter associations representing the interests of identical workers.

The Ceylon Workers' Congress claims 367,469 members. Formed in 1940, it draws members mainly from Indian Tamil plantation workers. It is an ICFTU affiliate. A breakaway body, the Democratic Workers' Congress, was formed in 1956. This claims 398,165 members, making it the country's largest union.

Other trade union members are divided between a number of labour federations. The Ceylon Federation of Labour is the trade union aim of the Trotskyite Lanka Sama Samaja Party. Formed in 1948, it claims 305,639 members (1976) in sixteen affiliated unions. Its sister organisation for public servants is the Government Workers' Trade Union Federation. The Ceylon Trade Union Federation (1941), with 35,271 members in twenty-four unions, is aligned to the Ceylon Communist Party and the WFTU.

The All Ceylon Federation of Free Trade Unions (1958) is affiliated to the WCL. It embraces the National Workers' Congress, which claims 60,000 members. The Sri Lanka Independent Trade Union Federation was founded in 1960 and forms the trade union wing of the Sri Lanka Freedom Party. It claims 55,132 members in thirty-five affiliated unions.

In the public sector, there are also the Public Service Workers' Trade Union Federation, and the Union of Post and Telecommunications Officers.

SUDAN

The early trade union movement featured many small unions in rival national centres. Most present day unions were registered in the early 1960s, after independence, and in 1966 there were three national centres, namely: the Federation of Sudanese Workers' Unions (1963), the Federation of Workers Trade Unions of the Public Sector (1965) and the Federation of Workers Trade Unions of the Private Sector (1965).

In 1971 all existing trade unions were dissolved and a new organisation, the Federation of Sudanese Workers Unions, was set up, in accordance with the 1971 Trade Union Act.

SWAZILAND

The Swaziland Federation of Trade Unions comprised five registered trade unions, namely the Government Industrial Workers' Unions; the Miners and General Workers' Union, the Amalgamated Union of Ngwane Commercial and Industrial Workers; the Citrus Plantations, Agricultural and Allied Workers Union; the Swaziland Bank Workers Union. In 1973 trade union activity was suppressed.

281

TANZANIA (formerly Tanganyika and Zanzibar)

The first trade unions were formed in 1949, and a national centre in 1955. In 1964 the government introduced the National Union of Tanganyika Workers (Establishment) Act which dissolved the Tanganyika Federation of Labour and its eleven affiliated unions and created a single central union with eleven sections. The National Union of Tanganyika Workers covers some 330,000 members, about 80 per cent of employed labour. Its international links are with the Organisation of African Trade Union Unity. It is structured along both industrial and geographic lines, and NUTW has no affiliates but (nine) industrial sections and a network of regional and branch offices. The main sections cover East African community workers; transport, mines and domestic workers; teachers; government civil servants and agricultural workers. Under the Trade Disputes Act, a statutory conciliation procedure exists and strikes and lockouts are illegal if this system is not followed. The government controls wage level and increases.

On Zanzibar, the Workers' Department of the Afro-Shirazi Party undertakes trade union work. It was formed in 1965 to replace all existing unions.

TRINIDAD AND TOBAGO

Trade unions date from the Working Man's Association of 1919. They developed along broad industrial demarcations, such as the sugar industry, government service and the transport industry. More recently, however, the trend was towards the 'blanket' type union. There have been successive trade union federations, such as the Trinidad and Tobago Federation of Labour and the TUC. At present two national centres exist. The Trinidad and Tobago Labour Congress is recognised by government and employers as the most representative organisation. Founded in 1966, from the national Federation of Labour and the national TUC, it claims 60,000 members and it is affiliated to the ICFTU and the Caribbean Congress of Labour. A number of breakaway unions, having a more militant and political orientation, have formed the Council of Progressive Trade Unions. In 1973, a total of eighty-three workers' unions were registered, having a total membership of 95,000.

TURKS AND CAICOS ISLANDS

There is one active trade union, the St George's Industrial Trade Union, with a membership of about 250.

UGANDA

In 1948 there was only one registered trade union. The Uganda Trades Union Congress was formed in 1956 and claimed 102,000 members in the mid-sixties. Its affiliation was with the ICFTU and it had twenty-three member unions. The rival national centre was the Federation of Uganda Trade Unions, formed in 1964 and a much smaller organisation. It was affiliated to the All African Trade Union Federation. In 1973, legislation was passed to establish the new National Organisation of Trade Unions, which replaced the existing structures. All trade unions registered under the law belong to this organisation.

UNITED KINGDOM

Trade unions originated in Britain over 200 years ago, among craftsmen. They are now organised in part on the basis of a worker's occupation, but often all workers in an industry may join the same union. In Dec 1975, there were 111 trade unions affiliated to the Trades Union Congress with a total membership of 10,363,724. A further 1m. workers were members of unions not affiliated to the TUC. In 1973, there were 495 (registered) unions, but nearly 77 per cent of all members were in the twenty-four largest unions whilst under 1 per cent were in the 253 smallest unions. Under the Employment Protection Act, trade unions are given a certification of independence. The single national centre for trade unions is the Trades Union Congress. Founded in 1868, it is an ICFTU and ETUC affiliate, and many of its constituent unions are active in the International Trade Secretariats. Through its governing body, the elected general council, the TUC formulates the main policies of trade unionism and it represents the workers in the ILO, and in consultative machinery with government and employers, such as the NEDC, the Health and Safety Commission and the Advisory, Conciliation and Arbitration Service. Affiliated unions retain full autonomy, but the TUC may mediate in inter-union disputes in certain circumstances, and it aims to help settle unauthorised and unconstitutional stoppages of work. The TUC as well as many individual unions provides extensive educational services for members. Trade unions in related industries or occupations have formed these national federations: the Confederation of Entertainment Unions; the Confederation of Shipbuilding and Engineering Unions; the Federation of Theatre Unions; the National Association of Unions in the Textile Trade; the National Federation of Furniture Unions; the National Federation of Professional Workers; the Printing and Kindred Trades Federation; the United Textile Factory Workers'

283

Association. Forty-eight trade unions, with a total membership of 405,702, are grouped in the General Federation of Trade Unions, founded in 1899. There are eight TUC regional councils in England and Wales. Scottish trade unionists have their own national centre, the Scottish TUC (1899) with seventy-eight affiliated unions in 1976. Trade unions in Northern Ireland are represented by the Northern Ireland Committee of the Irish Congress of Trade Unions, although most trade unionists in the province belong to unions based in Great Britain and their organisations are usually affiliated to both the ICTU and the T.U.C. The T.U.C.-Labour Party Liaison Committee, set up in Jan 1972, discusses policies on industrial relations and management of the economy. The 'social contract' was agreed by this Committee in 1973, and the contract formed the basis of a voluntary wage restraint policy in 1975–6. The five largest unions are:

(1) The Transport and General Workers' Union. This was established in 1922, as the result of an amalgamation of fourteen unions on the initiative of the Dock, Wharf, Riverside and General Workers' Union in association with the National Union of Dock Labourers. Since 1922 it has absorbed a number of other unions, and in 1976 it had 1,863,670 members.

(ii) The Amalgamated Union of Engineering Workers. This was formed in 1970. It comprises the Amalgamated Engineering Union, which was formed in 1920 from the old Amalgamated Society of Engineers (1851) and other unions; the Amalgamated Union of Foundry Workers, formed in 1946 from several older craft unions; the Constructional Engineering Union, formed in 1924; and the Association of Engineering and Shipbuilding Draughtsmen, later known as the Draughtsmen's and Allied Technicians' Association, formed in 1913. In 1976, the AUEW had 1,211,000 members.

(iii) The National Union of General and Municipal Workers. This was formed in 1924 from the National Union of General Workers (1889), the National Amalgamated Union of Labour (1889) and the Municipal Employees' Association (1894). Many other unions have been absorbed since then. In 1976 it had 883,000 members.

(iv) The National and Local Government Officers' Association. This was formed in 1905. In 1930 it amalgamated with the National Association of Poor Law Officers, and in 1963 with the British Gas Staff Association. In 1976, it had 625,163 members.

(v) The National Union of Public Employees. This was founded in 1888 as the L.C.C. Employees' Protection Association, later the Municipal Employees' Association. A section of this body in 1907 formed the National Union of Corporation Workers, which adopted the present name in 1928. In 1976, the Union had 550,000 members.

ZAMBIA (formerly Northern Rhodesia)

The Zambia Congress of Trade Unions, the nation's only trade union centre, claims a membership of 141,977, about a third of employed labour. It was formed in 1965 to succeed the United Trades Union Congress. There are sixteen affiliated unions, of which the main ones are the Hotel, Catering Workers' Union of Zambia; the National Union of Building, Engineering and General Workers; the National Union of Commercial and Industrial Workers; the National Union of Plantation and Agricultural Workers, and the Zambia Railways Amalgamated Workers' Union.

The Civil Servants' Union and the Zambian African Mining Union (40,000 members) remain independent of the national centre.

INDEX

Most of the chapters in this book run in alphabetical sequence, and for this reason we have not attempted to produce a completely detailed index. The main aim has been to allow the reader to locate the country by page for any major subject included in this publication.